All the Joy You Can Stand

101 Sacred Power Principles for Making Joy Real in Your Life

Also by Debrena Jackson Gandy

*Sacred Pampering Principles: An African-American Woman's Guide
to Self-Care and Inner Renewal*

All the Joy You Can Stand

101 Sacred Power Principles for
Making Joy Real in Your Life

Debrena Jackson Gandy

THREE RIVERS PRESS

NEW YORK

The author gratefully acknowledges reprint permission from *The Lioness* for "Turning Points" © 1996 and "Psalm of the Twelve Gifts of Spirituality" © 1990 by Reverend Victoria Lee Owens.

Published by Three Rivers Press, New York, New York. Member of the Crown Publishing Group.

Random House, Inc. New York, Toronto, London, Sydney, Auckland
www.randomhouse.com

THREE RIVERS PRESS is a registered trademark and the Three Rivers Press colophon is a trademark of Random House, Inc.

Originally published in hardcover by Crown Publishers in 2000.

Printed in the United States of America

Designed by Cynthia Dunne

Library of Congress Cataloging-in-Publication Data
Gandy, Debrena Jackson.
All the joy you can stand : 101 sacred power principles for making
joy real in your life / by Debrena Jackson Gandy—1st ed.
1. Afro-American women—Religious life. 2. Afro-American
women—Conduct of life. I. Title.
BL625.2.G355 2000
158.1'082—dc21   99-85985

ISBN 0-609-80708-0

10 9 8 7 6 5 4 3 2 1

First Paperback Edition

To the "little women" who are the love of my life—
my daughters, Adera, Kiana, and Kenzie;
and to Joe, my husband, best friend, and life partner.
Thank you for opening my heart wider
and teaching me how to stand
more and more and more joy.

Acknowledgments

special thank-you from deep, deep down in my heart to those whose life stories and experiences inspired the chapters in this book. Because this book is made up of real-life anecdotes and vignettes—my own, and many, many more not my own—it is a quilt of stories I've had the privilege of sewing together and a tapestry I've had the pleasure of weaving.

Big THANK-YOU's to my literary agent, Denise Stinson, for continuing to believe in me and my work; to Kristin Kiser, my enthusiastic and encouraging editor; to Nat and Thelma Jackson, for being my proud parents; to my sister, Ericka, for being my sounding board; and to my little brother, "Little J," for being the apple of my eye.

Thank you to the sisterfriends who were part of the Sisterfriends Roundtable: Youlanda Allen, Angela Toussaint, Barbette Edwards, Sharon Allen Felton, Carol Blakley, Gotha Johnson, and Gayl Kirby, who helped me zero in on the themes for this book. Thank you to my sisterfriends in the *Beloved* theater party group, the Kindred Spirits, the pajama party divas, the pampering party crews, my Sisterfriends e-mail group, A Circle of Sisters, and the Wisdom Circle. Thank you for loving me, supporting me, and helping me to keep it real!

And thank you God/Goddess for allowing me to be on this planet, at this time, sharing this very necessary message.

Said the woman to her Inner Power,
"Come out, come out, wherever you are."

Would you like to know? . . .

- ◇ What gets in the way of feeling and experiencing your power on a daily basis?

- ◇ How to make space and free up energy in your life?

- ◇ How to restore, recharge, and renew your spirit?

- ◇ What brings you joy?

- ◇ Why you may feel restless, unfocused, and unfulfilled?

- ◇ Why you may easily get angry, upset, or defensive?

- ◇ Why you may be experiencing a loss of passion and enthusiasm in life?

- ◇ How to break the cycle of unhealthy or short-lived love relationships?

- ◇ Why judgment and guilt are so destructive to the spirit?

- ◇ Why forgiving yourself and others is so liberating?

- ◇ When your Purpose is tapping you on the shoulder?

- ◇ How to be more open to your agents and angels?

- ◇ Ways to heal your memories and emotions?

- ◇ Ways to heal your body?

- ◇ How to identify your "power pack" and create a support system?

- ◇ How to recognize seasons and cycles in your life?

- ◇ The connection between joy and power?

- ◇ The ways that God gets your attention?

- ◇ How to integrate renewal into your life?

- ◇ How to create a life that is gratifying and deeply fulfilling?

Contents

Preface

We are in a time when many, many women just like you are starting to feel a change come over them. A change that they can't quite explain because it's happening on the inside. A change that feels like a restlessness within, an inner quickening or an inner stirring. A change that may cause you to question things you've accepted for a long, long time; a change that is telling you "it's time for something different," even if you don't know what this "something different" is; a change that is letting you know that it is time to dig deeper and get in touch with your Divine Self, that immutable part of you that is spirit. This feeling is caused by your sacred inner power beginning to reawaken. These are also signs that your spirit needs feeding and is hungry for something more.

I believe that we each are created with an enormous capacity for having joy, peace, power, ease, and grace in our lives. We have an unlimited amount of divine potential that we have only *begun* to tap. We've experienced but the tip of the iceberg, brief snapshots of the brilliance, magnificence, and greatness that lies within us. There's more. *Much, much more.* And it is the awakening of this brilliance, magnificence, and greatness within that is causing this feeling, this inner stirring. I can relate to being in this space because being in this space is what prompted me to write this book.

All the Joy You Can Stand will help you learn how to access your sacred power and inner joy on purpose—*consciously and intentionally*—and "midwife" them from being inner stirrings to being more fully expressed. *All the Joy You Can Stand* offers you a process for birthing your divine potential and removing internal blocks so that real power and joy become permanent residents in your life instead of occasional guests.

This book presents you with new ways of thinking, speaking, acting, believing, and being that free you up and enable you to access and *in*sperience more joy, and thus *ex*perience more power, in your life.

In this book, you will find a collage of stories and experiences from lives of women who look like you and are like you—personal stories I've collected from my life and those of sisterfriends, mentors, readers, family members, elders, sistercircle members, and participants in my seminars, workshops, keynotes, and retreats from around the country. These stories are not made up, inflated, or exaggerated—they are real. Real stories that bring to light the untruths that keep us disconnected from our true selves.

These stories will help you bring joy out of exile in your life, joy that is already within you, and free up more of your personal power. These stories, which are organized into short two- to three-page "chapterettes," communicate the essence of the 101 sacred power principles. These sacred power principles share ways of knowing, feeling, creating, and expressing your authentic power, your sacred power. Sacred power is not power derived from a position, a job title, a degree, or how much money you have; not power that can be gained, lost, or taken away—but it resides within you, waiting to be tapped. This power is an inherent, unlimited inner resource available to you as part of your "divine design."

As you journey through the sacred power principles, you will come to understand how joy and power are inextricably intertwined, like braids. Each supports the other. Joy is the gateway, the bridge, and the raw material of your sacred power. *Joy is the fuel of your spirit—your spiritual nutrition.* Using each as a spiritual stepping stone, the 101 sacred power principles guide you on a journey that helps you remove the blocks of fear, lack, and limitation that are suppressing a fuller expression of Who You Really Are. This book is written to be a tool to assist you in your spiritual growth, to assist you in developing spiritual strength, and as a guide on the journey to personal empowerment and transformation.

My hope is that this journey helps you tap the wellspring of your joy and sacred inner power. It is also the story of how I got in touch with my own.

Introduction

In many ways, this book is a sequel to my first, *Sacred Pampering Principles: An African-American Woman's Guide to Self-Care and Inner Renewal*. It is a spiritual synthesis of my "learnings," insights, peaks, valleys, and triumphs and challenges on the journey to finding and expressing my own joy and sacred power.

I teach, speak, and write about joy, peace, power, ease, and grace because I am learning to bring them more fully into my own life, not because I have mastered them. And to the degree that I have been able to make them a reality in my life, part of my life's work is helping other women make them realities in their lives also.

Over these past few years, especially since becoming a national author, I've been striving to fulfill a pact I made with myself and God—to practice what I teach, to have my life represent a possibility of "having it all" with ease and grace. I didn't just want to write *about* it. I wanted to *live* it, using my life as the testing ground, the practice field, the living laboratory.

Over the course of the personal self-care journey that led up to my writing *Sacred Pampering Principles*, I sought to live-the-talk, walk-the-walk, and integrate into my life and spirit what evolved into the 24 sacred pampering principles that became the foundation of this first book. As each of these principles started to take root and become real in my life, I could feel myself starting to change—in a very, very good way. I could feel something starting to percolate and bubble up from a place deep down inside of me, something that felt like it had been trapped and held captive for a long, long time.

I've come to realize on my spiritual path that sacred pampering is a mind-set, a new paradigm, and a way of life, not just something I do. Yes, when I first started down the sacred pampering path, I thought pampering was about taking more bubble baths and treating myself to more pedicures, massages, and facials. I thought it was about eating more nutritiously, being sure I got my exercise, making "me time" a priority, and doing more activities that I really liked. At that time in my life, I thought pampering and self-care was only about *outer grooming* and doing a better job taking care of my body. I've come to realize that this is a very small slice of it, but by no means all of it. Sacred pampering means something much more, much deeper. It means living life from a place and in a way that nourishes and renews your mind, body, and spirit *ongoingly*.

Sacred pampering, as I define it, is about (1) aligning your life with what brings you joy; (2) choosing to do what energizes and renews you; and (3) doing what nurtures and fortifies your mind, body, and spirit. *Sacred* means "important, highly valued, worthy of reverence and respect." So sacred pampering is about honoring and practicing self-care *first*, instead of last or least.

Little by little on my journey, I discovered that as I made sacred pampering a way of life and as I started aligning my actions, interactions, choices, and behavior with what brought me joy, I started triggering a release of power from within that seemed to have been buried. I was becoming more and more aware of a deep inner reserve of power that I didn't even know was there. I was coming to realize that pampering was but the beginning of the journey, not the final destination.

Making sacred pampering an integral part of how I live and move through life has not been easy, because it has required personal transformation. I've had to roll up my sleeves to do some serious spiritual and emotional housecleaning. I've had to clean out old beliefs, behaviors, and words, and get rid of the clutter, chaos, confusion, and stinkin' thinkin' that lingered in the hard-to-reach nooks and crannies of my life. Making the shift from self-care last to embodying a *self-care first* approach to living has required that I overhaul and reshape how I use my energy, and how I see my life, myself, and my body. Making sacred pampering real in my life completed just the first phase of my personal transformation process. The next part of the process involved my more fully accessing, channeling, and expressing the inner power that was itching to be released and set free.

And I wasn't alone. As I read letter after letter and card after card sent from readers of *Sacred Pampering Principles* from all across the country, other women shared that they, too, were experiencing something similar—a bubbling up of something inside as they started internalizing and applying the sacred pampering principles to their lives. As they began to integrate the principles, they, too, began to experience this awakening of a deeper inner power and inner joy.

It was at the fifth session of the Annual African-American Women's Advance (not retreat) in 1998, For Sisters Only: Sharing, Healing and Renewal, for which I am founder and executive director, that I finally made up my mind to write about this power and joy I was (re)discovering and beginning to set free. During the opening circle of introductions, I listened intently as each woman shared what compelled her to attend this transformational, all-sistahs event. I listened as a common theme began to emerge from this diverse cross-section of women who were attending from the local Seattle area and from cities across the country, and who ranged in age from 25 to 70. Women felt disconnected from their power and were hungry for reconnection. They came to the event with a spiritual thirst; they wanted to feed their spirits; they wanted to drill deep and tap into their well of sacred inner power and joy that they knew was there but didn't know how to fully reach. They came to the Advance hoping that this experience would help them reach it. It did then and continues to do so for the women who attend.

It was then and there, as I sat in the opening session of the Advance listening carefully to women share their stories of what brought them to this event, that I decided that my next book, the one you are now holding, would guide women on a journey of, one, accessing and expressing their sacred power, and two, of experiencing more real joy in their lives. I've learned that our sacred power naturally emerges when we reconnect and get in synch with the positive energy force of life. Our sacred power is divine power that seeks to be expressed—and indeed, must be expressed if we want to experience a more deeply fulfilling life.

My hope is that as you journey through the pages of this book you will begin to understand what is at the essence of being able to manifest the desires of your heart, and you will get clear on what has been getting in your way. *You will begin to see joy as the natural expression of your spirit, and power as your ability to affect and shape yourself and your reality.*

Remember this: you were created to play big, not small. Playing big is your innate and inherent right—your birthright. *All the Joy You Can Stand* introduces you to dimensions of your joy and sacred power that, until now, may have been partially hidden, buried, or eluding you. *All the Joy You Can Stand* invites you to blow the lid off, to play bigger and to more fully step into your joy, your power, and your greatness.

God heaps on you all the joy you can stand, but we keep giving God an itsy-bitsy cup to fill. So if you want more but aren't experiencing and receiving more, it's *you* limiting *you*, not God limiting you. *I invite you to trade in your cup for a bucket.*

I pray that you accept my invitation.

With peace, love,
and more power to you,

Debrena Jackson Gandy

January 25, 2000

All the Joy You Can Stand

1. Clear the silt

I am sitting at Afrikando, a chic West African restaurant in Seattle on a Monday evening in January 1999, enjoying my monthly dinner and dialogue with my mentor, Miss Maxine, a bodacious and sassy 70-year-*young* wise woman. Miss Maxine and I convene on the third Monday of each month for what I call our Wisdom Circle. The Wisdom Circle is my opportunity to "sit at the feet" of one of my elders and ask questions about life, relationships, marriage, sex, money, raising kids—whatever my heart desires. As my mentor, she helps guide, nurture, and prepare me as I mature deeper into womanhood, into wisdom, and into myself. She also acts as a sounding board for my ideas, projects, and aspirations.

This particular evening, I brought along the proposal draft of this book. I had been working on it for the previous couple of months and it was finally completed. I was very pleased with it. I wanted Miss Maxine to read it before I put the finishing touches on it and shipped it off to my literary agent.

After we had placed our dinner orders, I proudly slid the notebook containing the draft of my book proposal to her across the table. She put on her glasses and took her time carefully studying each line of the double-spaced, thirty-page proposal. Fifteen minutes later, she closed the notebook abruptly with a loud *snap*, took off her glasses, and leaned toward me across the table with an intense, penetrating look on her face. She asked, "So what is it that *All the Joy You Can Stand* really *provides* for women? I'm still not sure after reading through your entire proposal."

I thought to myself, "What do you mean, *still not sure?*" I was caught off guard and a little taken aback, to say the least. I had expected to hear glowing compliments on how well the proposal was written, how descriptive the writing was, and how well it captured the message and intention of the book. Well, I should have known better. Miss Maxine doesn't play. She shoots straight from the hip. No holds barred. She then instructed me to answer her question using a metaphor.

She sat in silence waiting patiently as I looked down at the table, trying to gather my thoughts and develop a response. After a couple minutes of pondering her question, I looked up and explained, "What comes to mind is a river. Life moves with a flow and a rhythm to it like a river, and when we know how to go with the flow, our lives work." I went on, "I believe that all of us want our lives to work. We want to know how to go with the flow, but instead, many of us are swimming upstream against the current. Or we have gotten lost in a side stream somewhere, caught in an undertow, or the silt in our lives is weighing us down, muddying our vision, clogging our spiritual channels, and impeding our ability to flow."

"Yes! Go on, go on," Miss Maxine said excitedly. "Say more about the silt!" "Well," I said, pausing again as I struggled to find the words that would most clearly convey my thoughts, "silt is sand, dirt, rock, and mud that accumulates in the bottom of a river and clogs it up. Many of us have accumulated mental, emotional, and spiritual silt in our lives, and we don't even know it. Or if we do know it, we don't really know how to clean it out."

I was feeling it now. The words were starting to spill out of my mouth. I continued, "Our internal silt can take the form of denial; drama; struggle; not being true to ourselves; self-sabotage; self-doubt; and self-defeating thoughts of lack, limitation, and fear, while the external silt can take the form of toxic relationships, negative judgment, destructive criticism, psychic attacks from others, depletion of our spirits, invalidation, and physical or emotional abuse. This silt needs to be dredged, cleared out, and removed so that our lives can become clear and we can experience the flow again."

"Mmmmm. Very good, very good," Miss Maxine replied. I exhaled and leaned back in my chair, glad that my explanation had sufficed. Miss Maxine wasn't done with me yet, though. "What you just explained," she rebutted, "tells me *why* you are writing this book. Now tell me what *All the Joy You Can Stand* is actually going to *do* for women." I furrowed my brow as I struggled to articulate what, up until a few minutes ago, I thought my proposal did quite well. Then slowly, like a morning fog lifting as the sun rises in the early morning hours, I began to really get it. "*All the Joy You Can Stand* is a journey through 101 principles that help you dredge your life, remove the blocks, and clear away the silt so that you can experience more joy, free up your power, and get back in tune with your true self!" I exclaimed.

Leaning back in her chair with her hands clasped across her lap, Miss Maxine beamed a big smile of satisfaction and responded, "Bull's-eye, my dear! That's it! We must first dredge out our lives and clear away the silt before we can fully tap into, rediscover, and reclaim the power and joy that is trapped beneath the layers of sediment, rock, and mud. And *All the Joy You Can Stand* gives us the dredging tools and the dredging process. Is this what I hear you saying?" she queried. "Yes, Miss Maxine, it is," I replied with new resolve and clarity. *"It certainly, certainly is."*

For me, this conversation with Miss Maxine shed a whole new light on the purpose of my book. And it also let me know that my proposal needed some more work. Yes, I thought to myself, this book is about recovering our joy and our power, freeing them up, and retrieving them from places where they've been buried for far too long. But first we must become aware of the silt and acknowledge that it exists.

Silt can be dangerous because it doesn't descend on you in one fell swoop—it kills your spirit quietly, gradually strangling and depleting it day after day. We quietly suffer from the symptoms and telltale signs of the silt creeping into our lives and sneaking up on us, a little bit here and a little bit there. On the outside, we may look like we're doing fine, while on the inside, we are hemorrhaging spiritually. For many of us, this erosion has left *holes in our souls* and a trail of other effects: loss of motivation, procrastination, loss of energy, loss of passion and enthusiasm; feeling unfocused, unfulfilled, disorganized, always on the go, off center; being unsettled, anxious, nervous, indecisive, irritable, fidgety, or feeling as if your life has become one rushed, hectic, stressful routine.

All the Joy You Can Stand offers a process for increasing the presence of joy in your life and the expression of your inner power in your love relationships, in your friendships, in your work, in your marriage, in your behavior and your choices, with your kids, in your business, with your finances, and in your body. You will learn how to increase your "joy tolerance" and your "joy threshold."

By the way, *how much joy can you stand?* I'd like to suggest that it's much, much more than you are currently experiencing. Having a fulfilled life is the Creator's intention for you and for me. We must remember: we are created with an innate right to fulfillment, joy, health, and prosperity. Manifesting a fulfilled life means making real a life that is complete, optimal, deep, and rich. Manifesting a fulfilled life is not a pie-in-the-sky notion or an exceptional reality to be experienced by a select few. We should know that it is available to each of us. The more joy you can *stand*, the more God gives you. The more joy you can stand, the more of it you experience.

I believe that if we knew *what* silt needed to be cleared in order to recover our joy and power, and if we knew *how* to clear it, we would. Now you have a process—a process for tapping into and actualizing more of your divine potential, more of Who You Really Are.

So sisterfriend, get out your shovel, your backpack, and your traveling shoes. I invite you to join me on this journey of coming into your power, to standing in it, speaking from it, feeling it, knowing it, and expressing it, *ongoingly*. It's time to do some dredging, some serious dredging that is long overdue. It's our time. It's your time. It's your appointed hour, and this silt has got to go!

2. *Learn self–love*

> *You are already living*
> *with the love of your life.*
>
> —Richard McWilliams

ourteen floors above Madison Avenue, I was sitting in the lounge at the lovely Gazelle Day Spa in Manhattan, New York, leading a sacred pampering seminar for some of the spa's VIP clientele. About halfway through the seminar, Cherie, one of the patrons, walked in and sat down to join the discussion. We were in the midst of discussing the signs and symptoms of pampering neglect, and the unhealthy and self-defeating behaviors we exhibit when self-care is a low priority or no priority in our lives. After listening for a couple of minutes, Cherie spoke up and asserted, "It's really very simple. All you have to do is love yourself."

I nodded my head in agreement. "Yes, this is true. I agree wholeheartedly," I replied, and then added, "But knowing that you've got to love yourself doesn't mean that you know how to do it. And saying you love yourself doesn't necessarily mean that you do." A hush fell over the room as the ladies went deep into thought pondering the implications of this statement.

I LOVE MYSELF seems to have become the black woman's national anthem in the past few years. We are quick to say it and quick to assert it, especially in the company of other sistahs. However, as I have traveled around the country talking with women in my workshops, seminars, retreats, and keynotes, one of my realizations is this: many of us *say* we love ourselves, but if we pay close attention to our words and thoughts, and observe our behaviors, actions, and choices—how we treat our bodies, each other, our kids, our mates, our money, and how we invest our energy and use our time—we would see a contradiction, an incongruence, a *gap. Many of us are not there yet.* We've been *told* to love ourselves and we know it's a good idea, but many of us haven't been shown or taught *how* to love ourselves. We haven't seen it modeled and it hasn't been "exampled" for us. It exists as a good idea in our minds, but is not yet a reality in our lives.

Taught how to maintain and groom our bodies? *Yes.*

Taught to love our selves? *No.*

If we'd truly been taught self-love, we would believe unwaveringly in ourselves instead of doubt ourselves; have faith instead of have fear; feel free instead of feel obligated; feel innocent instead of guilty; play big instead of small; accept each and every part of our bodies, instead of rejecting the parts that we don't like; acknowledge instead of deny and avoid; be at peace instead of stressed out; be complete instead of complain; and see perfection instead of finding fault. So we literally must *unlearn* self-loathing and relearn self-love. We must practice it. Become familiar with it. Experience and *in*sperience it. We must learn to *assign* a high value to ourselves and then *demonstrate* a belief in this high value. We must learn how to plant, cultivate, nurture, and grow self-love.

This is no easy task, however. It took me several years to get my self-love act together. It required rigorous self-evaluation, truth-telling, forgiving, releasing, and lots of self-reflection. When I flipped back through certain scenes in my life, I looked for signs that indicated either self-loathing or self-loving. What my reflections revealed was that I, as positive and spiritual as I *thought* myself to be, had evidence of self-loathing sprinkled throughout my life. The evidence was in the times I had dishonored my time, my body, or my energy. The evidence was in the times I had over-committed myself, said yes when I really wanted to say no, or allowed myself to be put in uncomfortable situations out of feelings of obligation or guilt.

Self-loathing showed up on occasions when I had eaten snacks late at night when I *knew* it was not good for my body, or I had not given my body enough rest or a much needed break. The evidence was in the times I'd mis-managed my money and allowed myself to get into positions where my financial debt weighed on me like an anchor; when I felt compelled to always be on the go, in the mix, or at all of the professional networking and social functions. The evidence was in the times I would agree to go out with friends even when I was dead tired after a rough week at work; when I didn't feed my body enough fresh food or drink enough water; and when I allowed men with questionable character and negative energy into my body in the form of sex. Yes, there were many signs and much evidence to confirm that there were a lot of holes, rips, and tears in the fabric of my self-love.

As I began to steadily make my way toward this place called self-love, many things began to change. I began to change. My thoughts, words, actions, beliefs, choices, and interactions began to change. Self-love started to take root and grow in my life. I was learning to truly love my *self* for the first time, and "love my cells," as Rachel Bagby encourages in her book *Divine Daughters*. I was now beginning to *show* and demonstrate high regard for my mind, body, spirit, energy, and time.

So as we begin the dredging process, we don't want to beat ourselves up. We don't want to flog ourselves for poor choices we've made in the past, or for our bad habits or problems. But we do want to tell the truth: *collectively, and thus, individually, we are not doing as good a job of loving ourselves as we may think we are.* And in this acknowledgment lies the beginning of our healing, the beginning of the journey, and the first step toward learning self-love.

3. *Make space*

*W*hen I'm feeling stuck, unclear, indecisive, or unable to move forward in a particular area of my life, it's often because I'm feeling mentally cramped and crowded. Usually this means there is some place in my life that has gotten too cluttered or is out of order.

When there is clutter, chaos, and confusion going on in our external world, it is often a function of feeling cramped, cluttered, and congested in our inner world. Being "out of order" in our external world is usually an indication of something's being "out of order" in our inner world. Yes, your outer environment affects and reflects your inner environment.

Is it that box of books I've been meaning to take to the used book store for weeks? Those outfits hanging in my closet that I haven't worn in over a year? That pile of papers I haven't touched in six months? That junk in my car trunk or the spare closet? Or those old coats that have been hangin' in the hall closet for over two years? Once I stop to clean out or bring into order a physical space that is "out of order," something starts to happen. Making space in your outer world has the effect of creating space in your inner world.

Making space is not about cleaning up, it's about cleaning out. Making space is a form of releasing and letting go of things that are no longer serving you. Making space sets in motion a process that dislodges your mental logjams and gives you a jolt that loosens up your thinking and provides a "clearing" in your mind. Too much "stuff" in your physical space can suffocate your spirit, stifle your creativity, clog your mental channels, weigh you down, and make you feel "heavy." Too much stuff creates stagnation.

Ever notice how much lighter you feel after you clean out your underwear drawer, bedroom closet, desk, guest room, garage, purse, sewing box, cupboard, or refrigerator? There is a definite connection between our outer spaces and our inner mental space. So we must stop and learn to *make space.* We often don't have enough room or space in our lives for the joy and the blessings to come in, so they keep waiting patiently in the wings of our lives for a little room of their own. In other words, *you have to make space so that joy has a place.*

One of my "making space" challenges is with papers. I hang on to too many papers "just in case." Just in case I need them for future reference. Yet 90 percent of them sit there untouched and "unreferenced," just piling up, taking up space. So I have to go through my papers once every three months to get rid of those that I can't identify a *specific* future need for.

Making space is not the same as getting organized, becoming more efficient, or simplifying. Making space requires that you *clear it out, move it out, release it, get rid of the excess.* To be successful when you make space, be sure not to just *relocate* stuff. You must do it completely. For example, you clean out your bedroom closet, put the clothes in a big garbage bag, and then proudly set the bags in the garage, the closet, or the guest room until you can deal with them later. *You did it.* You finally cleaned out your closet. But then the sacks of clothing sit around for weeks or months before they are hauled away or donated to the Salvation Army, Goodwill, or a women's shelter.

This is not making space. *This is a relocation program.* When you move stuff around or relocate it, it's still taking up space, just in a different place. If this is what making space has tended to look like in your life, take notice. This can be indicative of the way you handle conflict, unfinished business, your anger, or uncomfortable situations or individuals in your life that need to be addressed. Instead of handling the problem or truly resolving it, you relocate it.

So right now, do an inventory of the physical spaces in your life. Is there a place that has excess, is too cluttered, or is "out of order" and needs clearing out or cleaning out? Choose one place to focus on first that you know you can complete victoriously within the next thirty days, and get to it. Then get out your calendar and mark the date that is thirty days from today. As you make space you'll notice yourself feeling lighter, thinking more clearly, feeling more focused, and even attracting new people and new energy into your life.

Make space so that joy has a place.

4. *Free up energy in your life*

The more I learn about energy, the more I realize that physical energy, spiritual energy, and Life Force are different expressions of the same source. Do you experience stress, inner conflict or inner tension, or feel unsettled, upset, restless, angry, resentful, or overwhelmed? Or are you frequently tired at the end of your workday? These are signs that your energy is blocked and needs freeing up. Other signs that your energy needs freeing up are that your life feels "heavy" or constricted; much of what you do in the course of your week doesn't bring you joy; you are held hostage by a lot of "shoulds" and "have to's" in your life; or you are often disappointed, upset, frustrated, or defensive. Any of these can indicate that your energy is constantly being depleted and drained in the course of your day, and not being adequately replenished, restored, and renewed. Any of these symptoms can indicate that your energy is being suppressed and stifled by circumstances or relationships that are weighing you down.

Where your energy is trapped or bound is also where your power is being blocked, compromised, or diminished. A power-full woman recognizes that her energy is precious, and she is committed to keeping her energy freed up. Your energy remains freed up when you are true to yourself. Being true to yourself means you honor your needs and desires, and you recognize and honor your boundaries. In order to free up your energy, you may need to say no, decline an invitation, forgo an event, decide to resign, step down, not renew your membership, bow out responsibly, or take your toys and go play somewhere else.

My friend Jeanine was an executive at an upscale, international day spa. She had a work environment to *live* for—plush chairs; soft, sensuous lighting; tranquil music floating through the halls; a great staff of friendly people; and relaxing scents of lavender and jasmine wafting through the air. The spa was growing, becoming more and more profitable, and gaining in prominence and notoriety.

There was just one problem: *her boss.*

Her boss, who was also the owner of the spa, had a way of interacting with her and others on staff that Jeanine found abrasive, disrespectful, and downright rude. Because she worked closely with the owner on a day-to-day basis, she was often on the receiving end of her boss's yelling fits and blow-ups. On several occasions, she attempted to meet with her boss to discuss her concerns, but her boss flat out denied any abrasive behavior or disrespectful treatment of Jeanine or any of the other employees.

Jeanine loved her job, her co-workers, and the clients, but her spirit was suffering from her boss's abuse. She would drag home at the end of her workday feeling as if the life force had been sucked out of her, as if her spirit had been beaten up. The positive aspects of her job were soon outweighed by her boss's volatile behavior. Going to work every day started to take a serious toll on her, first emotionally and spiritually, and then physically.

She knew things had gotten out of hand when her doctor informed her that she had developed fibroids, or hardened masses, on her uterus. She had been doing some reading on the mind-body connections of disease and knew that the spiritual and emotional cause of fibroids were related to nursing long-standing hurts and resentments. Fibroids also indicated that her feminine power had been under attack for far too long. She knew she had a decision to make: to stay or to go. Honoring her energy and well-being, and keeping her sanity and peace of mind, had become more important to her than her executive position or a big paycheck.

Two weeks later, she gave her resignation notice, much to the shock and utter amazement of the staff, and most of all her boss. With the decision to leave her job, she also decided to schedule herself to have her fibroids surgically removed after her last day. Though she had only a couple months of savings stored up, and no new job waiting, she knew she'd made the right decision. The day she walked away from her job, she felt lighter, as if spiritual shackles had been broken and as if someone had taken a 100-pound weight off her shoulders. She knew she'd made the right decision because she felt *free*.

Joy becomes more and more real in your life as you free up your energy.

5. Manage your energy

Have you noticed that our spirits don't operate according to Timex, Rolex, Greenwich Mean Time, or Daylight Savings Time? Time is a frame of reference that applies to the physical realm. It is a dimension that applies to our bodies but not our spirits. Our spirits operate according to an *energy* reality, not a time reality. Energy is Life Force in motion, the "stuff" that all matter is essentially made of. So in order to have more experiences of joy in your life, you must understand your relationship to energy. To have more experiences of joy in your life requires that you first make the shift from managing your time to *managing your energy*.

I made a decision to become self-employed and go full time with my training and consulting company in 1994, partly because I wanted an avenue for the fuller expression of my creativity and fuller use of my natural gifts, talents, and abilities. But most of all, it was a decision I made because I knew it would allow me to have more control of my time, money, interactions, and most importantly, my *energy*.

When we are constantly in situations in which we feed others' energy but are not fed in return—giving, giving, giving but not receiving, repeatedly making energy deposits in other people's lives but not getting decent returns—it's time to make some serious shifts in how we manage our energy. This way of living is dangerous because it erodes our spirit. These dynamics can indicate that we are mismanaging our energy. And eventually, if these patterns of behavior in our relationships and interactions go unchecked long enough, they will begin to kill the body. Hence the degenerative diseases such as cancer, diabetes, arthritis, lupus, multiple sclerosis, chronic fatigue syndrome, fibroids, and cysts that are spinning out of control in our community.

We are constantly exchanging energy throughout our day through handshakes, hugs, conversations, in meetings, and in person-to-person interactions with others. And the most intense energy exchange of all is sexual intercourse. Even in a handshake, the energy flows from the energetically stronger person to the energetically weaker person. The one with the weaker energy field will draw from the one with the stronger energy field.

And we don't even have to make contact with someone to exchange energy. We exchange and absorb energy with other people *all* of the time, whether we are aware of it or not.

Ever notice how you feel drained around certain people? You can find yourself becoming a twenty-four-hour filling station or a dumping ground for the toxic energy of other folks. Managing our energy this way negatively affects our minds, bodies, and spirits. So having more joy in our lives requires that we first do an inventory of the content and substance of our lives, particularly our interpersonal relationships, to assess how we are using our energy. When we are not honoring our energy, when it is being misused, abused, forfeited, held hostage, or not recycled, our capacity for joy is greatly diminished.

Are there clues, cues, and indicators that let you know that you need to balance or better protect your energy? The answer is a resounding yes! The following quiz will help you know if your energy or Life Force is being mismanaged or drained. Get out a pen or pencil and put a check mark next to the statements that apply to you. If *any* of the following are true for you, consider it a signal to pay closer attention to how, where, and with whom you are investing your energy.

ENERGY QUIZ

◇ You feel worn out or drained after talking in person or on the phone to a particular friend, acquaintance, family member, or client, customer, or patient.

◇ You rarely are able to manifest what you say you want.

◇ You set goals or start projects that time and time again do not come to fruition, or don't work out.

◇ You are a chronic procrastinator.

◇ Your thoughts or your speaking is often scattered and disjointed.

◇ You overgive or overnurture others in your life, particularly in your family or close relationships.

◇ You often have crazy, off-the-wall thoughts run through your head.

◇ You rarely sit down to take a break, rest, or chill out.

◇ You're stuck in a pattern of trying to people-please.

◇ You feel compelled to always be on the go or *doing* something.

◇ You feel unappreciated at work, in your household, or in your close relationships.

These are all possible signs that your energy is "off," out of balance. These signs indicate that (1) your energy is being *overinvested* in other people or other things; (2) too much of your energy is being lost and not recycled; (3) you are giving too much of your energy away and not keeping enough for yourself; (4) there is not enough "reciprocity of energy" in certain relationships; or (5) you are not incorporating enough renewal into your life.

As a speaker and national seminar leader, I have the opportunity to travel around the country, meeting new people and coming into contact with lots of different energies. I have worked on fine-tuning my sensitivity to other people's energy so that I can now literally feel when someone's energy field is "off," or depleted. Three particularly memorable encounters come to mind.

My girlfriend Monica, who was a self-esteem class instructor in a program at the downtown Seattle YWCA, was going to Kenya to visit her husband's family and asked me to substitute for her for three weeks while she was away. During my second week, I was walking down the hall with Tina, one of the program staff members, and she stopped to introduce me to Marie, who was passing by. Marie was a psychotherapist and one of the on-site counselors. As soon as Tina mentioned my name, Marie broke into a huge smile and reached out eagerly to shake my hand. She explained that she had read my book, *Sacred Pampering Principles*, and that we also had a mutual friend.

As Marie continued talking, I could feel something starting to happen. It felt like my energy was being vacuumed right out of my body and sucked into hers. I could literally feel the chaos swirling around in her energy field. It felt like she had thunderbolts, lightning, and a spiritual tornado swirling around her like the dust cloud that surrounded the character Pigpen in the comic strip *Peanuts*. I wanted to get away, and *fast*. I felt like I was suffocating.

Now don't get me wrong. Marie was pleasant, delightful, nice, all of that. She wasn't evil or mean. It wasn't her personality I was picking up on, it was her *energy* field.

On another occasion, a women's organization invited me to come to Chicago to lead a sacred pampering seminar. Prior to making the trip, I had several telephone conversations with Annette, the president of the organization, but I wouldn't have the opportunity to meet her in person until the day of the seminar. When I had been at the seminar site for about fifteen minutes, one of the women in the organization came over to where I was setting up to let me know that Annette had arrived and was anxious to meet me. A few moments later, I turned around and was greeted with an enthusiastic hello and a big hug from Annette.

Right away, I could tell that Annette was a good-hearted, hardworking person. But I could also feel her energy field tugging at me, especially when she hugged me. I could feel her energy field gasping for help. I could sense that her spiritual energy tank was running on "E." I could feel that she was depleted, probably from doing too much, feeling pulled in too many directions, being always on the go, constantly rushing, and feeling as if she never had enough time or energy, especially for herself. Not only was she broadcasting these messages through her energy field, she was also broadcasting them through the way she carried her body. I could tell that she expended a *lot* of energy giving to others, probably overgiving, while, at the same time, feeling underappreciated. I could tell that she was probably shouldering too much responsibility in her life by the way her shoulders were hunched, the way she moved, and her shallow breathing pattern.

After the seminar, when Annette and I had a chance to talk one-on-one during the ride back to the hotel, she shared some of the challenges and frustrations she was dealing with in her life—frustrations with her kids, her live-in boyfriend, her mother's illness, and her job. What she shared confirmed the message her energy field and her body had been broadcasting.

On another occasion, I was having a kickoff planning meeting with a new consulting client, a state agency that had called my company asking for assistance resolving some intense, interpersonal conflicts they were experiencing within the all-female management team of one of their medical programs. There were two managers in particular on this team who were experiencing serious problems with one another. The conflict had escalated into an ugly power struggle that was beginning to consume the entire office. One of these women was an African-American doctor. And as she spoke, filling me in on her perception of the source of the conflict, it was clear that she was brilliant, very accomplished, and very good at what she did. She disclosed that the conflicts and power struggles that had been going on within the management team for several months were really taking a toll on her. She was stressed out and had a hard time focusing. I could tell the conflict had taken a tremendous toll on her spiritual and emotional energy, too. It was obvious that her energy field was depleted and out of balance, *big time*.

If it were possible for this doctor's energy field to speak to me in words, I think it would have told me "I'm not getting the respect I deserve, no matter what I do; I feel unsupported, under attack, overloaded, and overwhelmed. I'm about to lose it. I need a break." Her energy field would have told me a story that revealed deeper truths about the effect of the conflict on her spirit. She may have described herself as about to have a nervous breakdown, while really, she was on the verge of having a *spiritual breakdown*.

I had to work hard to stay focused when one of the other three women in the meeting spoke, because the negative pull of this doctor's energy field was so engulfing. I could feel her energy field reaching out to me across the small conference table like the suction tentacles of an octopus trying to latch on and pull me in. Her spirit was starving for renewal and replenishment, even if it meant subconsciously feeding on my energy field during the meeting.

I share these stories not for the purpose of implying that we're all walking around with our energy fields shouting "Help me!," but to point out the effect on others around us when our energy field is depleted or out of whack. There are decisions we make and actions we take every day that either honor our energy or dishonor it. This is why we must learn to manage and attend to our energy in more healthy and empowering ways. We can become dangerous to be around when our spiritual energy gets depleted. When we don't manage our energy properly or responsibly, we can start to become needy, high-maintenance, overly emotional, or "energy parasites."

To better manage your energy, begin by checking in with your body. Check in with your *energy center*, your gut, which is located in your lower abdomen, also the location of your *womb*. Your womb is the seat of your feminine power, and it is very sensitive to energy. Is your energy center telling you that a situation or relationship feels heavy, light, wrong, off, or right? Managing your energy involves evaluating a decision or situation not just externally but also internally. Honoring your energy also means establishing healthy boundaries. Don't allow yourself to be energetically or spiritually depleted. Don't be a martyr. And don't allow other people's crises and problems to become yours. You can help, assist, and support others without having to adopt their problems or take on their burdens as if they were your own. This is a big energy depleter.

Notice if you feel anxiety or tension when you are asked to commit your energy and time to an effort, project, or event. When you are asked to volunteer, help out, or give of your time, energy, or money, tell the truth to yourself about whether or not you really want to participate. Are you saying yes out of obligation because you feel you *should* say yes? Or will you feel guilty if you say no? When we are asked to do something we *really* don't want to do, we tend to say things like "I'll try to make it"; "Maybe"; "Probably"; "I'm not sure." Instead, try using these clear-cut responses: "No, thank you. I'm going to decline." "I'll pass." "That doesn't work for me." These responses have certainty. They are definite. They take a clear stand. If one of these responses is fitting, and it is a true reflection of how you feel, then use it.

When you say no in response to a request, notice that you may feel compelled to explain why you've said no. *Why is this?* I think we feel compelled because we still carry around internal messages and old mental tapes and scripts that whisper "Nice girls don't say no," or "Good girls are helpful." Or we secretly think we won't be liked or accepted anymore or will lose favor with someone if we say no. This may sound overly simplified, but it's true. We carry around old, limiting scripts that tell us: a good woman gives of herself unceasingly; nice girls are always cooperative and accommodating. It is the residue from this deeply rooted conditioning that kicks in and creates the urge in us to explain ourselves when we say no. We think, if we can just present enough evidence to justify saying no, then maybe the person doing the asking will understand and not get mad at us!

As you learn to better manage and honor your energy and your boundaries, you will find yourself having more vitality, having more physical and emotional energy, thinking more clearly, being more decisive, being less defensive, and getting irritated and frustrated with others less and less.

Your energy is precious. Manage it accordingly.

6. *Know what brings you joy*

What brings you joy? Such a simple question, but how many of us have given it any deep thought? What brings you joy is a question that deserves your serious attention because it holds the key to experiencing more joy, peace, pleasure, and ease in your life. This is a carefully chosen question—a question that, when answered, helps you reconnect with what nurtures and renews your spirit and feeds your soul.

In the sacred pampering seminars I lead for women around the country, I pose this question in the seminar, pair women up, and give them a few minutes to share their responses while their partners write down their answers for them. This question is often met with a blank stare or a perplexed expression as women struggle to come up with specific responses. As women prepare to share with their partners for the exercise, they often repeat the question out loud to themselves. I've listened as they vocalize their interpretation question. They usually say, "Hmmm, what do I enjoy?" or "Hmmm, what do I like doing?"—*neither* of which is the question they are supposed to be answering. I gently remind them that the question at hand is: *What brings you joy?*

In the seminar, there are women still struggling with the *what brings me joy* question and looking at a blank piece of paper after several minutes have gone by. There are also those who, after a couple of minutes have gone by, have been able to come up with only three or four responses. As a way to help women get unstuck, I encourage them to think back to their girlhood, remembering those experiences that brought them joy then, and probably still do now. Truth be told, many women struggle with the question because not much joy is present in their lives right now. Joy has been displaced by frustration, stress, constant activity, busy-ness, perpetual motion, and routine.

I have had the chance to interact with over 3,000 women through my seminars, lectures, and keynotes. And I have been paying close attention. When joy is missing from our lives, it shows. Many of us are experiencing symptoms of a "joy shortage" in our lives, but don't realize that the symptoms we've been experiencing have anything to do with not having enough joy in our lives. Here is a list of some of the most common telltale signs of not having enough joy in your life. Get out a pen or pencil and **check off the items that apply to you, *some* of the time or *most* of the time.**

JOY SHORTAGE QUIZ

◇ Unfocused

◇ Unfulfilled

◇ Easily angered

◇ Frequently upset or "pissed off"

◇ Feel overwhelmed

◇ Very critical of yourself

◇ Restless

◇ Constantly rushing

◇ Poor listener

◇ Have a hard time holding still

◇ Patterns of self-sabotage

◇ Fear of success

◇ Drama, struggle, and crisis make regular appearances in your life

◇ Always on the go

◇ Minor body aches and pains

◇ Bad complexion

◇ Loss of passion and enthusiasm

◇ Overweight

◇ Underweight

◇ Very defensive

◇ Chronic procrastinator

◇ Constantly behind schedule

◇ Prone to gossiping

◇ Loss of intimacy in love relationship(s)

◇ Your life feels like a routine

◇ Difficulty sleeping soundly

◇ Have an addiction (i.e., drugs, alcohol, working, sex, food, shopping)

◇ Get irritated easily

◇ Mild depression, very low motivation

◇ Many regrets and resentments

◇ Constantly seek approval from others

◇ Indecisive, difficulty making up your mind

◇ Muscular tension in your body

◇ Feelings of loneliness or isolation

◇ Lack of vitality and vigor

◇ Blame others for how you feel

◇ Inability to relax

◇ Have few close friends

◇ Feel like a victim

◇ Frequently frustrated

◇ Workaholic

◇ Feel guilty

◇ Jealous of other women whom you perceive as "having it all"

◇ Feel shameful about your body

◇ Unwilling to try new things

◇ Low motivation

◇ Frequently feel tired and worn out

◇ Difficulty expressing love or tenderness

◇ Frequently say yes when you really want to say no

◇ Frequently complain and criticize

◇ Lack of sexual energy or loss of interest in sex

◇ Feel like something is missing in your life

◇ Need drugs or alcohol to relax or have a good time

◇ Difficult to enjoy yourself alone

◇ Compulsive overachiever

Notice that I did not include any type of rating scale with this checklist, or an interpretation for particular scores. This is because the intention of the checklist is not to have you feel bad or beat yourself up if many of these signs apply to you, but to have you acknowledge *what is so*—to provide you with a "snapshot" of the symptoms of a "joy deficit" that may be surfacing in your life. Transformation begins with telling the truth, acknowledging what is so—something so many of us try so hard to avoid. You probably weren't aware of the many ways that *not* having enough joy in your life can express itself. Having a joy shortage in your life shows up in real, observable ways in your thinking, choices, actions, and behaviors. *Joy is the fuel of the spirit,* and without enough of it in our daily lives, we begin to suffer in numerous ways—our spirits start to dry up and get brittle like a water-starved plant. When you feed your spirit a healthy diet of joy, it stays filled, radiant, and renewed.

Some of the responses women in my seminars have "excavated" in the What Brings Me Joy exercise have included singing in the shower; reading a good novel; receiving a good, long hug; sleeping in on Saturdays; relaxing in front of the fireplace with a mug of hot chocolate on a chilly evening; sunbathing; sipping a cup of herbal tea while enjoying stimulating conversation with a group of close girlfriends; sewing; quilting; painting; playing the piano; getting a massage from a masseuse with "good hands"; taking a long bath without interruption; traveling to a tropical destination; savoring a delicious home-cooked meal that someone else prepares; or staying in pajamas all day.

A woman from a seminar I led in San Diego wrote me afterward to share the effect the seminar had on her. She drove by a park on her way home from the seminar, a park she had passed on many occasions. Instead of passing on by this time, however, she pulled over, got out, and treated herself to ten minutes of swinging on the swings with the little kids. She had a ball! "Swinging at the park" was one of the experiences she'd written down during the What Brings Me Joy exercise in the seminar. She explained that she had always justified *not* stopping to swing because she didn't have enough time. She had places to go, people to see, things to do. Out of 840 minutes (based upon fourteen awake hours) in her day, she hadn't managed to invest even *ten minutes* of it in something that brought her so much joy—something as simple as swinging.

When joy is not a priority in our lives, we argue that it's an issue of "finding the time" or "making the time." I think joy is scarce in our lives because we don't understand or realize how critical joy is to our spiritual, emotional, and physical well-being. Therefore, we don't consider it important. After all, we "make time" for what we *think* is important. We haven't realized that joy can save our lives. We haven't realized that not having enough joy can kill us—at least kill our spirit. Joy makes life worth living.

To begin getting in touch with what brings you joy, get out your journal, a piece of paper, or use the space below, and take a full ten minutes to *write down* your answers to this question: *What brings me joy?* It's one thing to think about it, it's another to crystallize your thoughts into something you can write down.

You may notice that you run out of responses after the first three or four minutes, or that your responses are too general. I urge you to be clear and specific. Over the next three days, take this exercise even further and ask yourself: *what kind of job, business, relationship, interaction, project, hobby, activity, or expression of my talents brings me joy?* Write your responses down for each arena of your life. After all, if you don't know what brings you joy then there is a slim-to-none chance of joy being real in your life.

WHAT BRINGS ME JOY?

_____   _____
_____   _____
_____   _____
_____   _____

7. *Feed what you value*

A little over ten years ago, as I was beginning my journey to integrating sacred pampering and self-care into my life, I thought that having more joy and deep satisfaction in my life was a matter of "getting my priorities straight." A priority is something we regard as more important than something else. But I discovered that having more joy in my life didn't come about as a result of getting my priorities straight, but from having my actions and behaviors be *consistent* with what I *said* I valued. What you value is what you consider significant or important.

An assessment of where, how, when, and with whom we invest our time and energy is an accurate and telling barometer for where our priorities lie. We *think* that we act in accordance with what we value. This is usually not the case. Most of us are actually doing the opposite—our actions and behaviors are supporting something very different from what we *say* we value, something very different from what we *say* is important to us. Unfortunately, this is the norm.

When your behavior is at odds with what you value, you experience anxiety, dissatisfaction, "spiritual constipation," and internal conflict. These are by-products of the head-on collision of our behaviors and our values. What you value is a function of your beliefs. Someone's values, and thus his or her beliefs, show through a person's actions, behaviors, and choices. In other words, *demonstration* is the vehicle through which our values are revealed. When you say your values are one thing yet your actions and behaviors demonstrate another, you undermine your power, integrity, and spiritual energy.

Let me give you a general example. The United States of America was founded on a set of beliefs. Among these are that "all men [and women] are created equal." Additionally, it was established on a declaration to its citizens that they had certain "inalienable rights." Among these were "life, liberty and the pursuit of happiness." Yet the past and present track records of this country's treatment of *certain* of its citizens, particularly those with more melanin (pigment) in their skin, has been *far* from equal. Actually, the *actions and behaviors* of individuals and institutions in the Caucasian majority have demonstrated and continue to demonstrate the belief that this declaration did not apply to dark-skinned people. We have seen, through actions and behaviors, that the belief is *not* justice for all, but justice for *some;* certain groups of this country's citizens *can* have their "inalienable rights" alienated, or taken away.

America *says* it is a Christian nation and values democracy and "liberty and justice for all," yet the white majority has perpetuated heinous acts of brutality against other human beings in the form of chattel slavery, and continues to treat other American citizens inhumanely with blatant and condoned racism and overt discrimination.

I use this example *not* to point an accusatory finger but to tell the truth and to expose a very sick and unhealthy condition, a cultural condition that pervades our individual thinking and behavior. This same type of dynamic occurs at the individual level. You give energy and attention to what you value, whether you are an individual or a nation of people.

It is clear to me that this country does not value all of its citizens equally. It seems to actually devalue groups of people according to the amount of pigment in their skin. This is a condition that leads to intense denial as the white majority projects its ills and insecurities onto other groups, and demonizes other groups of people because they can't face up to their own demons. There is a gap between what the people of America *say* are their values and their *actual* behaviors and actions. So we must recognize that we are living in a culture with a schism between what it says it is about and what it is really about.

Learning to tell the truth about your actions and behaviors is the path to freeing your spirit, and thus your sacred inner power. To expose the contradictions between what you *say* you value and the actions and behaviors you *demonstrate* takes courage. To feed what you value, to align your energy, attention, time, and resources with what you say is important to you, starts to bring your power out of hiding. It takes courage because most people are in a cultural trance where contradiction is the norm. There is a *lot* of cultural validation for living a life where you feed what you *don't* value instead of what you do. There is a lot of validation for remaining in the trance.

To what degree are you feeding what you say you value? Many of us are feeding what we *don't* value instead of what we do. We are feeding what we think we should value, what we have been told we should value—by our parents, or our peers, or in the relentless assault of advertising, the media, or the Euro-American culture. Learning to feed what you value isn't easy, but it is power-full.

Feeding what you value can be *difficult*, not because it is inherently so but because there is a strong undertow to the contrary. We are feeding what seems to provide financial security, what protects us from facing the truth, what keeps us comfortable, what keeps things familiar. When you are feeding what you value, you begin to crack the code to the combination lock on your sacred power.

To feed what you value, first you must get clear on what you *really* value. Ten years ago, I looked up and realized I had some big gaps. I said certain things really mattered to me, but my actions and behaviors didn't match; they were incongruent. I had things I *said* I wanted in my life, yet I continued to *do* what sabotaged my having them. I said there were certain things I believed in, but my actions and behaviors demonstrated that I was operating from an opposing set of beliefs and values. I would condemn certain behavior in other people yet continue to exhibit this behavior myself.

Finally I asked myself, "What am I feeding with my attention, energy, time, and inner resources? Is it consistent with what I say I value? What are my actions and behaviors revealing about what I *really* value?" After telling the truth to myself about myself, what became clear was that I had some serious alignment issues. Instead of feeding what I say I valued, I was feeding the very opposite.

MY PROCLAIMED "VALUES"	MY ACTIONS AND BEHAVIORS
(What I *said* I valued)	(What I *really* valued as demonstrated through my actions and behaviors)
Investing money. Building wealth ⟶	Financial struggle. Living paycheck to paycheck, investing zero. Accumulating credit card debt. Spending my money on things that depreciated in value instead of what appreciated in value.
Saving money ⟶	Expending and spending. My "outgo" exceeded my income. Not paying myself first. Not saving even a small percentage of each paycheck.
Honoring my body ⟶	Eating a lot of fast food, rushing when I ate, not drinking enough water, snacking on empty calories throughout the day, being always on the go and not giving my body enough rest.
Exercising ⟶	Was inconsistent with my workouts, was easily demotivated, was often too tired to exercise. Talked a lot about *needing* to do it, but didn't.
Being fit and trim ⟶	Didn't think fit or act fit, ate for taste not nutritional value.
Relaxation, taking it easy ⟶	I was constantly rushing and always on the go.
Being in a healthy love relationship ⟶	Instead of understanding that I *attract* healthy love as a reflection of *having* healthy love for myself, I was *in pursuit, looking for and trying to find* the elusive "good man."

The first step in stopping my insanity was to call myself out—tell the truth to myself about the values I was *really* holding. My values at that time, truth be told, demonstrated a commitment to buying and spending, not to investing and saving; to dishonoring my body, not to honoring it; to being in perpetual motion, not relaxing; and I was on the hunt, trying to *find* a healthy love relationship externally, instead of first establishing a healthy love relationship internally, with myself. The gaps of contradiction were alive and well in my life.

One evening, I was having a conversation with a good friend who is an African dance instructor, seminar facilitator, and entrepreneur. She is the person I first heard use the term "feeding what you value," as she was sharing her observations about the place and space she felt a lot of women were in who she'd been working with lately in her dance classes. She explained that many women were hypocritical, saying they were about spiritual growth, their health, sisterhood, supporting one another, or being in a healthy love relationship, while their actions and behaviors were feeding something very different—jealousy, gossip, abuse of their bodies, and acts of relationship desperation. "We've got to break this cycle," she shared. "Living a lie slowly kills your spirit and undermines your power. If we're going to save ourselves, we've got to start telling the truth. We have to start feeding what we value."

Yes, it *is* possible for your life to be aligned, for your actions and behaviors to reflect what is meaningful, significant, and important to you. But you have to get out a fine-toothed comb and be willing to scratch up the contradictions. Face the gaps. Tell the truth about your own hypocrisy. Tell the truth about the inconsistencies and incongruencies in your life. The sooner you stop denying or ignoring these inconsistencies, the sooner you can be free of the gravitational pull of self-deception.

Feeding what I value means that I've had to take a stand in many areas in my life, lining up my choices and actions with what I say is important to me. Once I got married, and my husband and I had our first child, Adera; I then adapted a value of honoring family time. One of the ways I support and feed this value is by not answering the phone after 8:30 on weekday evenings. Those calling for me have to leave a message on the answering machine. The world has to wait until the next day. This is family time.

At first, friends and family still called at 9:00, 10:00, and some even at 11:00 at night. It took about a month, and then they began to get the message. Call Debrena before 8:30 P.M. and she'll answer the phone. Call after 8:30 and you'll get the answering machine. This action was one of the ways I demonstrated valuing family time as sacred time. To further "feed" and support this value, I stopped agreeing to attend meetings or volunteer activities held on Sundays. For me, Sunday was family day and a sacred day of rest.

I discovered that the path of ease begins to unfold as we close the gaps and eliminate our contradictions, and as we begin to feed what we value by aligning our actions and behaviors with what we say is important to us.

8. *Invest your energy in what brings you joy*

Many of us are dying quietly, dying because we are living lives of "quiet desperation," devoid of joy, devoid of full self-expression, devoid of authenticity. When we examine the content and substance of our lives, we don't find enough joy there. When your investments of energy in your life are not aligned with what brings you joy, your spirit is slowly eroded.

Your physical, mental, and emotional energy are expressions of your Life Force, your spirit. Do a scan of your life and ask "In who, what, where, and how am I currently investing my Life Force?" *Is your life aligned with what brings you joy?* Or is there a gap between what brings you joy and the experiences, relationships, friendships, and line of work that currently make up the content and substance of your life? Many of us are ensnared in the "gap trap" and our spirits are being worn down and depleted, making us vulnerable to spiritual, emotional, and ultimately, physical *dis-ease*. This is when joy gets displaced and your spirit starts to suffocate beneath heavy layers of stress, constant busyness, anger, anxiety, disappointment, unfulfilled expectations, and perpetual motion. It's enough to have you teetering on the edge. And that is exactly what many of us are doing—teetering precariously. Many of us feel like we are living on the edge of our sanity. We feel lost, out of control or almost out of control.

You become dangerous to others, particularly other women, when your spirit isn't being fed enough joy. You're more likely to criticize, judge, complain about, and be jealous of other women when you are not having enough experiences of joy in your *own* life, especially those that you perceive as being happier, slimmer, or prettier than you. If we don't have it, then we don't want another sister to have it, either! *Uh-huh. Who does she think she is?* When joy is *scarce* in your life, you have a hard time embracing it when you see it in someone else's.

For me, learning to invest my energy in what brings me joy has been an unfolding process over the course of the past nine years, and still continues. Five years ago, I came to realize that one of the major factors contributing to my life's being "unaligned" was my job—being an employee, working for someone else. After much agonizing and hand-wringing, I decided to stop being an employee and go full time with my own business, instead of doing my business "on the side" as I had been for four years. But there were also other arenas of my life that also needed a "joy check." So I asked myself:

What kind of mate brings me joy?
What kind of marriage relationship brings me joy?
What kind of relationship with my children brings me joy?
Use of what gifts, talents, skills, and abilities brings me joy?
What kind of close friendships and acquaintances brings me joy?
What kind of activities, interactions, and involvements brings me joy?

And in turn, I've also had to ask myself, "Who do I have to *be* in order to attract and create these types of experiences and relationships? What choices do I need to make in order to have my entire life, not just parts of it, aligned with what brings me joy?"

Did it require that I think differently? *Yes.* Did it require that I believe differently? *Yes.* Did it require that I make different choices? *Yes.* Did it require that I tell the truth to myself about how and where I'd been using or misusing my energy? *Yes.* Did it require that I increase my capacity for joy in my life? *Yes!* Did it require that I learn to consider myself worthy and deserving of a joy-full life? *Yes!* Did it require that I be willing for my life to work in all areas? *YES!*

Having your life aligned with what brings you joy is not an unattainable pipe dream or an idyllic fantasy—it's doable and achievable. It *is* possible. I believe this is how we are designed; this is how we are intended to live—

joyfully. Some of the results you can expect to experience when you begin to align your life by investing your energy in what brings you joy are:

- Having more energy and vitality in your body
- Attracting more positive, like-minded people into your life
- Feeling more on purpose
- Having more enthusiasm and passion
- Feeling more at peace
- Feeling like you have enough time
- Rarely feeling stressed
- Feeling more at ease and relaxed
- Feeling more focused
- Finding that minor body aches and pains disappear
- Attracting more abundance and blessings with less effort
- Being more clear and decisive
- Complaining and criticizing less
- Looking and feeling more radiant and energized

9. Learn to hold still

"Hold still, girl," my mama would warn every five minutes while she pressed my hair with a hot comb heated on the stove. My hair would crackle, sizzle, and smoke as Mama ran the hot comb through its parted, greased sections and I squirmed around in the chair trying not to get my ear or neck burned. *Hold still* now has a whole new meaning for me as a grown woman. As I look around, I see a lot of us squirming. We have a hard time holding still, being still, sitting still, relaxing, or chillin' out. Notice how easy it is to get caught up in rushing here and there, always being on the go? Constantly rippin' and runnin'?

To hold still means to stop moving, to take a time out, to halt the ride for a moment so that you can get off, get your bearings, get re-centered, and "be still and know." Our society has become a frantic "instant" culture. We want everything quick, fast, and in a hurry—instant pain relief, instant photo, instant gratification. We need to learn to hold still. Learning to hold still helps you to stay sane.

It is easy to get caught up in states of perpetual motion—going, going, going—from the moment your feet hit the floor in the morning until you lay your head down on your pillow at night. Holding still is about being gentle and kind to your spirit by giving it a break, a chance to recuperate, instead of abusing it and rough-handling it. We must recognize that our spirits thrive on peace, quiet, stillness, and calm, not chaos and constant activity.

Establish personal practices that keep the world from invading your every waking moment. That's right. Let the voice mail or answering machine answer your phone calls for the first hour after you get home from work. Keep the TV turned off for at least the first half-hour. Give yourself at least ten minutes to transition and decompress before shifting into second gear—preparing dinner, straightening up, checking phone messages. Give yourself ten minutes to just sit down, put your feet up, hold still, and exhale—in through your nose and out through your mouth.

A single sisterfriend, Yvette, was always rippin' and runnin',' going from "crazy-busy" at work to "crazy-busy" after work: volunteer meetings, social functions, helping out with programs at church, meeting friends for happy hour, or doing a litany of miscellaneous errands that required her to drive all over town. It was routine for Yvette to make it home around 10:00 P.M. though she got off work at 5:00, and then tumble into bed exhausted. And her weekends were no different. She was in nonstop, always-on-the-go mode. And her whole routine would begin again on Monday.

One Friday evening in late fall, I was lucky to catch Yvette at home. On the spur of the moment, I called, reached her, and invited her over to join me for a cup of tea while we chatted, listened to some jazz, and enjoyed the cozy fire I'd built. My husband had taken our three daughters over to his sister's house to visit, so it was one of those rare occasions when I had the house all to myself. While we were talking, Yvette shared that she felt dead and empty inside. After doing some soul searching, she had come to realize that being in perpetual motion and always on the go was an attempt to outrun the emptiness she was feeling. She figured she could avoid her feelings of emptiness if she could just keep herself distracted, if she could just stay busy enough, she'd escape it. She was now coming to realize that the only way to make the deadness and emptiness go away was to stop, acknowledge it, and search within for the answers to why she felt compelled to be so busy. But first, she had to *hold still* long enough to reflect and explore her interior. She first had to get herself off of this insane, high-speed treadmill she called her life so that she could look within and save herself. It worked.

For fourteen straight days, Yvette decided to come home directly after work. She bought a blank journal and three motivational books. She held still for an entire two weeks—a record for her. Through a combination of self-reflection, holding still, reading, and journaling, Yvette literally stumbled on the source of her "busy-itis." While she was holding still, she discovered that she had not fully recovered spiritually or emotionally from her boyfriend's breakup with her seven months earlier. With all of her other boyfriends, *she* had always been the one to initiate the breakup. But not only had she been in love with this boyfriend, she'd even entertained serious thoughts of marrying him. She now realized she was still carrying around feelings of emotional devastation and abandonment from the breakup, though on the outside, she appeared to be functioning normally. Once again, the breakup exposed some old, unhealed wounds she had from her relationship with her father, who had left when she was seven years old. In her mind, she couldn't keep her father around—he had "broken up" and "broken off" his relationship with her and left—and now this boyfriend had done the same thing. This fragile, unhealed wound had been oozing for years; her spiritual and psychic energy had been slowly seeping out since her dad left, the time when she first felt empty and dead on the inside. She felt as if she had failed, as if she wasn't capable of keeping a man.

Learning to hold still and go within was the beginning of her healing, the beginning of her personal breakthrough. Now Yvette is a transformed woman. She even looks different. She's at peace. She has pep in her step and a smile on her face; she laughs frequently and easily; and she is "releasing" the 15 pounds of extra weight she'd picked up since the breakup. She radiates positive energy. She has returned her attention to her goals and dreams. She spends more time at home relaxing instead of always runnin' the streets, and she's attracting men like bees to honey. Yvette now enjoys her own company. She's learned to be comfortable *holding still*.

10. *Simplify your life*

$\mathcal{E}$-mail, cellular phones, voice mail, answering machines, pagers, meetings, grocery shopping, laundry, housecleaning. It's enough to make your head spin. I know mine sure did.

We now have more technology in our lives than ever before. Technology can be insidious and very seductive, though; it can appear to make our lives easier, but it does not make the *quality* of our lives better. It has the illusion of saving or making time, when really it creates a sense of time speeding up and thus we feel we have less time, yet more to do. In turn this generates pressure and perpetuates a cycle in which we feel compelled to do more and more while feeling that we have less and less time to do it in.

You know that things need to be simplified if your life feels "heavy," too complicated, too complex, or like an arduous process. So these past few years, I've been on a mission to scale back, cut down, and make changes that yield a simpler, purer, lighter, more gratifying life.

Last year, my sister forwarded an anonymous e-mail message to me that she found on the Internet. It carried a powerful message: "We have more conveniences, but less time; more experts, but more problems; more medicine, but less wellness; we've become long on quantity, but short on quality; we have multiplied our possessions, but reduced our values; we build more computers to hold more information, but have less communication; we've conquered outer space, but not inner space." *Can I get an amen?*

The first place I looked to simplify was my personal appearance. I calculated that over the course of a month, my hair alone was costing me around $150 for appointments every two weeks, plus five hours at the salon and an additional eight hours spent prepping and curling my hair in the mornings. Then when I added in the time and money spent on my acrylic nails and nail appointments, I added another $50 a month and an additional two hours. And this didn't include the emergency "fill" appointments I had to make when I broke a nail.

With the dramatic increase in my travel schedule after the national release of my first book, I decided to make what, for me, was a drastic change. I worked up my nerve to get rid of my "relaxed look" and cut my hair into a short, two-inch, texturized style, and to get rid of my acrylic nails. What a relief it was. I felt liberated. With my short hairstyle, it took me all of five minutes in the morning to do it. I bought an inexpensive set of hair clippers from the beauty supply store and had my husband trim it for me every couple of weeks. No more worrying about the rain making my hair "go back" or the curls falling as I was on my way to a speaking engagement or appearance. No more having to put a scarf on my head at night before going to bed, waiting for curling irons to warm up, burning the tops of my ears, or being concerned about sweating out my relaxer during my workout.

More liberation came with getting rid of my acrylic nails. My fingernails had been badly damaged and weakened by five years of wearing acrylic nails, so it took me three months to rehabilitate them. But it was well worth it. No more having to be extra careful not to break a nail when putting on pantyhose or opening the car door, or avoiding certain activities, like bowling, for fear of breaking a nail.

I feel freer now, more uninhibited. I spend less money and time on my personal appearance, not because I care about it less but because I've simplified. It wasn't until *after* I simplified my personal appearance that I felt the full impact of my new freedom. Less money and time also means less maintenance needed to look good. Many of us have a high-maintenance look that we've become slaves to because we feel we don't have a choice, we don't know anything different, or we think lower maintenance means you have to look raggedy. Not so. For you, simplifying may not involve your hair and nails. *It may be something else.* The point is to evaluate your life and identify areas you can scale down and simplify. Free yourself up. Uncomplicate things. Lighten up. You can retrieve precious time, energy, and attention and direct and channel it elsewhere. I was so tickled by the sense of being more freed up that I looked for other places in my life that could be simplified. My hair and nails were just the beginning.

To simplify my workday, I started scheduling client appointments, consultations, and training sessions only on Tuesdays, Wednesdays, and Thursdays, leaving Mondays for in-office administration and followup and Fridays for relaxation and play. I stopped trying to cram so much into my day and started giving myself more time between appointments. The old way I organized my schedule had me rushing from one appointment to the next. Now I build an additional fifteen minutes into the commute time between appointments so that if the first appointment runs a little over, I still have ample time to get to my next appointment without rushing. I now arrive at appointments on time, calm, cool, and collected (most of the time!) instead of harried and ten minutes late.

One sisterfriend who is a single mom decided to get rid of her TV set completely, not just cut down on the amount her daughter was watching. She reported that her daughter started sleeping better, was less hyper, better behaved, and her schoolwork improved. Around our house, Wednesday nights are now known as "No TV Wednesdays." We've replaced the TV with reading time or a family activity.

Another sisterfriend scaled back her business and decided to work four days a week instead of five. Another friend got rid of her pager. Having to promptly return phone calls in response to everyone's pages to her throughout the day was creating too much stress for her. So she simplified others' access to her by getting rid of her pager and directing people to leave a message on her answering machine, where she would then return phone calls at *her* convenience.

I decided to let my health club membership expire, though the health club was close to home. I wanted to find something I could do without having to leave home, something that didn't require any special equipment or a workout facility. One night, my husband and I were up late watching TV and I saw an infomercial for Billy Blank's Tae Bo. This was just what the doctor ordered. I could exercise in my living room, in the comfort of my own home. And working out at home allowed my daughters to actually *see* me working out. They now join me when I do my Tae Bo workout.

Another way I simplified my life was to take a bath the night before instead of a shower "the morning of" to give myself a few more minutes of prep time. I don't talk on the phone after 8:30 at night during the week. I let the answering machine take messages and I return calls the next day. This is time for my husband and me to relax and unwind after getting the girls to bed.

Pause for a few minutes to identify three areas in your life that could use some simplifying. Come up with three things you can *start* to do or *stop* doing that would simplify your life.

K. I. S. S.—Keep it simple, sistah.

11. *Solitary refinement*

"Solitary refinement" is improving and refining your thoughts by developing your ability to be at ease being alone, doing things alone, or being by yourself. For the past ten years, I've been integrating more solitary refinement into my life, and it has been a powerful ingredient in my spiritual growth.

As women, we often feel compelled to always be doing something with someone else. We'd rather not go at all than go to a restaurant or movie by ourselves. *What would other people think?* We also have a hard time indulging in quiet pleasures alone without getting antsy, restless, distracted, or self-conscious. Yes, there are times to be with friends and family, but there are also times to be alone.

Alone time builds up your spiritual muscles. During alone time, you're able to hear yourself think. You start to hear the inner voice of your Higher Self and recognize it when it speaks to you. You are able to calm the incessant mental chatter of your mind. I think many of us have a hard time distinguishing the inner voice of our intuition from the inner chatter of our ego because we haven't spent enough time experiencing solitary refinement and becoming familiar with the "sound" and feel of our own inner voice.

Solitary refinement is a way to cultivate your intuition and tune into your heart and your gut feelings. Solitary refinement also nourishes your spirit and feeds your soul. For your awareness to grow, your clarity and peace to increase, your consciousness to expand, for patience to take root in your being, and for your intuition and discernment to become more refined, your spirit needs solitary refinement. The most desirable woman to be with is the one who can thoroughly enjoy herself, *by herself.* She treats the company of others as a bonus, as the cherry on her sundae.

Solitary refinement is also an opportunity to bring value to the simple pleasures in life. My solitary refinement time consists of experiences such as journaling, reading, writing, praying, meditating, browsing through bookstores, strolling through boutiques unrushed, walking on the waterfront pier near my home, browsing in upscale stationery stores, deciding on which fresh bouquet of flowers to buy at the Pike Place Market, or relaxing on one of the comfy couches at a Barnes & Noble bookstore with a good spiritual self-help book and a delicious Starbucks latté.

My mom's solitary refinement takes place when she quietly works in her garden pulling weeds, watering her multicolored hanging flower baskets, or reading her daily newspaper in the morning while sipping a cup of coffee at her dining room table after my little brother has been shipped off to school. Another girlfriend loves to sit under a certain tree at a park near her apartment, meditating or reading.

After I moved back to Washington State to live in Seattle after living in Los Angeles for several years, I was feeling restless, "ungrounded," and a little off-center, like a plant whose roots had lost their grip on the soil. I had grown up in Olympia, Washington, the capital of the state, a much smaller city about an hour south of Seattle. So going to college in Southern California and then living in Los Angeles for a couple of years was a big change from the calm, community-centered life I lived in Olympia.

L.A. living was not only a culture shock to me, but, as I was to realize later, also a major shock to my mind, body, and spirit. L.A. was life in the fast lane. As a culture, to me, L.A. represented excessive materialism and excessive concern about appearance, sex, and money. After only two years of living in L.A., I could feel myself beginning to change and becoming "infected" with the shallow values and beliefs of the fast-paced Southern California culture. I started absorbing more of the culture and getting more wrapped up in the lifestyle than I cared to admit. In many ways, I was starting to think and act like the same L.A. folks I would judge in a heartbeat as being selfish and superficial. So when I moved to Seattle, I was feeling the effects of my L.A. living—and it didn't feel good. I needed an antidote. My spirit was restless.

At first, I thought the logical remedy to my restlessness was to join an organization, volunteer, take some classes—channel some of the restless energy I was feeling into something "constructive" or pile more on my plate so that I didn't have time to think about being restless. Maybe I could create such a huge distraction by staying busy that I wouldn't notice it. Better yet, maybe the restlessness would just go away if I pretended it wasn't there.

Why is it that we think ignoring something will make it go away? Actually, ignoring or denying something feeds it and makes it grow bigger and loom larger in our minds. This "create distractions" strategy in the form of staying "crazy-busy" seemed logical at the time because, back then, I didn't yet realize the critical importance of quiet time, me time, alone time . . . solitary refinement.

One morning as I was driving to work, it hit me. The *last* thing I needed was more activity in my life. What I needed to do was settle down and reground myself. My spirit felt like it was floating a few feet outside of my body. I needed some solitary refinement—quiet time with myself and by myself so that I could come back down to earth, get some clarity, do some reflection, refine my focus, and come back to myself. This was the antidote I was seeking. Ideally I wanted to get away for several days and take a short vacation. But I had been working in my new position with our family business for only one month and I did not have any vacation time earned yet. So instead I decided to vacation without going anywhere.

My vacation was a two-week period during which I practiced some serious solitary refinement. This solitary refinement period involved my coming straight home from work every day for two weeks, sprawling out on the floor or across my couch, keeping the TV turned off, and replacing it with journaling, listening to jazz, sipping a cup of herbal tea or a glass of wine, and reading, reading, reading. I almost went nuts the first two days—the quiet almost drove me crazy. As soon as I'd settle down to start reading, I'd think of a reason to jump up to get something or do something. The phone would ring and I'd jump up and answer it.

At first, I had a hard time easing into solitary refinement for more than ten minutes at a time. Thoughts kept streaming through my head and bumping into one another. I was surprised at how wired and revved up my inner system was. I was a restless mess! I learned that being comfortable and at ease with my self and by my self was not as easy as I thought it would be. These two weeks of solitary refinement turned out to be two of the most powerful weeks of my life. My solitary refinement had the effect of "reanchoring" and "rerooting" me and getting me back on track. I learned to exhale, calm down, slow down, and savor solitude.

There are times in our lives when we have to roll up our sleeves and do the *self work* that no one else can do for us. Solitary refinement is one of these types of self work. You have to go this portion of the road alone. Just you and God. This is a part of life that develops character and inner peace. It tones your spiritual muscles. You learn to develop an internal point of reference for your joy. You learn that joy *already* exists inside of you. *Joy is not found outside of you.*

Perpetual motion and nonstop busy-ness erodes and depletes your spirit. Most of us wait until we feel we're almost at the end of our rope before we call a *time out* to recenter and reground ourselves. Or we can *integrate* solitary refinement into our lives, as a way to *stay* rooted and grounded instead of trying to regroup once we feel ourselves starting to float away, lose touch or get overwhelmed.

Solitary refinement is food for your spirit. Eat it up.

12. *Get back to nature*

I felt the tree scream.
          One morning around 10:30 I was about to get in my car to head to a client appointment, and I heard, *no, I felt* a high-pitched gut-wrenching scream of anguish and agony. I walked around the parking lot of our condominium looking for the child who screamed in pain. Maybe a knee had been badly scraped from a fall off of a bicycle or a little hand had gotten slammed in a door. No signs of any kids in distress. It was quiet and still since it was midmorning and most of the kids in our complex were in school.

The only activity was across the parking lot. My neighbor, Matt, had the door open and the lights on in his garage turned wood shop. Matt was quite the handyman around our condo complex, and also president of the condo association. On any given day you might see Matt changing a bulb in one of the sidewalk lamps, replacing the fluorescent lights in the carport area, or planting new shrubs in the bark bed. This particular morning, as I walked toward Matt, I could see he was bent over, concentrating on saw strokes as he cut down a young pine tree in the center bark bed with his handsaw.

As I walked closer, the screaming got louder. *Oh, my God. It's the tree that is screaming. I can actually feel it.* I dropped my purse and bag in the middle of the parking lot and started running toward Matt. As I ran toward him, I shouted, *"Matt, why are you cutting down that little tree!? It's not hurting anything!"* Looking up nonchalantly without missing a lick with his saw, Matt replied, "This tree has gotten too big and it's limiting visibility. We're going to plant some small shrubs here instead." Five seconds later, the little tree flopped to the ground with a dull thud. *And the screaming stopped.*

I stood there almost in tears looking at Matt, looking at the tree, feeling frustrated and helpless, and suddenly, very, very sad. "Matt, you didn't have to cut that little tree down," I said weakly. "Oh well, it's done now," he replied casually, as he shrugged his shoulders. Then he turned on his heels and strolled back to his wood shop.

This experience affected me deeply. It changed my mind and my beliefs about the consciousness of trees and plants. I could hear and actually feel that little tree screaming as it was being sliced down by Matt's saw. I didn't hear the scream with my ears; I heard it *inside* of my body. That little tree could feel and communicate.

I've read numerous metaphysical books that discussed people who could communicate with trees, plants, dolphins, whales, their pets, even rocks and minerals. I didn't find it weird or far-out, I just didn't understand how the communication occurred since it wasn't vocalized as it is when two people talk. Now I understood.

As we have disconnected from nature, we have gotten more and more disconnected from ourselves and our own true nature. In many instances, we've used distorted interpretations of the Bible to justify our rape, pillage, and abuse of Mother Earth. Genesis 1:26 says "Let us make man in our image, after our likeness, and let him have dominion over . . . all the earth and over every creeping thing that creepeth upon the earth." Herein lies the origin of the problem. The word *dominion* has gotten us in big trouble. I believe that God's intention, which probably was intact before the various revisions, alterations, and distortions of the Bible took place, was for man and woman to *steward* the earth, not dominate it. I believe, as humans, we are to recognize ourselves as caretakers of Earth, not conquerors and exploiters.

Indigenous cultures of color have a legacy of honoring and respecting Mother Earth, treating her as a living entity, and seeing themselves as *part* of nature, part of Her, cohabitants with the other creatures of the Earth. Not dominators. There is a correlation between how we treat Mother Earth and her dark body, and how we collectively treat our own bodies.

America calls itself a First World country, yet we are the sickest of the industrialized nations. We continue to pollute our bodies with preservatives and chemically treated food, just as we continue to dump chemicals into Mother Earth's body, burying nuclear waste beneath her crust and dropping other waste into her bloodstream—her rivers and streams. We rape her of natural resources without honoring her sacredness, or considering the damage it does to the habitat or the wildlife, just as we rape one another of spiritual energy or sexually violate one another. The rain forests, woods, and jungles we are destroying and clear-cutting represent her lungs. The topsoil that is being washed away or eroded when we remove the trees and plants that hold the soil together represents her skin. Her oceans represent her digestive system.

As our culture has gone more and more high-tech, we've gotten more and more out of touch with nature. We worship technology like a savior, like a god. We worship with our microwaves, cell phones, digital pagers, electronic planners, fax machines, and voice mail systems. "Our Machine Culture," as Malidoma Somé calls western culture in his book *Ritual: Power, Healing and Community*, "generates a force field inside of which one is enslaved." Meanwhile, we sell our souls and become slaves to the technology we've created—all in the name of "progress."

So we must get back to nature, and in doing so, we also get back to ourselves and our true nature. There are small steps you can take to reconnect with nature. Count the number of live plants in your home. Do you have at least three? If not, increase the amount of living greenery in your home. Plants have the ability to purify the energy in our homes, absorbing our toxic, negative energy and transforming it into fertilizer for their roots. If you have plants in your home, touch and talk to them when you water them. Visit a park, or go to your yard if you have one, and sit *on* the grass or the ground—not in a lawn chair, chaise lounge, or at a picnic table, but on the ground. Feel the earth. Make direct contact. No yard or park nearby? Then try sitting down on the floor in your home. Sit on the floor while you do your bills, watch TV, play with your kid(s), or talk on the phone. Having contact with the ground has the effect of actually grounding you.

As a special treat, our family will sit on the floor in the living room on a big blanket and eat dinner. I get out the paper plates, paper cups, and plastic forks just as if we were outdoors. Our daughters love it! When we hold our family conferences, we sit on the floor in the living room while we talk and share.

The Women's Advance held every year in March takes place at a private retreat home site about an hour and a half outside of Seattle, in a rustic, natural setting overlooking Puget Sound. This natural setting facilitates and actually accelerates the healing that takes place and also contributes to the powerful effects the experience has on the minds, bodies, and spirits of the women that attend.

In the middle of the back porch of the retreat home stands a huge evergreen tree with a trunk that is ten feet around. The woman who owns the retreat home tells the story of how the tree helped her to heal herself of uterine cancer. She hugged that tree every day, giving it the accumulated anger, resentment, remorse, regret, guilt, and wounded feminine power that were the spiritual and emotional root causes of what grew into her uterine cancer. During this time of recovery, she also worked on changing her food diet, her *thought* diet, her *belief* diet, and on forgiving herself, her ex-husband, and other loved ones in her life. And she was able to heal herself. This was ten years ago. To this day, her cancer has remained in remission.

Before participants leave the Advance, they are encouraged to hug the tree. For many of the women, particularly those who live in urban areas, hugging this healing tree is one of the more powerful experiences of the day for them. It's been a long time since many of the women have touched a living tree, not to mention hugged one. Many shed tears as they feel the tree graciously absorbing and receiving their melting resentment, anger, fear, and pain, and returning love. Women have described the feeling of the tree returning its love as a wave of warmth spreading throughout their bodies as if someone were pouring warm oil over them.

My mom and dad live on eight acres of lakeside land in Olympia, about an hour south of the part of Seattle where my family and I live. After the birth of each of our three daughters, the proud grandparents planted a tree for each one to commemorate her arrival. My oldest daughter, Adera, went as far as to name her tree Harvin Melville (Yes, Harvin with an "H"). When I asked her how she came up with the name, she told me that she could feel that it was a boy tree. On those special occasions when our daughters go to visit Grandma and Grandpa for the weekend, they water their trees and talk to them. I wonder if my mom and dad know that this is also an old African tradition. And during the summer, they help Grandma cut chrysanthemums and dahlias from her flowerbed, and pick fresh collard greens, tomatoes, string beans, peppers, carrots, and onions from her garden. They have a chance to touch living plants, put their hands in the soil, touch the earth, and get back to nature.

Look around and come up with ways you can get more reconnected. Get back to nature, and you get back to yourself.

13. *Take a personal retreat*

*F*olks who know me well know I *love* to host sisterfriend gatherings. I think it is crucial to our spiritual and emotional well-being to gather with other sisters. But I think it is just as important to be able to gather with *your-self*—to be able to feel at ease spending quality time with yourself. Have you ever taken a retreat by yourself, not with a friend or a group? In February 1994, I decided to do just that—take my first personal retreat. No husband, no kids, no girlfriends. Just me, myself, and I.

In a phone conversation months earlier, I met a wonderful woman who had seen an advertisement for the original self-published version of my first book, *Sacred Pampering Principles,* in a newspaper she subscribed to. She was so excited after seeing the advertisement for my book that she tracked down my phone number using directory assistance and called me. We had an instant connection and rapport.

After a series of telephone conversations and letters back and forth over the course of the next six months, a new friendship budded. My new friend, Debra, invited me to come and visit her in Sedona, Arizona. Over the years, I had heard many stories and read books about the mystique and allure of Sedona. It was considered a very powerful sacred site, much like the Egyptian pyramids I had visited in North Africa. I told her I'd give her an answer to her invitation as soon as I had a chance to talk it over with my husband, Joe. I decided that this trip would become a personal retreat. It would also be a great way to kick off the new year.

Though I hadn't physically met Debra yet, I'd met her in spirit. I knew she was a good, loving person. Joe, on the other hand, was not so convinced. He had his doubts. He asked how I could feel comfortable going to stay at a stranger's house in another state for four days. I assured him that Debra was no longer a stranger but had become a friend. He could see that taking this trip was something I really wanted to do. Finally, Joe agreed to the trip and sent me off with his blessings.

To get to Debra's in Sedona, I had to fly into Phoenix, Arizona, and then travel by van for another two hours. Debra knew what time the van was to arrive and was waiting outside of her condo for me when the van pulled up. I jumped out of the van and ran to give her a big hug. The way we hugged each other, giggling and swaying in delight, you would have thought we were two long-lost sisters who had finally been reunited.

The next three days of my life were magical, like heaven on earth. Debra had a lovely home that had me feeling like I'd entered a queen's chamber. Her home was decorated in soothing combinations of shell colors in sea foam green, aqua, and mauve, with a large comfy couch and chaise lounge sprinkled with lavish oversized pillows. Out of any window in her house I had a breathtaking view of the red rock formations Sedona is so famous for, jutting into the sky like the silhouette of a city skyline. She had a crystal-clear sound system and an extensive collection of angelic, high-toned music that softly floated out of her stereo and filled her home. She encouraged me to sleep in every day, wake up naturally, stay in my pajamas as long as I liked, play her CD collection, and read her metaphysical books to my heart's content.

Each day she'd prepare delicious, mouthwatering meals with freshly picked organic vegetables and herbs from her garden. Then around 1:00 P.M. we'd set out for the daily excursion she had planned. The second day we drove to the hilltop plateau where the city's tiny airport was located, for a bird's-eye view of Sedona's panorama of red rocks and stunning Grand Canyon–like cliff formations. The third day we paid a visit to the local metaphysical bookstore, where I bought a crystal that I swear I could feel pulsating in my hand. The fourth day, we went on a hike into the foothills of a nearby mountain to an ancient, sacred Hopi Indian site. We stood in the middle of a medicine wheel that had been assembled with rocks, held hands, and prayed together for an hour. From time to time while we were praying, I'd peek out of one eye and look around; it felt as if someone was staring at me. The presence of the energy of the Hopi that used to dwell in the hillsides of this particular area was so intense that it felt as if the hills had eyeballs that were watching our every move.

At the end of each day, I'd spill my thoughts, reflections, and insights onto the pages of my special personal retreat journal. When I returned home, I was a different woman. I was renewed, relaxed, and rejuvenated. While I was in Sedona, I did a lot of praying and meditating, trying to soak up the energy that was so highly charged it hung in the air like it was throbbing and pulsating. I absorbed so much energy into my body while I was there that, for a week after I had returned, my cordless phone would go haywire with static when I put it to my ear and my radio couldn't transmit a clear signal if I was within ten feet of it. I even blew out a light bulb in one of our lamps when I reached to turn it off! You might say I was also reenergized after my trip to Sedona. I certainly had a new sense of clarity, focus, and vision for the new year.

It may not be possible for you to go away to such a destination for your personal retreat. You may have to get creative, as some of my friends have done, and take a personal retreat without leaving the city or town in which you live. A reader from Baltimore wrote me and shared that she now retreats and regroups by going on a "phone fast" for ten straight days. She does not make or take any phone calls once she arrives home from work for ten days. Another sisterfriend, Darlene, calls in to work sick once every six months and takes a "sick" day, though she isn't really sick. She knows that calling in to request a wellness day off would be rejected. But she knows that taking a periodic wellness day for herself actually helps prevent her from becoming sick. It helps keep her mind and body well so that she doesn't have to take a real sick day. On her wellness day, she turns her phone ringer off and retreats from the world and her hectic routine to nurture her spirit and feed her soul.

My friend Maureen was feeling as if she were on the verge of a nervous breakdown. Her five-year relationship with her live-in boyfriend was coming apart at the seams; her employer had notified her that she was going to be laid off at the end of the month; and her car had stopped running and needed $900 worth of repairs. Two months prior to the onset of this series of events, she had agreed to take on a publicity project for me. Halfway through the project, I began to notice that Maureen was taking several days to return my phone calls, and she wasn't following up on "to do" items she'd committed to. On one occasion, I finally made phone contact after the fifth attempt in three days. She seemed highly distracted, harried, flustered, and scattered in her thinking. I mentioned to her that she seemed to be "off, not herself" and "out of it." In a weak, despondent voice that sounded worn-out and heavy with fatigue, she explained the many challenges that had converged in her life. She just didn't know if she could take it. She felt overwhelmed and overloaded. She was worried about being able to satisfactorily complete the publicity project. I assured her I would find someone else to complete the work and suggested that she make her sanity and well-being her new priority project. She admitted that she needed a break, badly, but she couldn't afford to take a vacation. I suggested that she "vacate" without taking a vacation by taking a sabbatical. I knew that a sabbatical was typically a leave of absence taken by a teacher or professor to study or write a book, but it seemed like the best word to describe what Maureen needed most right now—a leave of absence from her life, from its drama, and from her usual responsibilities. She really liked the idea.

She decided to begin her sabbatical after her last day of work in two weeks. She took the time during this interim to notify her family and close friends of her decision to take a thirty-day "leave" so that they wouldn't worry about her when she didn't return their phone calls. Maureen didn't leave town. She didn't go to a hotel. She just went underground and incognito for a month so she could take a break from her life, recenter and reground her spirit, and get back to herself.

A powerful woman recognizes that she must take breaks. She needs to retreat once in a while for a well-being break. She recognizes that stress suppresses her spirit and her vitality, so she takes regular breaks to allow her spirit to rejuvenate itself. Are you due for a personal retreat? After all, you deserve a break today.

14. *Practice self-care first*

*P*racticing *self-care first* isn't selfish. It's smart, and it makes good sense. Practicing self-care first means nurturing, renewing, and fortifying your mind, body, and spirit first, *before* attempting to nurture, renew, and fortify others. Self-care first means replenishing your well and refilling your own tank before trying to fill someone else's.

Why does practicing self-care first serve both you and others? *Because you can only give away what you have.* And if you are not filled first, you will subconsciously look to someone or something else to "fill" you. This dynamic is at the root of many of our addictions, codependent tendencies, "parasitic" relationships, and intense need to receive approval from others.

If you're constantly rippin' and runnin' and "burning the candle at both ends," you're probably suffering from a joy shortage and "spiritual malnutrition." Spiritual malnutrition sets in when you don't stop to refuel, reenergize, rejuvenate, and renew regularly as part of your life routine. Self-care first is about countering the effects of spiritual malnutrition and making renewal of your mind, body, and spirit a nonnegotiable, uncompromised part of your life.

When you operate from a place of renewal instead of being worn out, tired, and depleted, there is more of you present and available to meet all of your responsibilities and commitments; there is more of you present and available to share and give to your relationships, friendships, work, and family. The best news is that everybody wins when you have a self-care first approach to living your life. A self-care first approach creates a win-win situation for you and your loved ones.

There is a sequence to self-care. But for a long time, I had it all wrong. I thought that the way to have it all work was to tend to and take care of other people and other responsibilities in my life *first*, then salvage some time for self-care and "me time" from what was left over. More often than not, there were no "leftovers."

Guess what happens when you continually put yourself last? Others get very used to taking all that you are offering. Others get accustomed to using up all of the energy you make available to them. Not because they are cruel and malicious, but because our actions and behaviors encourage and allow it. We give others permission through our behavior. We *train* others how to treat us, and our behavior and way of being establishes boundaries to honor or dishonor; and others respond accordingly. When we have the self-care sequence out of order, and think *self-care should be last*, we set ourselves up to be taken for granted, underappreciated, overextended, overworked, and undernurtured.

There are many unhealthy by-products to living our lives in a self-care-last mode. Physical diseases can start to manifest in our bodies as a result of neglecting our inner renewal needs. Some of these diseases include diabetes; upper respiratory illnesses of the throat, sinuses, chest, and bronchial tubes; chronic fatigue; cancer, or being twenty pounds or more over the weight that works best for your bone and body structure.

The sequence that is most empowering for you *and* for others in your life is *self-care first*. I'm not suggesting that you care *only* for yourself, but that you take care of yourself *first*. At its core, self-care is about wisely managing and using your energy—your physical, spiritual, and psychic energy—so that you can give more fully *of* yourself by first giving *to* yourself. This is particularly important to remember if you have kids. A tremendous amount of our energy is used just feeding and maintaining the bodies in our households. Just look at the amount of energy invested and time spent taking care of other people's bodies alone: shopping for food (to feed bodies); shopping for clothes (to cover bodies); washing, folding, and putting away clothes (for the bodies to wear); preparing meals (for the bodies to eat); and cleaning up (after bodies have made a mess)! As a mom, you can look up and be so absorbed in your mothering role that you lose yourself somewhere along the way.

If you've ever flown in a plane, you're familiar with the safety procedures demonstrated by the flight attendant or shown on the safety video prior to takeoff. If you are an adult flying with children or someone who needs your assistance, you are instructed to put on your *own* oxygen mask *first*, before assisting others. Why is this? It seems to make perfect sense when it comes to airplane safety. However, you will discover that it also makes perfect sense when it comes to your life. If you're wasting away, gasping for air while trying to help someone else with his or her oxygen mask first, not only will you probably perish but the person you're trying to help will probably perish, too. We have a lot to learn from this airplane safety procedure. What it reveals is the proper self-care sequence: *fortify yourself first*. Get your own "oxygen mask" on first before trying to help, tend to, assist, or save someone else. Yet, metaphorically, we continue to try and put oxygen masks on everyone else first in our lives, and then wonder why we feel so worn out, so tired, so "short of breath."

Put your oxygen mask on first. This is what self-care is about.

15. *Plug your energy leaks*

At one point in my life, my energy wasn't just leaking out, it was spilling out all over the place. At the time, I didn't know that the symptoms I was experiencing had anything to do with a loss of my *spiritual* energy—I thought I just needed to get more rest.

I was tired most of the time. Forty pounds overweight, eating too much fast food; I wasn't taking time out of my busy nonstop workday to eat a decent lunch, and when I did, I sucked it down. I was saying yes to too much. I had to hit the snooze alarm three times in the morning before I was able to get up. I got to bed late three to four nights a week, then I rushed getting ready for work in the morning. I had a hard time unwinding and relaxing. I was sexually involved with too many men. I was always on the go. My expenses equaled my income, and I wasn't saving or investing any of my paycheck. I was also squandering my spiritual bank account, and as a result, my account was constantly overdrawn and "tapped out."

You have a spiritual energy field that is real, and there are factors that cause it to either expand or shrink. Many of us don't realize that our thoughts, beliefs, words, emotions, interactions, and experiences either expand or diminish this energy field. Your energy field extends out from your body and surrounds it like a capsule. Another word for your spiritual energy field is your aura—normally your energy field extends eight to ten feet out from your body. And it's not just people who have energy fields; all matter is surrounded by energy fields. Some people have the ability to see this field.

In his book *How to See and Read the Aura*, Ted Andrews explains that "the more vitalized your auric field, the more energy you will have to do the things you need and wish to do." And even more important, "the stronger your aura is, the less likely you are to be affected by outside forces." In other words, when you have a weak auric energy field, outside influences are more likely to encroach upon you. You are more easily manipulated, and you get tired more easily. Your energy field starts to "leak"—or in my case, spill—when you are too outer directed, outer focused, and focused on others. The "others" at this time in my life were men and social activities and events. When your energy is leaking, it translates into restlessness, emptiness, frequently feeling "drained," boredom, being resigned, not being able to produce positive results in your life, or having health problems. As you start to plug and seal up your energy leaks and stop the hemorrhaging of your precious energy, you strengthen your energy field.

At that point in my life, I didn't know much about the nature of my energy field, let alone that I had one. I didn't know that certain types of thoughts, behaviors, words, and interactions could either weaken or strengthen my energy field. Yes, our auras ebb and flow, mingle, pulsate, and interact with the auras of others; they even have colors. Usually babies and kids can see and experience the colors of the aura—that is, before we socialize it out of them or shut them down by making comments that cause them to doubt what they are seeing. As adults we may ask "Why did you put a pink bubble around the flower you drew?" or "You shouldn't color your teacher green." Could it be that children are using the color to depict the aura they see?

When my third daughter, Kenzie, was born, I noticed that she looked intently at people, and looked *around* them before she would let someone hold her. I believe she was "reading" their aura, checking them out before she felt comfortable going to them. So now, I know to pause a minute or so before I let someone hold her. When she smiles or holds out her arms, I know she's ready. If I wasn't aware of auras and I didn't honor her get-acquainted process, I could unknowingly undermine her sense of security.

You have probably experienced the presence of energy fields before, but didn't know what to call it or didn't know you were interacting with someone's energy field. Read the following statements to find out. If you answer yes to any of them, you have experienced the effects of the energy field.

1. You feel drained around certain people.
2. You feel drained after talking on the phone to certain people.
3. You have felt someone staring at you across a room.
4. You have walked into a room and immediately begun to feel anxious or nervous.
5. You have felt attached to a particular object.
6. You feel more comfortable sitting in a particular place or seat.
7. You can walk into someone's home and sense whether it is a peaceful or a tense household.

8. You feel an instant rapport or connection with someone you've just met.
9. You have an instant dislike for someone.
10. You feel a special affinity for a certain plant, tree, pet, or animal.
11. You are able to sense how someone is feeling, even if they are far away.
12. You feel more energized, excited, creative, or self-expressed around certain people.
13. You can feel when a friend or loved one isn't feeling well or is upset, though you haven't spoken to or seen him or her lately.

These are all cases of reading or exchanging energy with someone or something. Even after people die, some of their energy field may linger for a while, explaining why you may still feel their presence in a certain place or space. Everyone and everything with an energy field has a vibration. Hence the comments we make about someone's "vibes" being good or bad. You are picking up on their energy.

Since our personal energy field is constantly interacting and intermingling with the energy fields of others, it's important to be aware of the types of thoughts, behaviors, actions, and interactions that weaken or drain your personal energy field and those that strengthen, energize, or expand it.

I offer this information to increase your understanding of the effects of what may seem like everyday trivial choices. I am slowly and gently trying to make changes in the daily choices I make about what I eat, what I do with and to my body, and how I choose to respond to situations. Where you sense energy drains in your life is where you must plug the leaks.

To plug or seal up energy leaks in your personal relationships and friendships, you may need to decrease the amount of time you spend and energy you invest in certain family members or friends. You may be in a marriage or romantic relationship that is toxic or stagnant and needs to be revitalized or brought to a close. You may need to move some friends to the balcony in your life who have had prime seats in the "front row" of your life, as Susan L. Taylor tells us. You may need to bring more balance to your relationships by making more requests, asking for help, deleting some names from your address book, going places that attract a different element of people, or making a point to connect with more like-minded sistahs on the grow.

Take a good, hard look at the activities, interactions, and relationships that make up the content and substance of your life, and assess where,

Actions, Behaviors, or Interactions That Weaken or Drain Your Aura	Actions, Behaviors, or Interactions That Strengthen or Energize Your Aura
Being sedentary—not moving enough	Moving and stretching your body regularly
Self-care last	Self-care first
Carrying extra weight on your body	Eating food in its most natural form (not treated, processed, milled, canned, etc.)
Breathing sealed, stale air (i.e., inside buildings, in homes, in malls)	Breathing fresh air
Consuming alcohol, including wine and mixed drinks	Getting in contact with the earth. Touching plants, grass, trees, rocks
Consuming drugs, whether prescribed or over-the-counter	Correct breathing from the diaphragm instead of from the upper chest
Smoking cigarettes, cigars, or a pipe	Sleeping soundly, being well rested
A negative thought diet—thoughts of negative criticism, judgment of self or others, thoughts of lack and limitation	Experiencing joy and pleasure
Stress	Stroking and touching your body
Anger or fear	Seeing or touching natural, live bodies of water (i.e., ocean, lake, river, pond)

energetically, there is an imbalance of give and receive, or reciprocity. An energetic imbalance can indicate an *inequity of reciprocity*, which creates spiritual leaks. An inequity of reciprocity exists when your energy exchanges tend to be give-give-give-give-receive, invest-invest-invest-no return, or feed-feed-feed-and not be fed. You experience equity of reciprocity when your energy flows out to others and then is returned back to you, when it moves in a circle and is recycled instead of going only in one direction—away from you. An equity of reciprocity seals up energy leaks and establishes a balance of give and receive.

Start to gently but diligently plug your energy leaks. Establish more "energetic equity" in your life, and watch your energy, vitality, clarity, intention, joy, focus, your ability to create, your ability to manifest, and your ability to attract what you say you want *increase* tenfold. Pampering, which is aligning your life with what brings you joy and peace, has the effect of actually acting as a *sealant* for your energy leaks. If you make pampering more real in your life you will also be making joy more real in your life. The more real pampering is in your life, the more joy is real in your life. Both self-love and joy seal your energy leaks. When self-love is real in your life, you make choices that honor and show high regard for your energy.

Your energy is precious. Plug your leaks.

16. *Get ready, get set, grow!*

⌒ We are designed and wired for growing, loving, expanding, and evolving. So why is it many of us resist? When we avoid stretching ourselves and growing and choose to stay in ignorance or denial, we stagnate. Stagnation is against our true nature. Growth is our true nature. Life asks us to grow since it is a journey and not a destination. When we resist growth, we create short circuits in our minds, bodies, and spirits that result in unnecessary suffering.

In her book *In the Spirit*, Susan L. Taylor urges you to remember that "all the daily affairs that engross you—your goals, your relationships, the blessings that delight you, the challenges that make you struggle—are the Creator's way of engaging you, focusing your attention so that you keep moving onward, keep correcting your course." Indeed, it is easy to forget that life is not a destination; there is no place to "arrive" at—it is a forever unfolding process.

How you move through this unfolding process called Life is up to you. Life has a bias toward your growth, whether you realize it or not. You can either resist it, avoid it, try to run away, grit your teeth and struggle your way through it, or *grow* through it. Remember: *life doesn't have to be about suffering.* Yes, you can choose to grow, to acknowledge and welcome it. It's your choice. You can "do" life however you choose. If you're not sure which way you've decided to move through it, take a look at the themes that have characterized your life. When we choose the path of resistance, our lives tend to be painful, overly effort-full, or a struggle.

Personally, I am striving to live my life as if it were a river—able to calmly flow over and around obstacles or challenges. When a river encounters a log or boulder in its path, it doesn't panic, freak out, come to a standstill, or start sweating bullets. It incorporates the log or boulder into its flow and continues to flow on. I haven't reached "river" status yet though; I'm still more like a little stream. But I'm working on it. I still find myself seeing "logs" or "boulders" in my path, and I get worried, anxious, or concerned. I am striving to develop an unshakable faith. I am working on being able to see a log or boulder in my path, remain calm, cool, and collected, and think "Nooooo problem."

Often there are places in our lives where we are trying to *force* the logs and rocks out of the way. But if we step back for a moment, take a deep breath, exxxxxhale, and ask ourselves *"What purpose does this log serve? What is the learning here?,"* then what we previously perceived as an obstacle can be transformed before our very eyes. It becomes part of our growth process, propelling us onward, instead of seeming to stop it or slow it down.

Are you ready? Are you set? Well, then GROW ON, GIRL!

17. *The pleasure principle*

*How willing are you to give yourself
permission to experience pleasure?*

$\mathcal{I}$ n their book *Inner Joy*, authors Harold Bloomfield and Robert Kory make a poignant observation: "For most of us, pleasure is a highly regulated reward we believe we must earn. . . . The belief that pleasure is harmful arises from confusion between the experience of pleasure and excess in the pursuit of it." So true, so true.

As a little girl, I remember receiving confusing messages about joy and pleasure in church. What I thought I was hearing was that to experience pleasure was sinful, ungodly. This didn't seem right to me. This didn't seem to make much sense, either. I couldn't understand why God would create us with senses that allow us to fully take in the world around us if She didn't want us to experience pleasure. I couldn't understand why God would create such a beautiful dwelling place for us, Earth, if She didn't want us to experience pleasure. If God didn't want us to experience pleasure, why would She create us with the capacity to experience love, joy, bliss, and delight?

The church was not the only place we may have received confusing messages. We heard "life is short so enjoy it" while at the same time we were told "life isn't just fun and games, it's also a lot of hard work" or "business before pleasure." We've consumed and absorbed images from TV and the silver screen that show the obsessive pursuit of pleasure on one hand and "good hard-working people" on the other who don't have the *luxury* or the time to be concerned with "idle indulgences" such as pleasure. You put it all together, and what do you have? A culture that has a lot of fear and contradiction with regard to pleasure.

Pleasure does not discriminate. And it does not play favorites. Pleasure is joy's first cousin. Authentic pleasure cannot be bought, sold or traded. We can receive pleasure from big things and little things alike. The pleasure that is experienced when taking a warm bath sprinkled with drops of soothing rose essential oil is not better than the pleasure experienced from completing a challenging project successfully. It's a matter of *allowing* your body to feel pleasure and giving yourself permission to experience pleasure.

I can experience pleasure while combing and braiding my daughters' hair every morning before they go to school; potting flowers every summer in my hanging flower baskets on my porch; riding in my car on a classic rainy Seattle day listening to the jazz station on the radio; enjoying warm Marie Callender's Cherry Pie topped with Breyer's Vanilla Bean ice cream on a Friday night while snuggling on the couch watching a video with my husband; looking at fresh flowers sitting in a vase on my dining room table; being able to sit and read without interruption for a good hour; standing at my kitchen sink washing dishes watching the girls squeal and giggle in delight as Joe gives them horsey-back rides around the living room; having a good laugh on the phone with a sisterfriend; good service, good food, and good company at a restaurant with great ambience; painting my fingernails without smudging any of the polish before it dries; inviting friends over for a home-cooked meal and enlightening conversation; or sitting around on the floor with a bunch of girlfriends sipping herbal tea or wine and talking about life, love, the black experience, healing, and spirituality.

Pleasure is readily available to you, regardless of the day of the week, how young or old you are, the amount of money you make or don't make, or the color of your skin. Your body is the channel and the medium for experiencing pleasure, so if you are tense and tight, pleasure has a hard time moving through your body. When your body is tense, rigid, and tight, it has the same effect that tying knots in a garden hose has on the water's ability to move and flow through the hose freely. The kinks in the hose keep the water from freely flowing through. Likewise, the "kinks" in our spirits and our emotions prevent pleasure from flowing freely through our bodies.

Our blockages to experiencing pleasure even affect our sex lives. I believe that the reason many of us have difficulty reaching orgasm is because our bodies are congested with tension, worry, anxiety, and stress, all of which squeeze off the flow of pleasure. You have a difficult time experiencing pleasure when the flow of feeling in your body is restricted. So you must more fully open your body to the flow of energy and thus the experience of pleasure.

In order to allow yourself to experience pleasure, you have to let go and allow your body to respond. One way to more fully open up your body to the flow of energy is through bodywork. Bodywork focuses on working with the body in a way that is therapeutic and healing. It involves working directly on the body, or working with the body's energy field. Bodywork, which is administered by a bodywork practitioner, helps to return the body to its natural state of grace, flexibility, and fluid movement.

Massage is the form of bodywork that most of us are familiar with, but massage is just one form of bodywork. There are many. Here is a partial list of bodywork you may want to consider having done. If you experience tightness, soreness, tension, constriction, weakness, restricted breathing, headaches, bodily aches and pains, or low energy in your body, these could be signs that blockages exist that are inhibiting or compromising your ability to experience pleasure more fully. Below is a general overview of some of the various forms of bodywork.

NAME OF BODYWORK MODALITY	GENERAL DESCRIPTION
Acupressure	*Method:* finger pressure at key points on the body *Purpose:* relieve tension, stress, aches, pains, and cramps
Acupuncture	*Method:* fine needles are inserted at key points along the body *Purpose:* stimulate and regulate the flow of the body's vital energy, relieve acute and chronic conditions
Alexander Technique	*Method:* hands-ons guidance and verbal instruction *Purpose:* relieve tension and pain, improve posture and balance
Bioenergetics	*Method:* physical movements and breathing techniques *Purpose:* relieve chronic muscular tension and free repressed emotions and desires
Deep Tissue Bodywork	*Method:* massage of deep connective tissue and muscles *Purpose:* relieve lower back and neck pain and treat degenerative diseases such as multiple sclerosis
Feldenkrais Method	*Method:* movement, touch and verbal dialogue *Purpose:* align the body, relieve stress, tension, and improve balance and coordination

NAME OF BODYWORK MODALITY	GENERAL DESCRIPTION
Hellerwork	*Method:* deep tissue muscle therapy, movement, and verbal dialogue *Purpose:* treat chronic pain
Myofacial Release	*Method:* hands-on manipulation *Purpose:* free the body's tightened connective tissue, especially good for chronic back pain and headaches
Reflexology	*Method:* pressure applied to specific points on the feet and hands *Purpose:* relieve stress-related ailments
Reiki	*Method:* hand placement on the body to direct healing energy *Purpose:* alleviate emotional and mental distress, and acute and chronic physical problems
Rolfing	*Method:* deep manipulation of the connective tissue *Purpose:* restore the body's alignment, good for treating body rigidity from an injury or emotional trauma
Yoga	*Method:* position and breathing techniques *Purpose:* align the body, promote the flow of energy to the body's chakras (energy centers). Note: there are many forms of yoga. *Yoga* is a general term.

If bodywork is a new concept to you, try starting with a simple massage. You will feel like a new woman after a massage. Inexpensive massages are available through massage schools where practitioners in training are looking to "earn their hours" for their license, through some beauty salons, and through day spas, physical therapy offices, hotel fitness centers, and individual practitioners, some who will give you a massage in the comfort of your own home using a special portable massage chair or portable table. If you are familiar with other forms of bodywork besides massage, I suggest that you try one of them.

In the meantime, here's a simple exercise you can do to increase the flow of energy throughout your body. If you feel a warm rush in your body after doing it, it's probably because it opened up some blocked areas. You need to stand up to do this exercise.

Stand facing forward with your hands hanging at your sides. Place your feet shoulder length apart with your knees slightly bent. You are going to inhale as you raise your arms out in front of you and up over your head, and exhale when you bring them back down. First, inhale sloooowly while raising your arms out in front of you and then up over your head so that they are extended up toward the ceiling. As you raise your arms up toward the ceiling, you should also look up to the ceiling. When your arms are raised over your head, *slightly* arch your back while your arms are raised, as if you were starting to do a back bend. As you exhale slooowly, keep your arms extended. Slowly bend over until your fingers are grazing the floor (if you can go this far). Repeat this entire inhale and exhale sequence three times. The key to doing this exercise is the arching of the back when your arms are raised over your head and you are looking at the ceiling. How do you feel? Do you notice any subtle changes? Is your heart beating a little faster or a little harder? Do you feel a little breathless, energized, or flushed? If so, *good*. This means you are experiencing a flow of energy. You opened up some blocked areas. This is a great exercise to do first thing in the morning, as soon as you get out of bed. Instead of moving sluggishly and taking 5–10 minutes to really wake up, you feel energized and alert almost immediately.

How much pleasure can you stand?

18. *Know the source of your personal power*

God. Allah. Creator. Divine Spirit. The Great Mother. Jehovah. Love. Divine Intelligence. Life Force. These are different names for what I believe is the same Source. This Source is the Force, Light, Love, or Vital Energy that moves through, around, and throughout every thing. In a rock, God is there. In a tree, God is there. In every cell of your body, God is there, too. There is *no where* that God isn't.

As you grow spiritually, this becomes more and more real to you, and less and less a conceptual idea. You begin to feel it in your bones and know it in your heart. In his book *Superbeings,* John Randolph Price explains that "to grow spiritually means the increase of one's understanding of the true nature of God, man and the creative laws of the universe." To grow spiritually also means to grow in your understanding of the source of your personal power, and in feeling and experiencing this source in your day-to-day life.

Did you know you have an innate, inherent right to health, prosperity, and fulfillment? Did you know you are born with divine potential that can never be taken away from you? Did you know that God has deposited some of Herself in your being? Did you know that you are an individuated expression of God, just as a sunbeam is an expression of the sun, individual but connected to the Source all at the same time? Hallelujah! Author Marianne Williamson reminds us that "we were born to make manifest the glory of God that is within us. It's not just in some of us . . . it's in everyone."

Contrary to popular belief and popular culture, we are *already* power-full. But we've forgotten. And in the process of forgetting, our power has gotten buried deep beneath layers of emotional, mental, and spiritual silt and sediment that has suppressed and stifled our sacred power. One of my favorite spiritual writers, Eric Butterworth, shares, "You are the Presence of God at the point where you are. . . . There is no place in all the world where you can get closer to God than where you are right now." This means there is nowhere to have to get to, nothing to earn, nothing to prove, nothing to pursue. You may become more aware of God, but you can never change the closeness which is the Presence of God in you.

This also means that human nature is not one of jealousy, judgment, competition, lying, cheating, stealing, and fear. These are *learned* behaviors. Human nature is one of joy, peace, pleasure, faith, ease, grace, mercy, compassion, and love. Yet we often hear people say, "Oh, that's just human nature" or "I'm only human." *Only* human? As if to say that mean, dishonest, or desperate behavior is our standard mode of operation, or that messing up, falling short, or exhibiting ugly or negative behavior is our natural tendency. Not so. This is a learned and conditioned nature, not our natural human nature. This is behavior that arises out of frustrated, unexpressed divine potential.

Tapping into the source of your personal power and expressing your divine potential lifts off layers of emotional, mental, and spiritual mud, dirt, and rocks that may be choking off your personal power. Tapping into your Source uncovers and sets free your personal power, releasing it from the bondage of conditioned, distorted, fearful thinking, and the suffocating undertow of limited, oppressive beliefs and "scripts."

I am a big fan of the Disney movie *The Lion King* and its sequel, *Lion King II: Simba's Pride*. One, because it's set in Africa; two, because it's filled with profound symbolism and spiritual themes like forgiveness, honoring your ancestors, karma, healing, rites of passage, and community; and three, because the songs carry some deep messages. One afternoon as I was sitting on the floor with my daughters watching the *Lion King II* video and listening to the opening musical segment, for the umpteenth time, I heard a message in the lyrics that I hadn't noticed before. I listened carefully to the lyrics, rewinding the videotape a couple of times so that I was sure to hear all of the words. It was clear that the words were supposed to be referring to Mufasa, the Lion King, who was killed in Lion King I. But I listened, closer, much closer, and even wrote the words down. To me, the lyrics had a double message. Yes, they could have been referring to the deceased Lion King, but what I heard in the chorus of the song was a message about God, a message about knowing the source of your personal power and understanding that God dwells within you. The song explains, *He lives in you, he lives in me,* and tells us that if we want to discover God's dwelling place, where God lives, look in the mirror.

Time and time again throughout my life, experiences have arisen to show me that God's dwelling place is in me, not somewhere "out there," and to reveal that *I* am not the source of myself—God is.

Be still and *know* that God is your Source.

> *Know that God is very proud of you*
> *Know that God cares about you*
> *Know that God wants you to experience joy and happiness*
> *Know that God wants the best for you*
> *Know that God thinks you are a gift*
> *Know that God loves you*

Be still and know that God is your Source.

19. *Define yourself*

The roles we play in our lives can either trap us in rigid boxes or provide us an opportunity for more and greater self-expression. We absorb so many "shoulds" and "have to's" in our lives that it's easy to forget that our roles don't have to be fixed, but can be forever changing and evolving as we grow, change, and evolve. Especially among women, there has been a negative backlash against roles as oppressive and limiting, probably because we've felt that many of our roles as women were imposed upon us instead of self-selected. Actually, we live our lives in terms of roles, not in the sense of role-playing but in the sense of authentic parts we have chosen to fill. As popular business consultant and author Stephen Covey shares in his personal leadership workbook, "roles become a natural framework to give order to what you want to do and be."

Having to take on a role isn't necessarily bad, either. From what I've seen, it's our *resistance* to a role that causes us the most strife or has us feeling like we have to conform to the ways that role has been fulfilled in the past. We resist naming and claiming our roles. For many of our roles, choice enters the picture when it comes to *how* we choose to take on the role. This is very important to realize. There is choice within the role even if you didn't choose the role for yourself. It's often our *perception* of what the role is supposed to be, or how others have fulfilled it in the past, that limits us. Many of the roles in which we find ourselves—mother, wife, daughter, employee, employer, female—have been assigned characteristics and ways of being by the culture that limit and suppress our growth and self-expression. This does not have to be. *The roles we've taken that don't work for us anymore need to be redefined.* You have to redefine the role, or someone else will define it for you. *Name and claim your roles.* When you redefine your roles, you redefine yourself. The naming part of naming and claiming your roles requires defining or redefining your roles, and the claiming part involves stepping into it fully—*owning* the role without reluctance, remorse, or ill feelings.

When you stop to think of all the roles you move into and out of in the course of a week, you quickly realize that your nature is one of flexibility, adaptability, and change, not one of rigidity and being change-resistant. What are the many roles you have played, play now, and desire to play in your future? Take a couple of minutes and list all the roles you fill. It can be quite eye-opening. Be sure to include the more "obvious" roles like daughter and woman. My other roles include mother, wife, entrepreneur, sister, sister-in-law, niece, friend, consultant, trainer, speaker, author, facilitator, change agent, transformer, founder, bridge builder, collaborator, mentor, mentee, big sister, oldest child, catalyst, big thinker, leader, group member, partner, and lover, to name a few.

I must remember that all of these roles are *aspects* of me, avenues for expressing myself, but they are not who I am. *I am not my roles.* It is not the whole of who I am or the essence of who I am. Confusion sets in when we begin to think that we are our roles, or we lose sight of who we are because a role is looming so large in our lives. You must be anchored in something larger than your roles or you will become a slave to the role. *You will be limited by the role instead of liberated by it.* This is why it is unhealthy to overidentify with any one role.

We need to shed or redefine our roles once we outgrow them or they've served their purpose. Five years ago, one of my roles at the time was employee. Since then that role has been shed and replaced by the role of business owner and entrepreneur. Up until a few months ago, being a board member of a newly formed foundation was one of my roles. When I initially accepted the invitation to be a charter board member, I anticipated that I would serve for about two years. After the first nine months on the board, the role started to feel "heavy." I was sharing, giving, and contributing my time, energy, and ideas, but wasn't being fed and contributed to in return. I decided that I would complete one year and then resign. Much to the dismay and surprise of the other board members, I made the announcement that I would be resigning from the board at the one-year mark. It was important for me to let them know my reasons for leaving without blame, accusation, or bad feelings on my part or theirs. It was a positive parting, with all relationships remaining intact. As I shed this role like a dead leaf falling off of a tree, it was replaced by a new, green one.

The energy that I freed up by shedding this board member role was used to start a women's business alliance. When you shed a role, it does not *have* to be replaced by another or you may find that you have taken on roles that aren't serving you, you're not serving them, you've outgrown them, or they need to change. Don't keep lugging around a role that has gone stale. Stale roles are deadweight on your spirit. Do you have a role that needs to be shed, renegotiated, or redefined?

Six years ago, I had the privilege of adding "mother" to my host of roles. I had observed many, many women in this role, and I had observed how this role was often played out. There were several aspects of the role that I wanted to redefine and fulfill differently. For instance, there were aspects of the role that didn't work for me, aspects that seemed either limiting, unhealthy, or stifling. The parts of the role I chose to redefine were: over-nurturer, overdoer, overgiver, martyr, self-sacrificer, victim of entrapment, giver of conditional love, and modeler of self-care last. The parts of the role I wanted to keep were as nurturer, supporter, giver and receiver, listener, giver of unconditional love, guide, inspirer, motivator, teacher, and modeler of self-care first.

I was a member of a small women's group called B.O.L.D.D (Bold Outrageous Leadership by Divas and Doers). We decided that we wanted the group to be "radical" and outside the box. So B.O.L.D.D. focuses on developing our unique leadership capacities as women by more fully tapping into our feminine power. At one of our monthly gatherings, I suggested a role-naming exercise, in which we went around the circle and shared our experiences and perspectives on what roles other group members contributed and brought to the particular group. When it was someone's turn to have her roles named by the other group members, she had to listen and receive as others shared their perspectives on the role she played in the group. It was a very enlightening process. Here is a sample of the roles we named for each other:

> Angela: prodder, stimulator, storyteller, humorist
> Shanti: listener, harmonizer, observer, energy holder
> Debrena: deepener, expander, clarifier, weaver, invoker
> Shamira: vision holder, catalyst, shifter, energy reader, teacher

Defining yourself requires naming and claiming your roles, *consciously choosing* how you are going to interpret and fulfill the roles that are part of you. How have you been interpreting and fulfilling the current roles in your life, whether the role be single mother, married mother, single woman, boss, employee, "older" woman, artist, or African American? Have you been either relinquishing or redefining parts of the role that don't work for you or have you resigned yourself to the "same old, same old"? Are you determining your roles or are your roles overtaking you?

Recognizing your roles and realizing you have some say-so and flexibility in how you choose to fulfill them means that you not only extend this same flexibility and permission to others, but that you take on the roles of designer and definer of your life.

Define yourself, or someone else will.

20. *Discover your sacred self*

acred means important, highly valued, and worthy of reverence and respect. To discover your sacred self, you have to uncover her and remove whatever it is that may be stifling her or hindering her emergence. When I was growing up, the grown folks didn't run around saying "Little girl, you are sacred." TV and the movies didn't send messages to me that told me I am sacred. Instead the messages seemed to say, "You're not okay the way you are. You're inadequate. Buy this car, wear this deodorant, put on this perfume, and *then* you'll be okay, or at least better off than you are now." As a little girl, there were occasions when I did things that *I* thought were particularly brilliant, bold, courageous, or inventive, and my mom's response would be "Who do you think you are? Grown?" She didn't say "Great, honey. This must be an expression of your sacred self." *Please.*

Sacred wasn't a word I used to describe myself, and I surely didn't hear other folks describing themselves as sacred. Use of the word seemed to be relegated to church. Up until my mid-twenties, I thought sacred was strictly a religious term. *I am sacred? I was born sacred?* This was news to me. There was nothing I had to do to earn it or qualify for it, like frequent-flyer miles. No tests to pass. I was *already* worthy, *already* sacred.

Scrolling back through the sound bites I recalled hearing in church, I didn't remember a single instance when I was told I was sacred *already*, by design. As a little girl and a young adult, my interpretation of the messages I received had common themes: I was flawed, damaged goods. I had messages reverberating through my head that claimed "all have sinned and fallen short of the glory of God." I thought I had to be baptized, saved, take communion, repent, come forward during altar call, adhere to the Ten Commandments, not curse, and not have sex until I was married, then I *might* be eligible for being sacred. Why didn't anybody tell me that I was *born* sacred? I was sacred by design. God made me this way. Maybe the authority figures in my life hadn't been told either, or they had yet to realize it for themselves.

When I did an inventory of my thoughts, words, behaviors, and interactions over the years, it was clear that not only did I not realize I was sacred but also there were many, many times when I didn't act like it, either. There were relationships in my life I was not treating as sacred. Like my relationship with certain creditors. I would pay some of my bills late and complain under my breath as I wrote out the check. Like my relationship with my body, when I carried around extra weight that I knew was taxing my joints and my heart; when I would go to bed late, wake up tired, and not drink enough water to keep my body adequately hydrated. Like the relationships with my kids, when they got on my nerves and I would yell at them because *I* was the uptight one; this was not treating my relationship with my kids as sacred or honoring their sacredness. When I was going to a job every day that was stressing me out and killing my spirit, but I continued to work there because I didn't believe that I could earn a living from marketing my own gifts, talents, skills, and abilities in my own business, I was not honoring my sacredness. When I was having sex too early in romantic relationships or having sex, period, because I didn't have deep confidence in myself and my ability to keep the guy around without sex being part of the "glue," I was not honoring my sacred self.

Today, in small ways, begin to act, think, and speak as the sacred woman that you are.

21. *Adjust your attitude*

ttitude is not just a disposition or how you act; attitude is a state of mind and a state of *heart*. Your attitude affects your perception, shapes your experiences, and actually affects outcomes in your life.

A couple of months ago, a sistahfriend from San Diego forwarded some anonymous pearls of wisdom to me off of the Internet regarding attitude. Contemplate these seven points every day for the next seven days. I encourage you to make a copy of these seven points and tape it to your bathroom mirror, the dashboard of your car, or on your refrigerator.

1. It is your attitude at the beginning of a task more than anything else that will determine your success or failure.
2. It is your attitude toward and about life that will determine life's attitude toward you. Despite many people's belief to the contrary, life plays no favorites.
3. Develop the attitude that there are more reasons you should succeed than reasons you should fail.
4. We become what we think about. Control your thoughts and you will control your life.
5. Radiate an attitude of confidence, of well-being, of a person who knows where she is going. You will find yourself attracting good things to you.
6. Attitudes are more important than facts.
7. Attitudes are based on assumptions. In order to change attitudes you must first change your assumptions.

Check yourself. What attitudes are you holding in your mind and, more importantly, in your heart? Do you have an attitude of caution, suspicion, and withholding because you think others are guilty until proven innocent, or that others will screw you over if given the chance, and can't be trusted? Do you have an attitude that life has to be hard? Life has to be a struggle? Life has to be difficult? Life is the school of hard knocks?

Your attitude either empowers you or disempowers you. If you are not sure about the attitudes you're holding in your mind and in your heart, just take a look at what comes out of your mouth, how you behave, how others treat you, and how you interact with and treat others. I promise you'll find some undeniable evidence.

Attitudes are invisible but they become visible through our words, actions, interactions, and behaviors. As you come to understand the process going on behind the scenes that is the source of the kind of life reality you have, you come to understand how to *change* your life reality. Here are the six levels that explain the connection between your attitudes and your experiences.

Level 1   Your core beliefs are the source of your values. Your core beliefs act as your "personal truths"
                 Examples: Life is a struggle. Money is the root of all evil. A good man is hard to find

Level 2   Your values reflect what you think is important
                 Examples: Going to church on Sundays is important. Everyone should have the goal of going to college

Level 3   Your attitudes arise from your values

Level 4   Your attitudes inform and shape your perceptions

Level 5   Your perceptions shape your experiences

Level 6   Your experiences make up the content and substance of your reality, and thus give you your quality of life

Your attitudes actually shape *what* you perceive and *how* you experience what occurs in your life. Adjusting your attitude is part of the process of in-powering yourself.

22. *Be present*

One sunny Thursday afternoon last year I was sitting at a table in one of my favorite cafés, doing some writing work on a project. My ideas were flowing, I was deep in my creative zone, and I had the place virtually to myself. From time to time, I'd glance up to see a customer walk up to the counter to order an espresso drink or pastry to go. After I had been sitting there writing for about forty-five minutes, I glanced up to see a man walk up to the counter and ask the cashier if he could use the phone book. Then the cashier turned around behind the counter to retrieve the phone book from under a shelf behind him. The man who had walked in leaned over the counter with his arm outstretched. Moments later, the cashier turned back around, tried to grab the man's arm, and started yelling "What are you doing?! Get out of here!" The patron yanked his arm free of the cashier's grip and dashed out of the door. This all transpired in a matter of ten seconds, while I looked on, puzzled by the entire scene.

The cashier came from behind the counter and ran out of the door after the man. But by then, through the window, I could see that the man had run north, up the street and around the corner. *What was that all about?* I thought to myself. When the cashier walked back into the café, I had a deeply perplexed look on my face. I asked him why he had shouted at the man and grabbed him, and he replied, "That guy just robbed us! He stole some money out of the cash register when my back was turned!" He went on to explain how the man had asked to use the phone book as a distraction so that he would have time to push the "sale" button on the cash register when he turned away, open the drawer, and grab some money. When the cashier turned back around, he saw the cash drawer open and the guy with some bills in his hand. That's when he grabbed his arm and yelled at him to get out. The cashier then excused himself so that he could call the police. As he walked over to the phone, he asked if I would agree to give a statement to the police as a witness. I agreed.

This is where being present became critical. Being present means that you are aware, alert, awake, and "here now." Before you can pay attention or give your attention, you have to be present, in the moment. Fifteen minutes later, when the police officer arrived, she came over to talk with me after talking with the cashier. The cashier was able to recall only one detail of the man—his race. When she asked me to describe any details of the man's appearance I could recall, I said, "He was about 5'10" and weighed 165 pounds, he had on a baseball cap, a dark blue sweatshirt, and a Members Only–style lightweight zip-up jacket." I continued, "He was wearing black jeans, black and white tennis shoes, and his right front tooth was missing." After she finished jotting down my comments, she looked up with an incredulous look of disbelief on her face and said, "This is amazing! I understand that this whole incident transpired in less than twenty seconds. When things happen this fast, it is very rare to receive such a detailed recollection of someone's appearance from a witness. Usually witnesses can recall only a few sketchy details, especially when it's a matter of seconds like this one was. The cashier could only tell me the man's race. You've got an incredible memory! Thank you for your help." Then she excused herself. After the police officer left, I put away my writing project and sat there a few minutes, sipping my latte, pondering the officer's comment about my memory and what had just happened. Two minutes later, it dawned on me. *No, it wasn't that I had such a great memory. It was that I was being present.* I was alert, awake, aware, and "here now." I was tuned in to what was going on around me.

When the TV news stations broadcasted special reports across channel after channel about the two young white men at Columbine High School in Littleton, Colorado, who went on a shooting rampage in April 1999, killing thirteen of their classmates, my question was: *Where were the parents?* How could they be so unaware? Both boys had two parents living in the home, and they came from "good" middle-class homes in the suburbs, the news reports continuously emphasized. Regardless of having two parents in the home, living in the suburbs, being white, or coming from a middle-class family, this tragedy still occurred.

The parents had been *physically* present, but had they been emotionally, mentally, and spiritually present? Were they paying attention? They were not present, or they would have noticed—*something*. Obviously, there was a serious breakdown in the relationship between these parents and their children. Maybe the parents were busy working, consumed in their daily routines, or so absorbed in the activity of their own lives that they didn't notice.

I became painfully aware of the depth of the denial—in this case, of white America—as it desperately struggled to create scapegoats for the heinous, horrifying acts committed by these two young white men. Yes, white, suburban, middle-class America also had skeletons in its closet, and Eric Harris and Dylan Klebold pulled the skeletons out of the closet and hung them in full view.

The nature of their relationships with their parents was *never* raised, not questioned, not even once, in a single one of the broadcasts and special reports I watched about the incident. Instead, the Internet was scapegoated as the problem, or it was the "Gothic" movement that caused the problem, rock star Marilyn Manson, or inadequate school security. Anything but to show that there could be ugly cracks in the facade of the idyllic, suburban "Leave It to Beaver" type images that white America has tried so hard to project.

To me, Eric Harris and Dylan Klebold held up a mirror to our faces that revealed the denial, hatred, and emotional neglect buried and suppressed in the lives of so many of us, not just our young people, and not just white people. If I left this as a condemnation of the parents of Eric and Dylan, then the deaths of all of the students they shot would have been even more in vain. I used this tragic incident to reflect upon my own life, and to think deeply about how present I was in my relationships, particularly the relationships with each of my three daughters. I asked myself, *"Where am I not present in my most important relationships? Where am I not present and not in tune to signs my daughters are sending to me but I am maybe too busy, too distracted or absorbed to notice?"*

You become more present by starting with yourself. Be more present to your own moods, emotions, effect on others, body changes, habits, motivations, behaviors, thoughts, interactions, and words. Be present to the messages and images you are absorbing from TV (since this is the form of media that we "consume" the most of), whether it be in the news, sitcoms, or commercials. Be present to what you are allowing into your body. Turn the package over and read the label on food items at the grocery store before you purchase them. Ask more questions. Be more observant. Be more present in your interactions during the course of a week; be more inquisitive and curious. Be more present to the moods, emotions, and energy of those with whom you live.

I think one of the reasons people don't smile more at one another in stores or when walking down the street is that we've been trained to be too self-absorbed, trained to have our focus be myopic—only on our own thoughts, problems, and issues. And herein lies an amazing paradox. Being self-absorbed and being self-aware are not the same. The more self-aware you become, the *more* perceptive and aware you become. The more self-absorbed you become, the *less* perceptive and aware you become.

Sacred power starts with self; it's not only about the self. Learning to be present helps you increase your sacred power. Learning to be present helps you be in the moment.

23. *Pay attention*

One evening in early 1998, I decided to go to the Langston Hughes Cultural Arts Center here in Seattle to hear my friend Phillip Aaron give a lecture on success. What my friend shared at his lecture that evening rearranged my thinking.

Instead of talking about success in terms of achievement, perseverance, having a positive attitude, and writing down goals, Phillip talked about *attention*. Webster's dictionary tells us that "to attend" means to "be present, to heed, and to direct oneself." And "attention" is defined as "concentration, observation and noticing." Another way to look at attention is to consider it "directed energy" or "focused awareness."

Ever notice how you can be in a noisy room where people are having many simultaneous conversations and you are still able to focus on the words of the conversation you are having with one particular person? This is the power of attention. The gist of Phillip's message was this: *change the quality of your attention, change what you are "attending to" with your energy and awareness, and you can change the quality of your life.* Change the quality of your attention and where you are directing it, and you can create what you desire.

The following passages are words of wisdom I distilled from Phillip that evening. Over the next twelve days, meditate upon each of the twelve passages, and notice the possibilities that open up in your thinking.

1. The *quality* of your attention determines your success.
2. We've misunderstood the power of our attention.

3. The circumstances in our lives are our attention in disguise.
4. Ask yourself, "What is drawing my attention? Where am I directing my attention?"
5. We've been paying attention to the *unuseful* things in our lives.
6. Redirect your attention and you can change your life.
7. There are two ways to *give* your attention: thinking *about* something directs your attention; this is how most people give their attention. Thinking *from* it, however, is the most powerful path to manifesting it. Reside in the consciousness of it. Feel yourself having it and experiencing it *first.*
8. You don't need to change yourself. You need to change your *concept* of yourself. You are already perfect. We define ourselves by our false selves instead of our true selves. A distorted view of yourself moves you out of alignment with your Highest Good.
9. The people you think the least of or who irritate you the most are your greatest teachers. They point out where you have blockages.
10. Everything in your life is a reflection of your consciousness.
11. A consciousness of lack cancels out a consciousness of abundance. A consciousness of lack has you believing and acting as if there is not enough.
12. Success is having what you desire in life. Success is a natural process. The natural flow and energy of life is always pulling you toward your Highest Good. If you are not experiencing success, it's because you are interrupting or blocking the flow, you've gotten off track, or you are perceiving yourself and others through a veil of untruth.

These twelve passages can be distilled into what I call the Four Laws of Attention: (1) We are what we give our attention to; (2) What we give our attention to becomes real for us; (3) What we give our attention to grows; and (4) What we find in the world reflects our self-concept.

> *Question of the Day:*
> *To whom, what, and where are you giving your attention?*

24. Get conscious about your B. S. (belief system)

Last year when I was in Colorado speaking at an African-American women's event, I had the opportunity to have a long one-on-one conversation afterward, at the home of my host, with Clarice, one of the women who attended the event. Clarice was a gorgeous, dark chocolate sister who had been very successful in corporate America. After ten years in corporate America, she decided that she wanted to leave the corporation she worked for to start her own customer service and sales training business. She had been researching and developing her business plan for over a year and a half, and it had been ready for the past five months. She even had potential clients interested in contracting with her as soon as she started her business. Everything she needed was in place, but she was still dragging her feet. She wanted to figure out what was at the root of her procrastination. She knew she had deeper issues than the customary fear of not having a steady paycheck. So before I left town, she wanted to have a conversation with me that would help her identify the root of the mental blockages that were paralyzing her ability to move forward with her business.

Clarice had an impressive track record of achievements and accomplishments that included a host of awards and honors, a full-ride scholarship to college, and graduation in the top 10 percent of her class. For as far back as she could remember, she'd been not just an achiever but also an overachiever. At first the reason she thought she was dragging her feet about starting her own business was laziness. She had gotten accustomed to the corporate life, her benefits package, and the guaranteed paycheck.

As she talked about her achievements, she admitted that there was one area of her life that had constantly plagued her, one area of her life where she had not achieved her goal—it was with her weight. Carla was about 95 pounds overweight. She had been successful in every other endeavor she'd put her mind to, except this one. She believed that her weight challenge was somehow connected to her procrastination about starting her own business.

Most of us are unconscious of the beliefs we hold. Why? Because our beliefs are *transparent* to us. They are invisible to us, yet we operate from them and they show up in our lives in visible ways—in our thoughts, behavior, language, and in what we've manifested in our lives. Too often we examine our behavior, but we don't go any deeper, to the root or source of our thoughts and our behavior—to our beliefs. Our beliefs are the root and the source of our behaviors. And just like the roots of a plant, our beliefs are usually buried beneath the surface.

When you can get conscious about your beliefs and your belief system, you access a reservoir of tremendous power—power that can be used to change your life and manifest what you want and desire. Uncovering your deep-seated beliefs is simple, but it isn't easy, because it requires rigorous self-reflection and truth-telling. It requires taking a step back to notice the outcomes and results you've experienced in your life and the behaviors you've been demonstrating. Dig deep and ask yourself: *What are the core beliefs I'm holding that give rise to these types of results, experiences, and behaviors?* This is the process I led Clarice through—a process that would help her uncover the core beliefs that were causing her to procrastinate with her new business.

I asked Clarice to go back in her mind, back, back, back to the point in her life where she remembered her weight first becoming a problem. She said that she could remember being "heavy" as far back as first grade. One of Clarice's close sisterfriends who was quietly listening to the conversation offered Clarice a question. Did Clarice remember any particular childhood experiences related to her skin tone? Clarice gazed off in the distance as she scrolled back through her mental archives, trying to recall any child-hood memories about her skin tone. "Yes!" she exclaimed. "I do remember. I was about three years old and I remember looking at a picture on top of the fireplace mantel of all five of us kids. I remember actually thinking to myself, *I am the darkest.*" I urged her on. "Clarice, do you recall why you hap-pened to notice this particular distinction? Was there something in how the adults in your household interacted with you or treated you that would have you lock in on your different skin tone?" She paused again, this time for a full minute, and her eyes started to well up with tears. "Yes," she said quietly. "I remember feeling not as nurtured as my brothers and sisters, not as attended to, not as special, not as loved. When I saw the photo on the mantel, I think I rationalized in my young mind that it was because I was the darkest. I think it was then and there I concluded, 'I am not as worthy; I am not as valuable.' This was also about the same time I started eating a lot and gaining weight. By the time I was in first grade, I was, by far, the biggest kid in the class."

I asked, "So the issue with your skin tone predates your weight issue, right?" "Right!" she confirmed as her eyes grew big at the realization. "Do you see the connection, Clarice? It sounds like you've been holding a belief since you were a little girl that says your skin tone was not okay, you are not worthy of being as loved, you are not good enough," I said. "In your mind, it seems that you concluded that being darker meant not being as special, not as lovable. These became your core beliefs about yourself, and have shaped your self-concept ever since. The reason you may be having such a hard time starting your own business is that those old tapes that shaped your self-concept are still playing in your head, beliefs that originate from decisions you made about yourself based on your skin tone, and later, your weight. When you consider starting your own business, all kinds of self-worth and self-value issues can come up. The notion of starting your own business threatens all of the old beliefs about yourself that you have been carrying around since you were three years old, because to start your own business is in and of itself a bold statement of confidence in yourself, in your abilities, and in your gifts, talents, and skills. To start your own business means that you value your knowledge and skills. You highly value yourself," I summarized. Tears were now streaming down Clarice's face. "Girl, it's okay to cry," I said. "Our tears let us know that we are beginning to heal and to purge; and you're beginning to do yours right now. You are just now beginning to get conscious about some deep-seated beliefs that have had a grip on you, that have had you in bondage since you were three years old."

Like Clarice, the first step in being free from old, limiting patterns and behaviors is to get conscious about your B. S. (Belief System). Do some digging so that you can first address the beliefs that are already there, then they will begin to surface; they will become apparent instead of remaining transparent to you. It may not be easy, but it's freeing and it's necessary if you want to move forward in areas of your life where you feel stuck. To get conscious means to acknowledge, recognize, admit what is so. These old beliefs were what had been keeping Clarice from having one of the greatest desires of her heart—owning her own business. The self-reflection and truth-telling work she was starting to do had the effect of chipping away at the "belief blocks" that had been keeping her from starting her own business.

Early the next morning, as I was preparing to leave my host's house for the airport, Clarice, who had also spent the night, was already up, sitting at the dining room table with her pen and writing pad, mapping out her plan for making the transition from her corporate job to launching her own business. Our conversation had created a breakthrough for her.

Our lives, no matter what they look like, no matter what reality we have, are a function of our beliefs. Our beliefs are the lowest common denominator. The core, inner beliefs we hold about ourselves, about others, about how life works, about our bodies, about things that have happened to us, manifest as our outer reality, as our lived experience.

I was having an individual coaching session with a female client who was seeking more peace, ease, and simplicity in her life, and we were exploring some of the beliefs she held about how life works. As she reflected on her life, she noticed that she had recurring patterns of high drama, struggle, crises, and emergencies. As we sat talking, she came to realize that she was holding these core beliefs: *for her life to be exciting, she needed high drama, crises, and emergencies. Things had to be complicated to be exciting.* And as a result, she had lots of "complications" in her life—in her love relationships, with her employees, in her past marriage, in her friendships, and with her body. She had to get conscious about the beliefs that had a grip on her, or else creating a life of more peace, ease, and simplicity would continue to elude her.

A conversation with another friend, Antoinette, provides another example. Antoinette realized what core belief was at the root of her fear of success. She had been holding this belief: *it is easier to play small than to play big.* As a result, she had been playing small in all aspects of her life, suppressing her brilliance and creativity. In her mind, playing big meant rejection by close friends and family, since success was looked upon with contempt in her family. Striving to be successful meant you thought you were trying to be better than everybody else. Over the past two years, she has been working to get conscious about her B. S., particularly her beliefs about success. As a result of starting to acknowledge and remove this "belief block," Antoinette has released thirty pounds of weight; updated her wardrobe in brighter, more flattering styles; changed her hair style; given herself permission to have more fun, laugh more, and try new things; and has secured the most lucrative contracts in the four-year history of her consulting business.

Get conscious about your B. S. Free your mind and the rest will follow.

25. *Demonstrate spiritual humility*

Spiritual humility is the opposite of spiritual arrogance. Spiritual arrogance sets in when you start thinking that you are a little bit better or "spiritually superior" than those who are not as far along on their spiritual journey as you may be. Spiritual arrogance can set in after you have a particularly powerful or insightful spiritual experience, after reading a certain book, or taking a certain class or course. Spiritual arrogance tends to set in when you have an expansion of your spiritual understanding, but you haven't yet integrated or embodied it. You talk about your new understanding or enlightenment as if it is a given that others haven't discovered it—that somehow you've been privy to something that is available only to some.

Spiritual arrogance can sneak up on you when you're not looking. For most of us, as we evolve spiritually, we pass through a temporary phase of spiritual arrogance. The phase will come and it will go. But some of us stay stuck here for a long time, because there are "learnings" that we must first receive.

Here are some telltale signs that you've caught the spiritual arrogance virus.

- You often say "I'll have to meditate on it" or "I'll have to pray on it," because it sounds very spiritual, but you rarely do.
- You often preface statements about an important decision you've made or a course of action you're going to take with "Spirit told me . . . ," to keep others from questioning or challenging your decision or course of action.
- You call yourself "sharing" your perspectives on spirituality with others and it comes off sounding like a lecture.
- You don't hesitate to let others know that you are "very spiritual."
- You find yourself judging others and thinking "I'm more spiritual than she is" or "she is not as spiritual as I am."
- You claim that you are very spiritual yet you are uptight, controlling, difficult to get along with, work with, or be on a team with.

- You claim that you are very spiritual yet you are rigid, inflexible, easily irritated, or often have a funky attitude.
- You claim that you are very spiritual yet you constantly make poor choices, have drama or crises in your life, or are constantly stressed out about your finances.

When you are spiritually humble, you let your life be your example. You let your life speak for itself. You don't have to keep *telling* others how spiritual you are—it shows in how you live your life, in how you treat your body, and how you deal with situations that come your way. You're not zealous; you don't force yourself or your beliefs on anyone; there is alignment between your values and your behavior. *You practice what you teach.* Others are naturally attracted to you because they can feel the radiance and alignment of your spirit.

To others, it may appear as if you flow gracefully through what life presents to you, or like you have the "Midas touch." When you are spiritually humble, it looks like you are able to handle situations and challenges without getting flustered or thrown off-balance. When you are spiritually humble, you have the ability to keep things in perspective. When you are spiritually humble, you don't complain about the circumstances in your life; instead you are grateful to be here to experience them

Spiritual humility is an attractive quality.

26. *Change channels*

⟋⟍ hat "station" are you listening to? In your head, that is. What "channel" are you tuned in to? What internal conversations and inner chatter are you broadcasting to yourself? About yourself? What's happening on your "inner talk show"? Did you know you can *change channels*? You can turn your mental dial away from channels that are broadcasting lack, limitation, struggle, drama, "victimitis," regrets, anger, resentment, fear, insecurity, self-doubt, blame, negative self-judgment, distorted beliefs, mistakes, not being good enough, guilt, and how others are doing you wrong. You can turn your mental dial to a new channel—a channel that broadcasts abundance, plenty, ease, grace, right perspective, release, forgiveness, self-love, high self-esteem, and worthiness.

One afternoon a couple of years ago, I was having lunch with a sistah-friend Edith, who is a psychotherapist. I was sharing with her that I was nervous about an upcoming speech presentation I had that was going to be videotaped in front of a live audience. I was nervous because it wasn't just any audience, but an audience of other professional speakers. As Edith listened, she must have been able to tell I was filled with nervousness and self-doubt. So she asked if it was okay for her to lead me through a simple exercise that would help me "reframe" my thoughts and feelings and change my channels from nervousness and worry to authentic confidence. Of course, I agreed.

She grabbed a paper napkin and a pen and drew four columns. From left to right, she labeled the columns "Current Channel," "Current Internal Conversation," "Desired Channel," and "Transformed Internal Conversation." First she asked me to describe the current thoughts and feelings I was having about my speaking presentation. I replied, "Nervous, insecure, uneasy, worried." She wrote these under the "Current Channel" column. Second, she asked me to look *beneath* these thoughts and feelings to the deeper conversation that was giving rise to these thoughts and feelings. I shared that I was nervous because I was afraid I'd forget the lines of my speech when I was on stage, and I would look bad in front of the other speakers. I was insecure and uneasy because I was afraid of not measuring up. I was afraid that my speaking skills would be far below those of the other speakers, and if so, it would become public knowledge when I did my presentation. I was also worried that I might freeze up or stutter because I knew I was being videotaped.

Third, she asked me to describe, in the *present tense*, how I wanted to think, feel, and be (my desired state) when I was on stage delivering my presentation, instead of being nervous, worried, and insecure. I responded, "I am at ease. I flow through my presentation. I remember every line. I deliver my speech with confidence and passion."

Fourth, she asked me to identify the transformed internal conversation that would give rise to my desired state and desired outcome. After pondering the question for a minute, I replied, "I know my subject matter well. My nervous energy is good, enthusiastic energy. It means I'm excited and antic- ipating my presentation. The audience wants me to do good. I know what I'm doing. I know I can do this. I am an effective, experienced speaker."

Lastly, she drew a big circle around the third and fourth columns. She then handed me the napkin and suggested that I shift my attention and energy from my current internal conversation to the transformed internal conversation. In essence, she explained, I needed to tune in to a different channel if I was going to be successful in my presentation. My current con- versation could lead to nothing but my messing up. Here's what Edith's napkin looked like.

Current Channel	Current Internal Conversation	Desired Channel	Transformed Internal Conversation
Nervous	I'll forget my rehearsed lines. I'll look bad in front of my peers.	I'll flow through my presentation, I remember every line.	I know my subject matter.
Insecure	I'm not going to measure up. My speaking skills are far below those of the other speakers in the room.	I am an effective, experienced speaker.	My nervous energy is good energy. It means I am excited about my presentation and anticipating the day.
Worried	I'll freeze up. I'll stutter. I'll mess up.	I deliver with confidence and certainty.	I know what I am doing. I can do this.

As she spoke, I could feel an internal shift taking place. As I sat there, I could actually feel the knot in my stomach relaxing, my breathing becom- ing smoother and more even, and my shoulders relaxing. Yes, I needed to change channels, to shift my attention to a more "in-powering" conversa- tion, instead of hosting an internal conversation that was keeping me in a state of nervousness and worry.

For the next two days, I kept this napkin in my purse and pulled it out to review it before walking out the door in the morning, and right before getting in bed. Two days later, the day of the videotaping, I was calm, cool, and collected. Ten minutes before I was to go on stage, I pulled out my napkin and reviewed my third and fourth columns, quietly reading them under my breath. My last thought was *I can do this*. Sure enough, my presentation went off smoothly. I didn't stumble, stutter, or freeze up, and I moved around the stage with confidence and certainty. Afterward, other speakers came up to me to compliment me on my presentation.

This "napkin" process was a powerful reminder of how empowering or *dis*empowering our thoughts can be. Our thoughts shape our actions, perceptions, behaviors, experiences, and interactions. The key question is: *What are the internal stations and channels your are listening to about love, your children, marriage, your job, yourself, your health, your money, your time, your energy, and your body?* I invite you to use the four-part process my girlfriend Edith laid out for me. Instead of using a napkin, you may want to use a full piece of paper—something that you can fold up and carry around with you. You might be surprised at what you've been broadcasting across the inner airwaves of Station N-MY-HEAD.

27. *Be aligned*

hen you are aligned, there is congruence between your words and actions, between your thoughts and behaviors, and between what you say you want and what is actually present in your life. When you are aligned, what brings you joy is evident because it is reflected in the content and substance of your life.

At first, being aligned may sound like a tall order—it may sound like being aligned is out of reach for most of us, almost impossible, or at least, improbable. At first, it may seem far-fetched. But only because so many of us are living lives that are "unaligned." Let me tell you, I've lived both the unaligned life and the aligned life, and I definitely prefer the aligned life.

An aligned life is more fluid, more gratifying, more peace-full, more joy-full, and more powerful. An aligned life has less stress, conflict, and tension. When your life is aligned, you invest your time, energy, and attention in what really matters to you, in what is of value to you. Things flow. Your inner power is maintained instead of being wasted or weakened. *You have enough time.*

Getting aligned can be a challenge, though, due to the gaps that exist in our lives. Gaps exist when there is space between what we say we want and what we keep getting, between when we say we deserve and what we keep settling for, between what we stand for and what we keep falling for. When you start to align your life, you have to face the contradictions, gaps, and incongruencies that have made themselves comfortable in your life. Because where you are out of alignment is also where you are leaking precious spiritual energy.

A business associate, Evan, wasn't just leaking spiritual energy—he was hemorrhaging. On the surface and based on appearances, he seemed to be this funny, warm, outgoing, gregarious, friendly, honest, good-hearted guy with lots of integrity. But when it came to running his twenty-five-person company, it was a different story. There were incongruencies.

Over the past few years, I noticed that Evan started to have more and more stories about how his employees had tried to rip him off, do him wrong, steal from him, or screw him over. The first few times he mentioned these situations, I didn't think much of it. I wrote it off as the headaches associated with having employees. But after the fourth and fifth times, I started to listen more carefully.

Something was off. Somewhere Evan was unaligned.

Evan seemed to keep attracting experiences in which employees were dishonest, distrustful, or malicious. Could it be that he was holding core beliefs that *brought forth* and invoked dishonest and distrustful behavior? I started to listen more closely to the "innocent" comments Evan would make about his employees. I heard him say "it's hard to find good people; your employees will try to rip you off if you don't watch them; all they do is complain about wanting more money; or you can't trust 'em." And sure enough, the situations he kept experiencing with his employees were perfectly consistent with the beliefs he was holding.

I suspected that if I'd been a fly on the wall at his company, I would have seen him interacting with his employees in ways that revealed his core beliefs. His goal, however, was to have one of the top companies in the region in his field. In order to be a top company, you have to have good employees. But in Evan's mind, good employees were hard to find. This created an incongruence. When there is an incongruence, the universe follows the energy of your *dominant* belief, whether it is good, bad, or ugly. *What you believe most strongly is what you get. It is what prevails.*

In one particular conversation, Evan was sharing the "creative" ways he had been able to secure large quantities of newspaper advertising for one of his business's new services. He had taken out large advertisements in several newspapers, based upon an agreement to pay for the ads by the end of the thirty-day grace period from the time the ads ran. When he took out the ads, he explained, he had no intention of paying the newspapers within thirty days. He explained how he had been able to "get over" on these newspapers by delaying payment of their advertising invoices month after month, until the invoices went to a collection agency. Then, shortly before it was time for the collection to post on his credit report, he would call up the collection agency, negotiate his payments down, and pay off the delinquent invoices. When he shared this scenario, it wasn't to acknowledge the thin line of honesty he was walking, but instead to boast about his "creative financing" techniques. Interestingly enough, Evan was always complaining about how *his* customers were often delinquent in paying their invoices to him. *Hmmmm. Go figure.*

Evan didn't know his gaps were showing, or that he even had gaps. He considered himself a hardworking businessman who was simply trying to achieve his goals, make money, and grow his company. He believed he was doing the right things. He believed he was doing what he needed to be doing to get ahead. The problem was that Evan didn't know that he was his company's greatest problem and his own worst enemy. He didn't realize that his contradictions and incongruencies would not allow him to have what he said he wanted, to be the top company in the region in his industry. Or if so, it would be accomplished with tremendous amounts of energy, stress, and personal sacrifice.

Being blind to our gaps is disempowering. And eventually our gaps can get so wide that we start to fall in, especially when we keep ignoring them, denying them, or trying to run from them. Evan's gaps were catching up with him and he was slipping. But he always explained problems away as someone else being the cause; something else being the reason he didn't seem to be able to get things to work out in his company. Over the course of the past three years, Evan began falling in. He could no longer cover up or hide his gaps. What had started out as small gaps had become huge canyons, and he was losing his footing and starting to slide in fast. His employees continued to leave his company, one by one, until Evan's company dwindled from twenty-five employees down to three in four years.

To this day, Evan has not stopped to really take a look at himself, to tell the truth to himself about himself, and to examine his integrity, the beliefs he is holding, his incongruencies and contradictions, and the less than honorable way he treats his employees and his creditors. He hasn't yet been able to see beyond his ego. He is having to literally rebuild his business from the ground floor.

For me, "gap analysis" has been an ongoing process. And often it's the gaps that are right under my nose, the ones that are the most glaring, that I have the hardest time seeing. Or I develop a blindspot over my gaps because I have justified them and rationalized in my mind so that I can tolerate myself. Oh yes, I had gaps with my body—saying I was committed to being healthy and fit and treating my body like a temple, yet I continued to make unhealthy eating choices and carry around pounds of extra weight. I had gaps with my finances—saying God was the source of my supply, God would supply all of my needs, yet I wasn't saving or investing any of my money, and my *outgo* exceeded my *inflow*. I had gaps with men—oh yes, I had my twenty-five-item "requirements list" of what I was looking for in a man, though I hadn't yet actualized these "requirements" in myself! I said I wanted A, B, and C, and kept getting X, Y, and Z, and I didn't think it had *anything* to do with me—in my mind it was the brothers that were the problem. These were all signs that I was not aligned in major areas of my life.

Telling the truth is an unavoidable step on the path to spiritual growth and freedom. To get aligned you start by telling the truth to yourself about yourself. When you tell the truth, you see your gaps for what they are, instead of denying they exist or trying to sugar-coat them. And you are also able to see which thoughts, feeling, actions, and behaviors have been out of alignment, which ones are moving you away from what you say you deserve. For example, the way I worked on closing the gaps in my love relationships was to first look at the thoughts, actions, and behaviors that were *not* aligned with the self-love I said I had. To get aligned, I had to start developing in myself the very qualities that I wanted to attract in a man.

Once I started to close the gaps *within*, the external gaps that were showing up in my love relationships started to close, too. I said I wanted to attract A, B, and C and I started attracting A, B, and C instead of X, Y, and Z.

As you close up the gaps in your life and get aligned, you may find that others may not be very supportive of you. Or they may get downright irritated with you. This isn't because they don't want to see you better yourself. Most often it's because they are out of alignment, too, and their "stuff" is slapping them in the face. Your efforts to align your life may be forcing them to face their own gaps. But instead of dealing, others will often project their discomfort on to you. Be not discouraged. The discomfort of others is temporary while the experience of a new level of peace, joy, and ease in your life will be permanent.

28. *Tell the truth*

Telling the truth should be one of the easiest things in life to do. So how did it get a reputation for being difficult? I think it's because in the American culture lying is an acceptable social norm, especially if it is to save face, look good, or avoid hurting someone's feelings. A "white lie" is okay, right? You can let things slide a little if the circumstances warrant it, right? Unfortunately, telling the truth has become conditional and situational. As we continue to free up our power and make joy real in our lives, we must recognize how much of our joy and power is trapped beneath layers of not telling the truth to ourselves and to others.

bell hooks (she intentionally uses all lowercase letters in her name), a black feminist and one of my favorite writers, reminds us in her book *Sisters of the Yam*, "a commitment to truth-telling is the first step in any process of self-recovery. . . . Healing takes place within us as we speak the truth of our lives." We are holding our tongues and silencing our voices about so many things—and it's killing us softly. We must acknowledge what is so and tell the truth. After all, you can't begin to change what you don't acknowledge.

One evening a few weeks ago, my sistahfriend Edree and I were sitting out on her deck sipping herbal tea, enjoying a glorious view of Puget Sound and talking about women's issues. Since Edree is a healer and teacher and also does a lot of work with women, I was particularly interested in knowing about the general attitudes that she had observed in women about joy. She began, "I'm amazed at how low our tolerance for joy really is. Instead of feeling truly worthy and deserving of joy, we seem to regard joy as a reward for suffering, sacrifice, hardship, and pain. We seem to believe that 'joy comes in the morning,' after a night of struggle." I sat back in my chair, quiet for a few moments, as I absorbed Edree's insightful comments. I thought to myself, *Yes, truth be told, many of us have been lying to ourselves. The reason joy is not more real in our lives is because, deep down, we don't feel worthy of more joy. We're not able to stand as much as we think we can.*

Lying is a form of deceit, and deceit makes us dysfunctional. It "encourages us to deny what we genuinely feel and experience." And as a result, we lose touch with ourselves and "we lose our capacity to know who we really are and what we need and desire," bell hook asserts. Are there areas of your life where you have not been telling the truth, either to yourself or to others? *Are you telling the truth about . . .*

What brings you joy?	Your job?
Your marriage?	Your spouse?
Your finances?	Your love relationships?
A friend?	Your body?
Your sex life?	Your sexuality?
Your weight?	Your fears?
Your bad habits?	Your addictions?
Your childhood?	Your little secrets?
How angry you may be?	How unappreciated you may feel?
What isn't working in your life?	What is working in your life?
The shoulds and ought to's that are suppressing your spirit?	The abuse you may be suffering?
	How good you feel?
How blessed you are?	How you're afraid of success?
How you're playing small?	How bad you feel?
The desires of your heart?	What you really want to do?

What we've been masking, hiding from, avoiding, and denying is quietly doing us in. The path to dis-ease and disintegration of the mind, body, and spirit is constantly doing what someone else wants you to do and not being true to yourself. Unfortunately, we live in a culture where telling the truth is considered a courageous act. Just as I am challenging myself to be more courageous, I'm challenging you, too. *Nourish your courage.* Because telling the truth is in and of itself an act of self-liberation. When you tell the truth you expose something to the light. When you tell the truth, you free yourself from illusions and distorted thinking. Telling the truth also opens you up to possibilities of deeper love and intimacy with yourself and others in your life.

My 5-year-old daughter, Kiana, helped me learn a powerful lesson about telling the truth. On a Saturday morning last year, I was in the kitchen fixing breakfast when she came in and asked me if she could get herself dressed to go outside and play. After I told her yes, she reappeared a few minutes later dressed in "high-water" flowered pants that were faded at the knee, and a striped hot pink and white T-shirt that was so tight her stomach was poking out. She had so many contrasting colors and patterns going on that I almost went cross-eyed looking at her. She was grinning from ear to ear as she modeled her outfit selection. She asked, "Mama, can I go outside and play now?" My first reaction was to say, *"Heck, no. You look like an orphan or a throw-away kid. I'm not letting you set foot outside of this house with that on. Go change into something that fits and matches, right now!"*

But I caught myself.

I thought, *so what's the big deal? My five-year-old daughter wants to go outside and play in a crazy looking outfit that* she *thinks is beautiful. So what is my issue with her clothes* really *about?* While I was pondering these thoughts for a few moments, Kiana asked again, *"Mommeeee, can I go outside now?"* snapping me out of my reverie.

I wasn't telling the truth to myself about why I was uncomfortable with Kiana's going outside in the clothes she had on. It wasn't about her clothes not fitting, not matching, or being too tight, or faded. The real problem with her going outside in what she had on was that I didn't want the neighbors to see her in her crazy outfit and then have it reflect negatively on me. I didn't want them to think I had my daughter looking "raggedy."

This was deep.

So it really wasn't about Kiana's clothes. It was about my needing to *look good* to my neighbors, even if it meant negating Kiana's choice and self-expression. I didn't want *her* appearance to reflect negatively on *me.* I was going to make her change so *I* could be comfortable, though she was already comfortable in what she had on.

By telling the truth to myself in this instance, several things happened: I agreed to let my daughter go outside in what she had chosen to wear; I validated her choice and, in the process, I also validated her. I let go of my fear of my neighbor's judgment; and I did not let others' *possible* opinions and judgments of me determine my decisions and behaviors. In the process, I became a little more free, and so did Kiana.

Kiana went outside and had a great time playing. And yes, there *may* have been some neighbors who saw her and thought, "Debrena's child sure is looking raggedy." Or maybe no one thought anything. Either way, it was okay with me. Someone else's negative judgment or opinion of you can only affect you if you believe that person's judgment has some truth to it. What others think about me is none of my business.

Nourish your courage. Tell the truth.

29. *Get clear first*

$\mathcal{I}$ was in an individual coaching session with one of my clients, a brilliant family medicine doctor, Ron Horn, who wanted to move out of practicing traditional Western medicine as he had done for years, and make a transition to incorporating more holistic, integrative, and spiritually based methods into his practice. He wanted me to help him design a personal transition plan, launch his speaking career, and get "unstuck" on a reference-style book he was writing on integrative medicine. He had been working on the book for a year and a half, but had completed only five chapters. He concluded that he had writer's block. In our third consultation, we discussed his book project. He thought the reason he wasn't making further headway was because he wasn't being disciplined enough in setting aside writing time. He thought he needed tips on how to make time to write.

I noticed that Ron's eyes lit up and his gestures got very animated when he shared stories about using holistic healing methods such as color therapy, guided imagery, energy balancing, and intuitive touch in his practice to help facilitate his patients' healing. As he continued to enthusiastically share healing stories from the lives of his patients, it became clear to me why Ron had been stuck at five chapters for so long. Ron was writing the wrong type of book. He was trying to write a reference guide to integrative medicine while what he needed to be writing was a book that would allow him to share the real-life healing stories of his patients. He needed to write a book that would come from his heart, not from his head.

I shared my observations and suggestions with Ron. Storytelling was obviously comfortable and natural for him. Writing a reference book didn't bring him joy, but telling stories did. This was why he had stagnated on the project. A reference book didn't allow him to express himself and his spirit. I also pointed out that, as an African American, he came from a culture based on the oral tradition of storytelling. Writing a book that told his stories was natural for him.

The following week, when we met for our next consultation, Ron told me that my insights and observations were right on. After our last session, he had had a dream that same evening that confirmed the insights I shared. Once he embraced and accepted this realization, he could feel the internal shift start to take place, the inner click that occurs when you get clear on something or arrive at the truth for yourself. He shared that he felt lighter and more energized since reaching clarity on his book.

Clarity is when your head, heart, and gut are in one accord, and you are in touch with what is true for you. You are in tune with your core motivations and all of you is aligned. Internal discord is what results when you are not being true to yourself. When you are not clear, you have to continue talking yourself into and through things—through an unhealthy or toxic relationship, through an unhealthy or toxic marriage, through a job that is killing your spirit, through things that you are doing out of guilt or obligation. When you are not clear, it leads to inner conflict. When you don't get clear first, you end up doing things for the wrong reasons or going down the wrong path altogether. Your motivations become impure. You can lose sight of Who You Are and what you really want.

Just the other day, I received a phone call letting me know my girlfriend's aunt Janet had dropped dead at work of a heart attack at the young age of forty-eight. Ironically, earlier that same morning on a phone call with her mother, Janet had mentioned that the stress of her job was killing her. She couldn't take it anymore. She had called to let her mom know that she had finally decided to take an early retirement and leave her job. Unfortunately, Janet's decision came too late. Her body had suffered too long under the strain of an intensely stressful job, and her heart gave out on her.

There are signs to let us know when clarity is needed. You need to stop and *get clear* if:

◇ A work situation, family situation, or love relationship is draining you.

◇ You are investing inordinate amounts of energy into someone or something, and you are not experiencing reciprocity or seeing positive results.

◇ You are feeling stuck or blocked.

◇ You are feeling scattered or unfocused.

◇ You have a hard time completing things.

◇ You are procrastinating.

These can all be clues and cues that clarity is needed. When you arrive at clarity, you feel it internally—it may feel like a release, a relief, a letting down, an easing of internal tension, or a sureness or lightness where there once was a feeling of heaviness or "spiritual constipation."

One afternoon a couple of months ago, my girlfriend Georgette called and wanted to get together for a cup of coffee. We hadn't seen each other in months. The last time I saw Georgette, she was going through some challenging changes in her life, trying to find a new job because her previous position had been phased out. Georgette was in her mid-forties, had a master's degree, and had been without a full-time job for the first time in her life. This was the first time in her career that she actually had to look for a job. And so far, she'd been at it for six months with no luck. She had been taking part-time consulting projects to generate income while she continued to job hunt.

When we met for coffee, I asked Georgette how she was doing. For the next thirty minutes, she expressed the frustrations she'd been experiencing trying to find a full-time job. It had been very hard for her and hard on her. She explained how she had been doing all of the "right things"—networking, letting friends know she was in the job market, doing research on the Internet, scouring the papers for opportunities, and submitting résumé after résumé. But it wasn't working. No job had materialized for her after six months of intensive job searching and interviewing. When she was finished talking, she looked at me and asked if I had any creative job hunting suggestions to give her. "No," I replied. And she looked at me in amazement. "*No?!* Why not?" she asked.

I paused for a moment then started to explain. "I don't think the real issue is your strategy or your techniques or your resources or that you aren't looking in the right places or talking to the right people," I explained. "You are highly educated, highly talented, highly skilled, and you've got great experience in a hot field. From what I can tell, you are doing all of the right things. You have been in the job market for almost seven months and nothing full time has manifested. It doesn't make sense. Something is off. I think you may be stuck." I paused for a moment to let Georgette absorb what I was saying, then continued. "Are you telling the truth to yourself about what you really want to do, in your heart of hearts? I suspect the universe is getting mixed signals from you and doesn't know what you want it to deliver. Do you really want to stay in the line of work you've been in, or do you want to pursue a different line of work, or maybe even start your own business? You've probably been trying to sort through and figure this all out by yourself. I think you're stuck, and you need help getting unstuck."

Georgette stared at me for a full minute with her chin propped in her hand. I didn't know if she was going to cry or curse me out. Then she said, "You know what, after almost seven months of relentless job hunting, no one has told me that. My family and friends have wanted to be supportive, so they've either been encouraging me to stay positive or given me yet more suggestions and leads to pursue in the name of helping me. But with all of these good intentions, what I've needed is someone to do what you just did—call it like you see it. Tell it like it is. Give me a wake-up call. You're right. I'm stuck, and I haven't wanted to admit it. I've been trying to be strong and perseverant. But what I need to do is get clear about what has me stuck. Girl, thank you for bringing this to my attention."

"Girl, you're welcome," I said, giving her hand a squeeze, "and if you're open to it, I'm glad to give you the names and phone numbers of three different women who may be able to help you get 'unstuck.' Each is an executive coach and this type of thing is a specialty. Give each one a call, explain what you need, and see which one is the best fit for you." As we got ready to leave the coffee shop, Georgette turned to me, gave me a long hug, and said, "Girl, you just don't know how much I needed to hear this."

> *Get clear first.*
> *See your course of action become crystal clear.*

Ponder the desires that lie deep within your heart
And trust your truth to steer

—djg

30. *Purge and cleanse*

God gave us tear ducts for a reason—
so that we would have a way to
release strong emotions, whether they be positive or negative. Our bodies
are not designed to harbor emotions such as sadness, anger, grief, or resentment. We are supposed to feel them and then release them, let them pass
on through our bodies. When we hold on to negatively charged, toxic
emotions for too long they create blockages or pain in our minds, bodies,
and spirits.

When we allow too much negatively charged emotion to accumulate,
it has the same effect as the buildup of silt—sand, dirt, rocks, and mud—
in a river. It clogs it up, slows it down, and kills the life in it. Thank God we
are designed with the ability to unclog ourselves, to purge ourselves of
the buildup from toxic emotions and to cleanse our minds, bodies, and
spirits.

Three years ago I attended the Whole Life Expo here in Seattle and mail
ordered a deep intestinal cleanse kit from a brochure I picked up at the
Expo. A deep intestinal cleanse is designed to deep-cleanse the colon—
your large intestine—and loosen and eliminate the mucus, fecal matter,
and in some cases, parasites that have become compacted on the walls of
the colon as a result of our modern diet high in white flour, white sugar,
processed meat, processed vegetables, chemicals, pesticides, toxins, and
preservatives. I received my deep-cleanse kit in the mail two weeks later,
and I put the kit in the closet. It sat there, untouched, for three years.

It took me three years to pull that kit out of the closet. I asked myself
why I had waited so long to retrieve it. Well, for one, I realized how easy it
was for me to put food in my mouth because it tasted good or looked good,

but it was not so easy to have to confront the effects of years of making poor eating choices.

The kit sat there untouched for three years because I had been avoiding taking full responsibility for what I had been putting into my body and I didn't want to deal with what was going to be coming out the other end. I knew that the cumulative effect of years of poor eating choices was *literally* going to move through my bowels and out of my body in the form of mucus, toxins, and putrefied food matter. During this cleanse I was going to have to confront the effects of poor choices from my past that were still affecting me in the present in very real ways. And from what the guidebook to the cleanse program explained, *it wasn't going to look or smell pretty!*

You may turn up your nose at this description, but this really is what happens when we begin to heal. When things happen to us, we can have emotions that we don't deal with. We think it's over and done with. Forgotten. No longer affecting us—*so we think.* But forgetting something doesn't mean it's healed. Ignoring, avoiding, or denying something doesn't mean it's healed. Not wanting to face the ugly doesn't mean that the ugly isn't there or that the ugly goes away. Actually the ugly gets worse, more funky and more smelly the longer it sits there, much like milk that goes sour when it gets left out on the counter for too long. You gotta clean it out; you gotta purge and cleanse.

Another reason I think the kit sat in my closet for so long is that doing a deep intestinal cleanse is a serious undertaking. It is about *release* and *elimination*—two issues that are major for women, and particularly for us as black women. *Lease* means to use or occupy in exchange for rent. To *release* means to "set free from confinement or restraint; to liberate; to let go of." What you harbor or hang on to in terms of negative thoughts, feelings, memories, and emotions will occupy you—*literally.* I had been renting my body out to poor nutritional choices and bad eating habits in exchange for comfort and taste, but not what was best for my body. It was time to evict the toxins and *re-lease* my body to the new tenants of health and vitality. On this cleanse, I would be releasing not only toxic physical waste from my body but also toxic emotional waste lingering in my system from old memories and experiences.

To *eliminate* means "to get rid of; remove; to eradicate; to purge." The cleanse guidebook explained that, "Most Americans have substances in their intestines that have been there since they were children. . . . As this old substance breaks up, you may recall incidents that occurred when you ate the substance that is now coming out. . . . As long as the substance containing these emotions, thoughts, or desires is still within you, you will be influenced by them." The guidebook stated that "the deeper you cleanse the mucoid substance from your body, the more memories, thoughts, feelings, desires, and even tastes and smells from the past come to your consciousness." "Wow, this is some deep shit," I thought (no pun intended).

One of the points the guidebook made that I found fascinating was the section on "cleanse reactions." While on the cleanse, as your body starts to release and eliminate the accumulated "pollution" that is in your body, you can experience physical reactions that can appear as if the cleanse is making you feel terrible. Cleanse reactions could include headaches, nausea, dizziness, rash breakouts, or a runny nose and eyes. The guidebook emphasized that the intensity of one's cleanse reaction is directly proportional to the level of toxicity in one's body. One's cleanse reaction is the body's response to the toxins, mucus, bad bacteria, fungus, chemicals, and other accumulated poisons finally being moved out. You could feel worse before you felt better as your body purges these things from your system.

When you are purging and cleansing old stuff from your life, a cleanse reaction of some form is also likely to show up. If you are working on breaking the yoke of financial worry and a mind-set of scarcity and struggle, then you may have a financial emergency arise, such as a car accident, just as you feel that you are getting your finances back together. You are working on bettering yourself and beginning to make some positive changes in your life, then one of your kids suddenly has a crisis.

When you are purging and cleansing, others in your life may be part of your cleanse reaction. Know that purging and cleansing causes stuff to rise to the top like the whitehead on a pimple. The very thing you want to move out or get rid of will come back to meet you and greet you before it exits. *This* is why I had been avoiding this cleanse for three years. I was afraid of what might come back to "greet" me. In *Acts of Faith*, Iyanla Vanzant forewarns us: "When the time comes for us to let go of the things that have been holding us back, all hell breaks loose."

When you are purging and cleansing your body, your relationships, your thinking, your language, your energy, and your thoughts and beliefs, cleanse reactions will show up in your life that can look like hell is definitely breaking loose. But when a cleanse reaction arrives on the scene, it should be a cause for rejoicing instead of woe. It is here to tell you that you are moving forward, that you are purging yourself of some old patterns, and breaking yokes. A cleanse reaction lets you know that your healing has begun. You are on your way .

31. *Write on*

I've kept a diary since I was 9 years old, when I received my first diary as a birthday present from my mom and dad. My first diary had a bright orange, fake leather cover with its own little gold lock and key. My diary became my confidante, like a good friend whom I could trust with my secrets, but I knew she'd never tell. Thoughts, poems, aspirations, the names of the boys I had a crush on for the week, and the beginnings of many great adventure stories filled its pages. To me, my diary was a private piece of the world that no one else could enter.

When I turned 16, I received my first journal as a birthday gift—fresh, lined pages with a velvety floral cover that I now refer to as my "Sweet Sixteen journal." I decided that this journal would eventually be passed on to my daughter (I was hoping that I would have at least one), when she turned 16. So I started writing passages to my future daughter in my Sweet Sixteen journal, telling her about events, milestones, happenings, thoughts, and feelings going on in my life. Today this same journal sits beside my bed on my nightstand, waiting to be passed on to my daughter Adera, when she turns 16 in another ten years.

Once I graduated from college, I started to keep several journals, each one for a different purpose. Now I keep up to five journals at a given time— one for creative ideas and potential projects; a second for recording memorable quotes and notes from books or magazine articles I read; a third for business ideas, projects, and client meeting notes; a fourth that sits on my altar in my bedroom for recording goals or capturing insights and reflections received during my meditation time; and the fifth is for keeping a log of my dreams.

Journals can serve several purposes. There are times when I use my journals to record general thoughts and ideas. There are times when I use my journals to get clarity or reflect, and there are times when I use my journals to process something that's happened to me, sort out a challenge, or release emotions.

One afternoon I was standing at the kitchen sink washing dishes and an idea hit me—to create a leadership summit for African-American women in the greater Seattle area. With my hands still wet, I grabbed a pen and ran to find my creative ideas journal so that I could record the ideas about the event that were pouring forth faster than my hand could write them down.

When I went to Egypt, in addition to taking pictures and having slides made, I kept a journal of my daily excursions, lectures, adventures, and experiences. At the end of each day, the last thing I did before my head hit the pillow was to write down my reflections on the day's activities and how they had affected me.

When I went on my national book tour with the release of my first book, *Sacred Pampering Principles*, I kept a daily journal. Every minute of every day of my book tour was scheduled, from 7:00 A.M. to 6:00 P.M. for two solid weeks. My tour was an exciting, whirlwind flurry of radio, newspaper, and TV interviews; book appearances; readings and signings; and appointments to meet and greet many new people each day. Every day I was on another airplane, flying to a new city, and every night I was sleeping in a different hotel bed.

I absolutely loved it!

To help me stay centered and grounded in the midst of this very fast-paced, demanding, and intense schedule, I integrated a few key rituals into my daily routine while I was on tour. No matter how hectic, no matter how late it was when I finally arrived in my new hotel room, I did two rituals. One was taking a relaxing bubble bath while burning a stick of African Love or Coconut incense, and the second was writing in my journal before going to sleep. Writing down my reflections from the day was my way of digesting the day's activity, clearing my mind, and contemplating insights, "learnings," or understanding gained about myself or other people. A journal can also be a very therapeutic tool—it can help you heal memories, release pain, work through issues, express yourself, or savor a very joyous moment or experience.

But maybe you've never really been a "journaler." That's okay. Now is a good time to start, or restart if your journal or diary has been gathering dust for a while.

If you've gotten a little rusty and want to warm up your journaling muscles, there is a technique called spontaneous writing or stream-of-consciousness writing that can help. You start with a simple lead-in sentence and write whatever comes to mind. Let it flow. You can make up your own lead-in sentences, or get started with the ones I've provided below. Some lead-in sentences that you can try are:

> I remember . . .
> His eyes . . .
> Her hands . . .
> I like . . .
> Maybe once I'll . . .
> If I was a fly on the wall . . .
> Once upon a time . . .

I signed up for a writing workshop at a women's spirituality conference several years ago, and the workshop leader, poet Vicky Edmonds, explained that much of our anxiety about writing is left over from our school years or it is because we think there is a right way and a wrong way to journal. When you journal, there is no right or wrong way—there's only your way. In Vicky's poem "Let Yourself Come Out," she communicates this sentiment by encouraging you to "let yourself spill out" when you write in your journal. You can get a nice journal for about $15 at stationery stores, bookstores, specialty boutiques, paper supply stores, and even your local drugstore. Get creative and use different colored pens, or add some doodles and drawings in the margins.

At a sisterfriends slumber party I attended at a girlfriend's house a few weeks ago, one of the ladies brought her journal. In her journal, she had pasted photos throughout of herself at different ages, so that she could more easily associate her journal entries with specific stages in her life. Do what works for you. Do what tickles your fancy.

Write on. Write on. Right on.

32. *Body esteem*

Q: Debrena, how long have you been in this relationship?

A: I've been in a relationship with this body for 33 years, however, I am just now coming to appreciate and love her fully.

To esteem your body means to honor and highly value it. Learning to esteem my body has been one of the "final frontiers" in my spiritual journey, and one of my most challenging. I was so busy "working on my spirit" that I neglected my body. I'd forgotten that my body was the vessel of my spirit—a divine vessel. But I also came to realize that I could not continue to grow and evolve spiritually unless I addressed my relationship with my body—the vessel that houses my spirit.

I had to *unlearn* that my body was my enemy and start treating it like a dear and cherished friend. One of the realizations in my spiritual journey has been that my body is divine, not sinful. But this certainly didn't jive with the messages I remembered receiving about my body in church, Sunday school classes, and at Wednesday night Bible studies. Though it may not have been the *intent* to create an image of contempt and disdain for the body, that was certainly the impression made by the content of the messages I received. I heard that my flesh (a.k.a. my body) was weak, sinful, and corrupt. I heard that to enjoy pleasure was sinful. I heard that my flesh was carnal and lustful.

These negative messages and images about the body I received at an early age did damage to my relationship with my body. I perceived my body as a nonspiritual object. I didn't treat it right. As a result of my interpretation of these messages, I carried body shame around instead of body esteem. I believe my interpretation of these messages along with the litany of unhealthy media messages to be at the root of my weight challenge that started in high school and continued up through the last couple of years. It wasn't until my adult years that I started hearing empowering messages about my body being a temple of God, as it states in 1 Corinthians 3:16 and 6:19.

I really thought that, overall, I liked and accepted my body. If you asked me, I didn't have many issues with my body. It was just *certain* body parts I wanted to turn in and exchange for something better. You know—thighs with no cellulite, toes with no corns on them, breasts that didn't sag after breastfeeding three babies, and feet that were a size 8 instead of a wide size 10. I learned, however, that I couldn't reject certain parts of my body yet say I accepted my entire body. I couldn't have issues with certain parts of my body yet say I loved myself. My self included my body.

I kept getting amnesia, forgetting that God gave me one body for this trip. This was it. This was the body I'd been *gifted* with. This was not a practice model. No trade-ins; no exchanges or returns. We were together for the long haul. Yet, I kept treating my body as if my *real* body was going to arrive any minute. Like this one was for a test run.

Why does it take us soooo long to wake up and realize *this is it?* Too often we don't wake up until we feel a lump in our breast; until we're on the hospital gurney being wheeled into surgery, or the doctor is diagnosing us with diabetes, lupus, high blood pressure, chronic fatigue syndrome, or fibroids. By then, it can be almost too late.

For most of us, what has been modeled for us is body shame, not body esteem. If we were taught and modeled body esteem instead of body shame, we'd treat our bodies very differently. We'd honor and value our bodies instead of abusing them. The media make matters worse by bombarding us with messages that say, "Your body is not okay the way it is. It needs deodorant, makeup, perfume, this particular relaxer, or the latest gear to be acceptable." To call yourself out on how much you have invested in "props" and products to feel acceptable, I challenge you to choose one day this week (excluding Saturday and Sunday) to go without putting on any makeup. Go natural. Does even the notion seem out of the question for you? Just try it once and notice if it affects how you feel. Does it affect your demeanor, your disposition, your self-concept? Does it affect how others react to you? Does it affect how others treat you? Are you self-conscious? You may discover that you are more invested in needing makeup to feel good, acceptable, or presentable than you realize.

And unspoken messages are the ones that do the most damage because they tell us that our bodies don't look good enough or smell pleasant enough without "beauty aids" or makeup. And we've bought into much of it, lock, stock, and barrel. This is a heavy head trip. And this head trip breeds embarrassment about our bodies, how our bodies are shaped, how our bodies function, how our faces look without makeup, and how our bodies look naked. Even the notion of having others see us in a swimsuit can generate feelings of insecurity and anxiety.

When was the last time you took a good look at your completely naked body? We take quickie showers, then hop out of the shower and are dressed in a matter of minutes. On a recent speaking trip, I stayed in a hotel room that had not only the standard mirror over the bathroom sink but also full-length mirrors on the bathroom door as well as on both sliding doors of the closet. With these four mirrors, I had a chance to view my body from all angles at the same time. I saw little marks and spots, and of course, cellulite, that I didn't even know was there. I had a great time studying my body like a scientist would study a specimen under a microscope. We had a chance to get reacquainted.

How would you do in the following scenario? If a plaster mold of your body was made and lined up with ten other plaster body molds, would you be able to identify your body's mold if you had to be blindfolded and could go only by feel? Take some time and get to really know your body. Get to know how it feels, what it likes. Get acquainted with your body's unique curves, bumps, moles, dips, birthmarks, shape, and textures. Talk sweetly to your body. Touch and stroke your body lovingly and adoringly, especially those areas that you are still working on embracing and accepting more fully. For me, I'm still working on embracing my feet, my knock-knees, and my postbreastfeeding breasts (but I think gravity has won out).

Tell your body what you appreciate about it. Your body loves positive bodytalk. Did you know your body listens to all of the things you say about it—in conversation with others or inside your head? Your body is *always* listening to you. In her book *Divine Daughters*, Rachel Bagby tells us to say to ourselves nine times a day: "I love my cells." Yes, body esteem requires that you, as Rachel Bagby describes it, "Love your cells with a deep, deep love."

I take a few minutes after my pampering baths to talk to my body. While I am rubbing grape seed oil on my thighs (grape seed oil is a natural skin conditioner) and either my homemade concoction of olive oil and ylang ylang essential oil, or passion fruit shea butter into my skin from head to toe, I speak praises and thanks to her:

Hands, thank you for all you did today, doing my daughter's hair, opening, closing, and locking doors, preparing dinner, washing dishes, carrying, reaching, touching, caressing. I appreciate you.

Feet, thank you for all you did today, supporting me while I did my exercises this morning, walking me to and from the car and to my appointments, walking me into the grocery store and through the aisles to shop for food for my family. Thank you for supporting me without fail. I appreciate you.

Thank you *eyes* for seeing clearly as I drove down the freeway, read a book, put on mascara, read my e-mail, saw an old friend. I appreciate you.

You can develop your own words of thanks and praise to your body, or you can use these. Wrapping your arms around yourself and giving yourself a big hug is something else your body loves. How do you express gratitude to your body?

Contrary to the beliefs we may be holding, the truth is that our bodies are *not* corrupt. Our bodies have ended up being the repositories of our unresolved emotional, mental, and spiritual issues; of swallowed anger; of hardened unforgiveness; built-up resentment; negative memories; and grudges held. Over time, if we don't release, address or discharge these emotions, they convert into sickness, illness, and disease that manifests in our bodies.

Body esteem also affects our sex lives. Many of us are demonstrating body abuse instead of body esteem. When you have sexual intercourse, you are not only joining bodies with someone else, but you are also joining spirits and co-mingling energies, thoughts, and feelings, whether you realize it or not. Are you demonstrating body esteem in your sexual expression and sexual choices, whether you are abstaining, celibate, or sexually active?

If we love ourselves as we say we do, then this includes our bodies. Does your body *look* well loved? Does your body *act* well loved? If we truly value and honor our bodies, what ways of thinking, moving, talking to, touching, interacting with, and feeding our bodies should we be demonstrating? What ways of thinking, moving, talking to, touching, interacting with, and feeding your body are you demonstrating right now in your life? Give yourself this quick assessment. If a stranger had the opportunity to "shadow" you for two weeks, how would that person rate you on the body esteem continuum below? How would the stranger rate you on how you treated your body using the rating scale below? Where would you rate yourself?

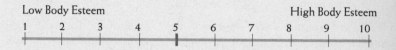

Low Body Esteem   High Body Esteem

1   2   3   4   5   6   7   8   9   10

If you were arrested for being kind to yourself,
would there be enough evidence to convict you?
—Peter McWilliams

33. *Your body is a communication tool*

*E*ver ask yourself why God gave you a body? She could have left our spirits free-floating. But then the experience of life on earth wouldn't be nearly as exciting. Life wouldn't be such a great learning opportunity if we didn't have a body for the journey.

I believe one of our assignments while we are here on Earth is to recognize that the body is a communication tool—a divine communication tool. It is a vehicle and a medium for taking in, processing, relating to, perceiving, and connecting with the world.

And the degree to which we use our bodies to communicate truth, integrity, acceptance, and love, we experience joy, peace, and deep gratification in life. To the degree that we use our bodies to communicate lies, deceit, anger, and untruths, we experience inner conflict, tension, aches, pains, disease, and deep dissatisfaction.

What is so fabulous about our bodies is that they are *wired* for telling the truth. Our mouths may lie, but our bodies always communicate the truth. To use our bodies unnaturally causes us to lose sight of God's purpose for us. So where there are inconsistencies, incongruencies, or unhealthy thought patterns in our minds, it reflects in our bodies in the form of disease and/or pain.

This is why pain is very important. Pain is one of the ways the body communicates. Pain is one of the body's forms of communication. Pain should be noted and noticed, not numbed and masked with Advil, Excedrin, Tylenol, Bayer, or Anacin. We are so quick to want to get rid of pain that we miss the message in the communication. In *Ritual: Power, Healing and Community*, Malidoma Somé explains that "illness is the sign language of the soul in need of attention." That headache may be communicating an internal conflict you are having about a decision. That queasy stomach may indicate a conflict between your conditioned beliefs and what you truly desire. That extra weight on your body may mean you've been *waiting* to pursue your dreams and aspirations, *weighed* down by years of taking care of others first and yourself last, *waiting* to follow your bliss, *weighed* down by "shoulds" and "have to's," or "insulating" or "padding" your brilliance, creativity, or sexuality.

A Course in Miracles tell us, "the body is beautiful or ugly, peaceful or savage, helpful or harmful, according to the use to which it is put." To what *use* have you been putting your body? To condemn, criticize, attack, judge, complain, manipulate, or dominate? Or to serve, bless, experience joy, forgive, rejoice, praise, respect, and appreciate?

If your body is a communication tool, what have you been using yours to say?

34. *What you feel you can heal*

Healing is not the same thing as curing. When you cure an illness, you stop the spread or progress of the illness, or you eliminate the symptoms. Curing an illness doesn't mean that the spiritual, mental, and emotional *sources* of the illness have been identified or eradicated; it means you've only addressed the symptoms. Curing is a passive process while healing is an active process that requires introspection, self-reflection, and a healing of also your attitudes, perceptions, and deep-seated, core beliefs.

To heal, you have to be an active participant in the process. Others can *assist* you in healing, but no one can heal on your behalf, or be your proxy. Ultimately, healing is a solo act. Healing is the result of removing blocks and healing your beliefs, perceptions, and attitudes—reversing the emotional patterns that gave rise to the illness in the first place. Healing is the process of restoring wholeness. As Iyanla Vanzant explained in her In the Meantime Tour I attended in November 1999, "healing is applying love to the places that hurt."

Notice that healing *restores* wholeness. This means that wholeness is your natural and original state. Thus healing is the process of getting back to who you are anyway. Healing requires that you have the desire, will, and energy to first be restored spiritually, mentally, and emotionally so that you can *then* be restored physically. Healing requires not only an internal willingness and an internal decision but also energy and initiative.

One of the ways our bodies communicate to us is through feelings. If we recognize that our bodies *always* seek to communicate the truth, then we can begin to understand how negative emotions or core patterns of denial, self-abuse, lying, self-hatred, anger, fear, jealousy, and self-doubt can lead to disease in the body. Once we begin to learn *how* and *why* disease manifests in our bodies, we can learn to decode the messages the body is sending, address what is really the source or the cause of our disease, and begin to heal.

To begin understanding what we need to heal, let's explore some of the diseases that women, and particularly black women, are suffering from disproportionately. In general, diseases that manifest in our distinctly feminine organs (i.e., breasts, uterus, ovaries, fallopian tubes, cervix) represent major losses of our feminine energy and power through overgiving and overnurturing, not honoring personal emotional boundaries, lack of self-care, practicing self-care last, suppressing our creativity or self-expression, or harboring anger and resentment toward men. As a result, our feminine power centers are drained and our spiritual and emotional systems become vulnerable to first spiritual disease and then eventually to physical breakdown in the form of disease in our bodies. Below are examples of some of the leading physical diseases among women and their associated spiritual and emotional causes.

- **Lung cancer:** Lungs represent the ability to take in the breath of life, to inhale and exhale through the process of respiration and inspiration. To *inspire* means to bring *in spirit* or breath. Over time, if your spirit is being suppressed, denied, depleted, or the breath is symbolically being knocked out of you, it can lead to complications such as lung cancer.

- **Heart disease:** The heart represents circulation, love, and the constant cycle of giving and receiving. Heart-related complications can occur when your ability to love, give, or receive has become blocked, or your heart has become "hardened."

- **Fibroids:** Fibroids are hardened masses of tissue that usually grow on an organ. They can be malignant or benign. Fibroids on your ovaries, fallopian tubes, cervix, or uterus can represent "hardened" anger or resentment toward a past or present male in your life. Or they can represent blows to your feminine power, serious blows to your creativity or your feminine self, or deep feelings of powerlessness.

To gain a better understanding of the mind-body connection of disease, read Louise Hay's book *You Can Heal Your Life*. It contains a complete alphabetical listing of the emotional, mental, and spiritual causes of "common" physical diseases, as well as affirmations to help reverse the emotional and mental mind-sets and beliefs that give rise to the disease.

In a sacred pampering seminar I lead in San Diego in June 1998, one of the participants, Karen, shared that she had almost decided not to come to the seminar owing to early bladder infection symptoms she had noticed earlier that morning. I suggested that she try to trace the physical symptoms back to their spiritual and emotional cause. Since it was the early symptoms of a *urinary* bladder infection, I suggested that she might be very *pissed off* about something or with someone. She sat pondering this possibility for a few minutes, then announced that there was no one in her life she was pissed with. A month after the seminar, I was having a conversation with a woman who was also in the seminar, and a good friend of Karen's. She informed me that Karen had finally figured out what her bladder infection had been about. Karen realized that she was still very pissed off at her dad and had some unresolved issues with him. Her dad had been weighing heavily on her mind around the time of the seminar. Interestingly enough, the day following the Saturday seminar was Father's Day.

Another friend was having problems with her feet. They'd been sore and achy for about a month, so much so that it was painful for her to walk. When she looked *beneath* the surface of her physical disease to examine what was the source of her pain, she realized that her sore feet represented her need to move forward, to "step out" in her life and to break up old, unhealthy patterns in her love relationships.

Another friend who is a director of a state agency department started experiencing stomach problems that forced her to take some sick leave from work. It turns out she was having some serious problems with one of her male managers, who was also a friend. For six months, it had been a continuous string of problems with him, and it was becoming too much for her to *digest*. She continued to allow him to stay on as a manager despite the chaos, confusion, and strife he was causing. Looking deeper for the emotional causes of her stomach problems, she realized her restless stomach was also probably the result of her ambivalence, of repeatedly denying her gut feeling—which was to transfer her friend out of her department—as well as the avoidance issues raised in making a decision that might result in her not being liked.

Listen to your body. It always *tells you your truth.* It will communicate with you in any way it can, even by using pain, if that is what it takes to get your attention. Instead of trying to escape the discomfort of the pain so quickly, stay with it, be with it, listen to it—talk to your body and ask what it wants you to know. Then *listen*. You'll know when you've unearthed the core spiritual, mental, or emotional root cause of your physical disease because your physical symptoms will actually begin to subside or dissipate.

What you feel you can heal—for real.

35. *Create sacred spaces and places*

Sacred spaces and places are those that we declare or consider "highly important" and "worthy of reverence and respect." Sacred spaces and places are those that invoke a sense of peace, rootedness, security, comfort, calm, and centeredness for us.

There are spaces and places around the world that are sacred to cultures or groups of people, like the ancient pyramids in Africa and Central America, the Taj Mahal in India, or the burial grounds of Native Americans. Here we are talking about creating places and spaces that are sacred to *you*.

My two oldest daughters love to build a fort in their bedroom using sheets and blankets tied between their bunk bed and the baby's crib. After their fort is draped and constructed, they proudly announce that Mama and Daddy are banned from entering their fort. They explain that it is only for little people—no adults allowed. To them, their fort is a special place because it has a boundary they've declared that big people cannot cross. The fort becomes their special space, their sacred place, at least until it starts to fall down. We all need to designate sacred space and to establish boundaries. This helps us know that we have a place in this world.

As I shared in my first book, *Sacred Pampering Principles*, "we need special spaces and places to take our bodies, minds and spirits to, where we can relax, nurture and love them." Sacred spaces and places are becoming increasingly important as technology invades our lives, minds, homes, families, and bodies, and the world seems to encroach on us. We need sacred spaces and places we can count on to provide us sanctuary and refuge from the incessant demands and pressures that modern living can bring. Special spaces and places help us maintain our sanity, inner security and stability, and well-being.

For me, my bedroom is one of my sacred places. I prop up on my bed with my back against my backrest, stretch out with a favorite book, sip on my Good Earth herbal tea, and put my Erykah Badu CD on "repeat" mode. My personal altar, which sits in a corner of my bedroom, is one of these such places. My altar serves as a spiritual focal point and the "table" at which I serve myself generous helpings of prayer, meditation, journaling, and self-reflection. When I retreat to my bathroom for one of my forty-minute pampering baths, my bathroom becomes a sacred space for renewal and relaxation. The Barnes & Noble bookstore in neighboring Tukwila about five miles from my home is also one of these such places for me. Heaven for me is ordering a nice, tall creamy Starbucks almond latte, staking out a spot on one of the cozy couches or oversized chairs in Barnes & Noble, and having an uninterrupted hour with a good book. For another sisterfriend, it's relaxing in the hot tub on her deck where she escapes to exhale and let the warm soothing water melt away the stresses of her day. For my mom, it's her garden as she quietly tends her vegetables. Over the course of the next two weeks, I invite you to identify two places or spaces that are sacred to you.

36. *Move more*

An inflexible body supports inflexible thinking. A rigid body supports rigid thinking. When you are inflexible and rigid, you are more resistant to change; change is more difficult for you. You have a harder time going with the flow, trusting Divine Order, and surrendering your ego when you don't move your body enough. See the connection? When your body, which houses your spirit, becomes tight, rigid, and inflexible, this is a sign that your energy, instead of moving and flowing freely throughout your body, has encountered blockages or become "frozen" or stuck in places.

When I'm getting Kenzie, our twenty-month-old, washed up or dressed for the day, I notice how loose and limber her little body is. There is no resistance. Her little arms and legs are limber—they bend, stretch, and turn with ease. As I watch my other two daughters wrestle and play together, I notice their high energy and high level of aliveness. They sparkle. They twinkle. They emanate Life Force. Their bodies bend and move easily. These are the natural and intended states for our adult bodies—loose, limber, agile, and full of energy. Not stiff and tight.

However, a very different picture has become our reality. We're feeling more and more tired, and moving less and less these days. As our society becomes increasingly high tech, we become more and more sedentary and we spend more and more time sitting in front of computer terminals. We need to shift from negative movement—rippin' and runnin,' rushing, always being on the go—to more positive movement. Negative movement increases stress while positive movement decreases it. Positive movement increases the flow of energy through your body, opens up your body's energy centers, increases feelings of calm, increases flexibility, and decreases body aches and pains.

Reflect on last week. Think about the *types* and *quantity* of movement your week consisted of. Most likely, it was movement around your home, movement that involved straightening up, cooking, doing laundry, cleaning, getting dressed and undressed, walking to and from your car, walking around your place of work, running errands or around the grocery store or the mall. Movement linked to getting you through your day-to-day routine is not enough movement to keep you loose, limber, flexible, and vitalized, though. This is not enough movement to keep energy moving fluidly throughout our bodies.

So we must move more.

You've got many forms of movement to choose from. Find the one(s) that work(s) best for you. To name a few, there are many types of African dance, walking, jogging, swimming, the treadmill, the Stairmaster, tai chi, qi gong, karate, kick boxing, aikido, and yoga. After months of searching, I've finally found a specific way to move more that works for me—it's Billy Blank's Tae Bo. Tae Bo is a combination of kick boxing, aerobics, and tai chi. In addition to Tae Bo, which I do for fifteen minutes, four times a week, I've tried to find other ways to move more in my life.

- Instead of searching for the parking space that is nearest to a store entrance, I purposefully park at a stall that requires me to walk at least seventy-five yards to the entrance.
- I start off with some basic stretches in the morning while I am brushing my teeth—side bends and leg lifts.
- When I travel through airports that have a People Mover (an escalator that moves horizontally), I walk to my gate instead of standing on the People Mover.

Make a commitment to move more in your life little by little. Start small and work your way up. Start with five sit-ups one night, and add just *two* more each night before you go to bed. By the second week, you can be up to fifteen sit-ups a night. Look for and *make* opportunities to move more. It will make a difference in your energy level, in your vitality and alertness, and in how your body feels.

Get your move on.

37. *Forgive yourself*

We hear so much about forgiving others that it's easy to forget that forgiving *yourself* is just as important. Forgiving yourself requires that you release regret, anger, resentment, disappointment, and/or guilt you are carrying around in your mind, in your body, and in your memories of past choices, actions, experiences, and relationships. Forgive yourself of what? you may ask. As Rachel Bagdy gently urges us in her book *Divine Daughters*, "Forgive all self-denigration you embrace to survive. . . . Free yourself of resentments' weapons and of regrets' breath-snatching shame."

Many of the degenerative diseases we women are disproportionately experiencing are, at their root, related to issues of forgiveness, fear, releasing, and letting go. These diseases include cancer, hemorrhoids, arthritis, urinary bladder infections, constipation, colon complications, irritable bowel syndrome, menstrual cramps, diabetes, headaches, gallstones, kidney stones, fibroids, cysts, liver problems, lupus, menstrual problems, obesity, multiple sclerosis, respiratory ailments, and skin problems.

Are you carrying around guilt about someone or something from a past situation? If so, you've got to let it go. Guilt is a distorted feeling, an illusion that arises out of a belief that you are unworthy, inadequate, bad, flawed, not good enough, deserving of punishment, or at fault, or to blame. Guilt is also the result of making negative judgments against yourself. Guilt does not serve you; it is not useful. These negative judgments become grievances you carry around about yourself, strangling your joy and making you fearful or doubtful. Forgiveness is what dissolves the grievances we hold against ourselves. When we forgive ourselves, we allow the disappointment, shame, or regret to be replaced by self-love, and re-leased to new tenants of compassion and peace.

But what often happens is that instead of treating guilt with doses of forgiveness and love, we try to give our guilt away to others. This is our attempt to get rid of our guilt. However, it has the very opposite effect. When we try to give our guilt away, it reinforces it and makes it *more* real. Actually, guilt perpetuates self-abuse. Because guilt creates internal discomfort, we try to off-load our guilt onto others in the form of criticism, negative judgment, condemnation, or being overly demanding. Since guilty thoughts and guilty feelings make us feel icky, we try to dump them on someone else.

We subconsciously exhibit these "guilt dumping" behaviors because we are still carrying around anger and resentment for something from our past, because we feel bad or shameful, or because we feel we have fallen short somewhere in our lives.

For those of us who are parents, we must be *particularly* careful. Our children can become the dumping ground for our projected guilt and unhealed *stuff*. You may unknowingly be trying to give your guilt away to them. Trust me: they don't want it.

In one of my favorite books, *The Dragon Doesn't Live Here Anymore*, author Alan Cohen explains why forgiveness of self is so necessary to our healing.

> We cling to our hurts, our grudges, our illnesses, our sorrows and our angers as if they offered us comfort or serenity. In truth, all they offer us is the solace of familiarity and the surety of a self-image that we can hold onto in the face of the insecurity of a changing world. We accept the meager rewards of sympathy, agreement, self-righteousness, and atten-

tion, which are not really rewards, but snares. The dear price we pay is that of inner tranquillity, joy and freedom.

We also like to hide guilt in "little secrets"—those things from our past that we say don't bother us anymore, or we say we've forgotten and moved on from, yet we're not able to talk about them openly to others. I had two of these "little secrets." I thought I had let them go, released them, and forgiven myself. I was to find out this was not the case. I had begun the forgiveness process, but I hadn't completed it. I thought I had healed and moved on, yet I was careful to keep my "little secrets" to myself. (Hint: If you still have an emotional charge around an issue, if you still "feel bad" about it, or hesitate in a safe setting to be forthcoming about it, then you are not healed.) If you are carrying around any shame, regret, anger, or guilt about it in your body, mind, emotions, and spirit, you still have some more forgiveness work to do.

I knew it was time to "come clean" and be completely free of my two "little secrets." God put it in my heart that I needed to confess them publicly to be free, and the March 1996 session of the annual women's empowerment event, The Advance, was to be the place. *Oh, no!* I argued with God, *not at The Advance.*

The Advance was my baby—I was founder and producer of this annual "experience" that attracted women from all across the country. I thought, *I'm the founder and executive director. I've got to look good. I can't go around confessing my secrets in front of women I don't even know!* God persisted. *You need to lay these burdens down for good, my child,* God whispered to my soul.

I didn't know when or how the opportunity to "lay my burdens down" was going to occur, but I knew that it needed to happen at The Advance. In my mind, to make the situation even more difficult, this was the year my mom registered to attend! *What would she think of me?* In the final days leading up to the event I would get a knot in my stomach every time I thought about the task I had before me.

The day of The Advance came. The Advance, which is a twelve-hour experience called The Day of Transformation, starts at 8:00 A.M. and ends at 8:00 P.M. It was now 5:00 P.M. and the event was well over halfway through. It looked like I was going to be able to get off the hook and get through the day keeping my secrets to myself. Fine with me.

It was time for the final presentation of the day. This particular presentation was being given by one of the wise women elders. *Wouldn't you know it?*

Her presentation was an exercise in forgiving yourself—publicly. She positioned herself in a rocking chair next to an old-fashioned full-length, oak-trimmed mirror she had placed in the middle of the main room. She told us to turn off all the lights and light the candles she had placed around the room. She held a big flashlight in her hand. She gave us our instructions for the exercise. She explained that we were each to come forward, one at a time, and stand in front of the mirror. While we looked ourselves dead in the eye in the mirror, we were to complete the statement, "I forgive myself for _____." She told us she'd ask us to repeat the statement if she could feel that we were saying it from our heads instead of from our hearts.

Women went forward, one by one, and each time, the presenter shined the flashlight up in their faces, peering at them closely to determine whether or not the forgiveness statement was coming from their hearts or their heads. Each time a woman finished at the mirror, my heart would start to pound in my chest. *Get up! Get up! Go ahead and get it over with,* I thought to myself, but I couldn't get my body to budge.

There were only a few of us left who hadn't gone up to the mirror. It felt like God and the devil were having a tug of war inside of me. Really, it was my ego being stubborn and resisting what I knew I needed to do—the devil had nothing to do with it. I started trying to talk myself out of confessing my "little secrets." *You don't have to share that secret. Say something else that will sound good.* While God kept nudging me. *Keep your word. Confess it with your mouth. Free your spirit fully.*

God must have noticed that I was having a hard time with this, because She sent over an angel to help me out. One of my sisterfriends came over, sat down behind me, and started rubbing my back. "You can do it," she said. "You can do it. It's okay." This was the exact kind of support and prompting that I needed.

I slowly rose to my feet and walked toward the mirror, passing by Mama as I went. When I arrived at the mirror, I could barely lift my head to look myself in the eye. Again the soothing voice of Spirit whispered to me, *It's okay. It's okay.* I took a deep breath and lifted my head.

I heard myself say, *"I forgive myself for having two abortions."*

There. I did it! My secrets were out. And I was still alive. I was still standing. No thunderbolts had struck me down. None of the other women had gasped in shock. My shoulders relaxed and tears started to well up in my eyes and roll down my cheeks now that my mission was complete. I turned around to walk back to my seat but didn't make it any farther than where Mama was sitting on the floor. I collapsed to my knees and put my head in that soft, safe spot between her breasts. She stroked my head and rocked me back and forth until my tears stopped flowing. I had completed my self-forgiveness process.

What secrets are you keeping that need to be set free? What is it you've told yourself is over and done with, yet is still festering in your mind or in your heart? It's time to forgive yourself. Pardon yourself. Extend mercy and compassion to yourself. Set yourself free.

We must remember, at any given moment in our lives, we are each making the best choices we know how to make, given our circumstances, our perspective, and our level of consciousness, information and understanding at the time. Yes, there are past choices you may have made out of anger, obligation, desperation, feeling scared, feeling boxed in, or because you were in survival mode. Nonetheless, it's what you chose at that moment given your level of understanding and the options you perceived yourself having at that time. You can forgive yourself now. Release yourself from the burdens of regret, guilt, and bad feelings.

We must also know that God gives us *unconditional* Love, not *conditional* Love. No matter what blemishes, blisters, imperfections, or scratches we may have in our lives, God sees perfection. There is *nothing* you can do that would cause God to stop loving you. Hallelujah! Even when you make serious mistakes, when you fail miserably, and when you make poor choices.

In the space on the next page, list at least four specific circumstances, relationships, or situations in which you need to forgive yourself. It doesn't matter how big or small; it doesn't matter how long ago. It is time to be free. It's time to give up the belief that God condemns you. We condemn ourselves, God doesn't. When you forgive, you "give for" your Higher Good. You make a choice to "give up" your pain for your power, and give up inner conflict for inner peace. You decide to replace condemnation with love and acceptance. As *A Course in Miracles* reminds us,

> Those who forgive are releasing themselves from illusions, while those who withhold forgiveness are binding themselves. . . . Fear condemns and love forgives. . . . For this reason, forgiveness can truly be called salvation.

I NEED TO FORGIVE MYSELF FOR . . .

_____ _____
_____ _____
_____ _____

Remember, when you make mistakes, when you mess up, when you are headed in the wrong direction, God allows unlimited U-turns. Meditate on this passage I recently read: *To love yourself for your goodness is easy. To love yourself, in spite of your errors and mistakes, is divine.*

38. *Forgive others*

That bitch. She betrayed me. She wronged me and stabbed me in the back. Someone who I *thought* was a close friend, a sisterfriend. She turned out to be a wolf in sheep's clothing.

The year was 1991 and I was the local founder and coordinator of a chapter of a women's spiritual growth and personal development group in Seattle. The monthly gatherings had become so popular that they were now held twice a month instead of once a month; and a men's group had started, too. My friend Tia was one of the charter members of the group, and also a part of my inner circle of close friends. She'd come to every meeting and be at all the events with several guests in tow. I thought she was the model of a good, supportive friend.

Word about the group was spreading, the group was growing, and we were averaging thirty women and ten men at each of the gatherings. But once the group reached its zenith, trouble began brewing and the "he said, she said" phenomenon kicked in. The gossip and rumor mill started turning. With the attention I was attracting as the chapter coordinator, I learned that my name would often be at the center of the gossip. On numerous occasions, individuals in the group who had my best interest at heart had pulled me to the side to let me know what was being said about me. I would ask who was spreading the rumors, and Tia's name would come up time after time. *What?!* Not my sisterfriend Tia! I thought she was down for me—in my corner. I thought she had my back. Little did I know she was stabbing me in the back, spreading rumors about me that cast dispersions on my character. Even my boyfriend at the time, who was in the men's group, told me how Tia had tried to taint him with gossip that was intended to drive a wedge between us.

It took me several months before I really *got* it. I was in denial. I didn't want to believe Tia was behind these vicious rumors. Each time I would get approached about her damaging gossip, I'd try to rationalize it. Finally, I got it. It hit me. It seemed that Tia was on a serious mission to turn people against me while continuing to masquerade as a good buddy. I started distancing myself from her, moving her further and further from my inner circle. No more invitations to come over and hang out. No more talking with her on the phone. I was seething mad on the inside, and I was shocked and deeply hurt. I felt betrayed.

It took me a total of four years to fully recover from Tia's betrayal. Forgiving her was a process that required me to invoke several methods of forgiveness, including writing what I called "purge letters" where I could rant and rave and get the negative thoughts and feelings I had about her out of my system. My purge letters were my means of spewing out the anger and ugly thoughts and emotions I had accumulated in my mind, body, and spirit. After I would complete a purge letter, I would rip it up and burn it. With each letter, I was clearing toxic emotions out of my body.

I also practiced forgiveness meditations during which I visualized Tia and I sitting face-to-face in chairs. In my visualization, I spoke to her, telling her how I felt betrayed and hurt by her gossip. How I couldn't understand why she would try to damage my character. At the end of the visualization, I surrounded her in a soft, golden light in my mind's eye, and said to her, "Tia, I forgive you and release you." Over the course of these four years, I wrote five purge letters to Tia and did three forgiveness visualizations. She was often in my prayers, too. When the anger and resentment had dissipated, when I could say her name without experiencing a negative emotional charge, or a tightness in my gut, I knew my forgiveness process was complete.

I learned that complete forgiveness can happen instantly or it can take a long time. *It takes longer when we aren't willing to give up being right about how you were done wrong.* We tend to draw out forgiveness when we perceive a payoff or benefit to hanging on to our negative feelings, or when the pain runs very, very deep. I didn't want to admit it, but in my mind, I was receiving a payoff: I was drawing out my forgiveness of Tia because I was quietly hoping that somehow it would cause her to suffer, or experience some of the pain and hurt she had caused me. Actually, it was causing me to suffer. Those parts of me that were withholding forgiveness of Tia were shut down and unavailable to love and joy. My forgiveness of Tia took a long time because I was *unwilling* to release and let go. I was unwilling to wipe the slate clean. Forgiving her seemed like it would let her off the hook, somehow.

Complete forgiveness means forgiving as well as forgetting. Don't fool yourself. Saying you forgive someone while still holding a grudge is not forgiveness. As Susan L. Taylor reminds us in her book *In the Spirit*, "forgiveness doesn't change the other person; it changes you." Forgiveness means that you heal the memory as well as your emotions.

Later, after my forgiveness process was complete, I realized that it took me so long to forgive Tia because my love for her ran deep. Otherwise, forgiving her would have been easy. Her betrayal would have been no big deal if her friendship hadn't meant anything to me.

As women, we often have some serious forgiveness issues with each other as well as with men in our lives. What women in your life do you need to forgive? We tend to have men in our lives—husband, ex-husband, father (whether absent or present), brother, or lover—who have caused us hurt, pain, or disappointment. Stop a moment and reflect. What men in your life do you need to forgive? Some of these individuals may even be deceased, but because someone has died doesn't mean that our feelings and memories died with the person. So go ahead and write down the names of people in your life whom you need to forgive. Remember: *Acknowledging that you need to forgive someone initiates the healing process.* It is the first step.

I NEED TO FORGIVE . . .

_____   _____

_____   _____

_____   _____

_____   _____

_____   _____

*Forgiving someone frees up your heart for receiving and experiencing
just that much more love and joy.*

39. *Go with the flow*

Have you noticed? *Life goes on, no matter what.* Life has a rhythm and a flow to it like a river. Life has a current. And part of our learning while we're here on Earth is to be able to recognize this current, feel it, identify it, get in tune with it, and move in the same direction it's moving—to learn to go with the flow.

So what is *the flow?* It is the energy, rhythm, and pulse of Love that is ever present around us, the forever unfolding living presence of God that moves through everyone and everything. It is the Force and Source of life.

When Life constantly occurs as hard and effort-full, you are not going with the flow. When Life has to drag you kickin' and screamin' forward through needed changes or necessary growth, you're resisting the flow. When you resist the flow, it feels like Life is hard; or you feel like you're taking two steps backward for every step forward.

As Eric Butterworth shares in his book *Discover the Power Within You*, "the best conductor of electricity is the substance that is least resistant to the flow of the electric current. Likewise, the best conductor of divine power is the person who is nonresistant to the flow of divine power." The person who *allows* herself to tune in to and then go with the flow. I believe one of the precious lessons we are to learn while we are here on Earth is how to keep surrendering and giving ourselves over to this flow, this current of divine energy.

Many times, we are trying to paddle our little Life boats upstream against the current, and we curse, complain, and scream about how rough the ride is. However, if we'd recognize that we are going against the current, turn our little boats around, and go with the current instead of trying to fight it, we'd expend a lot less energy and experience a lot more ease in our lives.

You can't go with the flow *and* be a control freak at the same time. You can't go with the flow while at the same time be plagued with worry, anxiety, or concern. You're either working with the flow or against it. And sometimes it takes capsizing your little boat and almost drowning before you get the message. You don't have to wait until a near-drowning to get it, though most of us do. *Life does not have to be a struggle. To go with the flow, you have to surrender your ego, surrender your need to control, surrender your obsessive attachment to things turning out one particular way, surrender your need to know everything, and trust God, trust your SOURCE.* This was the lesson Gail needed to learn.

Gail always had trouble stirring *somewhere* in her life. If she wasn't in a fight with her boss, she was in a fight with her boyfriend. If she wasn't in a fight with her boyfriend, she was in a fight with one of her kids. If it wasn't one of her kids, it was a co-worker or a family member. If all seemed relatively calm with her boss, kids, co-workers, and family, then her money would get funny. When things would get crazier than normal, she'd go to church on Sunday *and* on Wednesday, and put more positive affirmations up on her refrigerator. From the outside, it looked like Gail was really working hard, trying to better her life in spite of the ongoing flare-ups, but the dynamics in her life revealed that these toxic patterns kept recurring. Hint, hint. Yes, Gail was trying to "strong arm" change into her life with her will. She kept experiencing struggles because she wasn't willing to allow God's will to work in and through her life. She kept asserting her will, not God's will. She kept seeing others as the problem, instead of acknowledging that she was the common denominator in all of her troubled relationships. She wasn't flowing. For Gail, allowing God's will to work in her life meant that she had to humble herself, surrender her ego, stop trying to manipulate others in her life with her anger, begin releasing her pent-up anger, and admit that she didn't know how to create and sustain healthy, empowering relationships.

Nigel figured that if he could just make more money in his business, his troubles would evaporate. When asked about his life goal, Nigel's automatic reply was always "to make more money." That had been Nigel's response for years, even in the years when he made more money. Yes, he had the Lexus car, the designer suits, and all of the expensive executive electronic gadgets, but he wasn't at peace. He was caught up in the Pursuit Obsession. Yeah, he was able to make more money, but it was exacting a great price. It was taking a toll on his relationship with his wife and his teenage son.

Nigel had grown up in the Deep South, when the intensely discriminatory Jim Crow laws were in full effect. He was one of five sons of a hardworking sharecropper farmer. He'd watched his dad work hard to grow and harvest cotton, then have to sell his bales of cotton to the white landlord for prices far below market value. This perpetuated a cycle of financial hardship for his family in which his dad was always indebted to the landlord. As Nigel grew up, he promised himself that he was going to make a lot of money. He didn't want to be financially controlled by anyone else. He did not want to be in the same type of predicament as his dad. Money seemed to be the ticket to avoiding life's woes and struggles. As a young boy, he decided that not having enough money resulted in a lot of struggle in his life and that of his family. To him, making more and more money seemed to be the answer.

Over the course of his sixteen years in business, Nigel had drastically changed the focus of his business every four years, in an effort to follow the latest business trend that he thought had the greatest money-making potential. Pursuing a line of business that was a reflection of his true passions, a reflection of what brought him joy, was not even a remote possibility for Nigel. To Nigel, passion and joy were reserved for his hobbies, not for business. You couldn't make money doing what you loved, he believed. These two were mutually exclusive.

Nigel was selling his soul in the name of making money. And in the process he was paddling his little boat farther and farther upstream against the current. Yes, he was a successful businessman by society's standards, but it had been at a great cost. His spirit was restless and his soul wasn't being deeply satisfied. He had not only sacrificed a lot of blood, sweat, and tears but also the quality of his most meaningful relationships. Nigel kept persevering, however, though the waters were getting rougher and rougher and he was having to paddle harder and harder. Finally Nigel's little boat hit a log and capsized, and he had to declare bankruptcy. His bankruptcy was not a punishment; it was the result of his not being true to himself and trying to make things happen on the basis of his will alone. Nigel didn't realize there was another way.

When we don't listen, things continue to happen to us that appear to be bad luck or misfortune. When we don't listen, we get knocked upside the head or keep running into walls. Then we treat this "bad luck" as evidence that life is a struggle and we just need to try harder, work longer hours, keep our noses to the grindstone, or keep "pressing toward the mark." Really, what we need to do is take time out to hold still and get back in tune with the flow. We've been told time and again to "never give up." But sometimes this is exactly what we need to do. *Give it up and give it over to the Creator.* When we are neck deep in our own mess, we become oblivious to the flow. We have a hard time getting in tune. Our ability to discern gets dulled. What is a signal to stop and reevaluate our lives we interpret as a sign to persevere and barrel on through.

Some of us don't ever get ourselves turned around. We have stop signs and red lights all over the place in our lives, but we keep running them. We keep having head-on collisions with hardships, drama, and upsets. We resign ourselves to believing: *This is just the way life is,* or *life is hard.* Actually, it may be all we know, or it's the way we're most familiar with. This doesn't mean, however, that our way works. To learn to go with the flow, we have to admit that the rules we've made up about how to *do* life aren't working.

Thank goodness God is so gracious and patient with us. She doesn't force Her will upon us. She designed Life so that we could *choose* to *allow* Her will to prevail in our lives and affairs. God does not condemn us for the choices we make or how we choose to move through Life. How we choose to "do" Life is up to each one of us.

So begin today to recognize that you have a choice. There is another way. Do an honest evaluation of your life. Are there places where you are fighting the flow? Paddling against the current? Asserting your will, trying to do it *your* way, trying to *make* it happen or force it to happen? When things are meant to happen, they do. There is a natural convergence. You don't have to expend huge amounts of energy or keep pushing and pulling. These are indicators that you are *not* going with the flow.

When we observe women who seem to move through life with ease or come through challenges gracefully, it is usually because they have learned to go with the flow. They're in tune with its current and they've learned how to lift their feet and be carried by it. They've found that they don't have to rely only on their own strength or will. They don't have to do it alone. They recognize that there is a greater power available to them, waiting to be called on. *And they call on it.* These are women who tap into the flow ongoingly, as a regular part of their day-to-day living. Learn to go with the flow and experience more of ease and grace in your life.

One morning in November 1998, my publicist, Dee Dee, called me bright and early to share some exciting news. The producer of the top-rated Emmy award–winning national morning TV talk show *The View* wanted to have me on to talk about my book *Sacred Pampering Principles.* This was the big time.

Initially my appearance date was scheduled for December 6. Then the show's producer called back to inform Dee Dee that Starr Jones, the African-American co-host, was going to be out of town on December 6. Since they wanted Starr to conduct the interview, they needed to change the date to December 20. I confirmed December 20, and the new date was booked. I was soooo excited! I shared the news with family and friends, and then they got excited, too. I decided that I would have a viewing party after I was on the show, to watch the video recording of the airing and do a toast with friends.

One week later, I got a third call from my publicist. The producer of *The View* needed to change the date a *third* time—to December 16, a Wednesday. *Oh, no.* The middle of that particular week was terrible for me. I had two important client training sessions to lead the day before and after that date that had been scheduled and confirmed for over two months. In addition, it was in the middle of my kids' school week instead of at the beginning or the end, as the other dates had offered. I had a tough decision to make: should I bite the bullet and confirm the date, even if it meant seriously disrupting other people in my life? Maybe I could try to reschedule the training sessions with my client, though it risked inconveniencing lots of employees who had made arrangements to be there, as well as risk the possibility of damaging my client relationship. I knew I could *force* it to work if I absolutely had to. Maybe I could take a red-eye flight to and from New York and still make the training sessions. I would probably be exhausted and stiff after getting only a few hours of sleep on the plane, but wouldn't it be worth it? After all, this was a shot at being on a top national TV show. I decided to sleep on it. I thought about it overnight and then called my publicist first thing the next morning.

I decided to decline the date.

I concluded that it was going to require too much energy and effort for me to pull it off, and cause a tremendous amount of inconvenience to my client, to my family, and to me. My publicist checked and double-checked. "Are you *sure*, Debrena? Are you *positive* you can't do December 16th?" Dee Dee implored. When I firmly replied, "Yes," she sighed and responded, "Well, I'll try to get you rescheduled for January. National TV is a strange animal, though. And I can't make any guarantees." As it turns out, to this day, I have not been rescheduled for *The View*.

Many times over the next several months, I kicked myself for deciding not to accept the December 16 date. It took me four months to face the fact that the appearance rescheduling wasn't going to happen. The window of opportunity seemed to have closed—for now. But after four months, I was able to finally be at peace with my decision. I finally was able to lay it to rest. I believe that if it is meant to be, it shall.

Everything is in Divine Order, all of the time, whether we recognize it or not. For me, the flow at that time was honoring my family, my clients, and myself, instead of selling my soul for what I hoped would translate into a few minutes of fame and notoriety and increased book sales for me. I trust that this opportunity, or an even better one, will come my way again. And once again, I will feel it out, be true to myself, and *go with the flow.*

40. Surrender to divine order

There are no accidents in life. Period. There are no coincidences, either. It's when we have a narrow, self-absorbed, tunnel-like view of events and experiences in our lives that we fail to see the bigger picture, the intercon-nectedness. There is *no where* that God isn't. God is always moving and working behind the scenes and *in* the scene. What may look like chance, serendipity, or coincidence is the convergence of divine support, divine timing, divine synchronicity, divine intelligence, divine intervention, divine agency, divine placement, divine assistance, or divine resources working in your life. The more you acknowledge, open up to, and allow the presence of God to work in and through all areas of your life, the more you will experience divine order in your life.

Notice when something "good" happens to us, we label it good luck or a blessing? And when something "bad" happens, we label it bad luck or mis-fortune? *Divine order is in all of it,* including what we label as "bad." As the rap-per M. C. Hammer told us in one of his songs, "It's all good." It is our labeling, judgment, and short-sightedness that keep us from recognizing that it all is in divine order, despite how things may *appear* to us at the time. God has a bias *for* our positive growth, our evolution, our expansion, and our Higher Good. So even when Life doesn't seem to be working, it *still* is working perfectly.

I had a memorable experience of divine agency and assistance several years ago when I was living in Los Angeles. Around 6:00 on a Friday evening in the winter, I was driving home from work in Pasadena on the Santa Monica Freeway. It was an uncommon Friday evening because it was raining cats and dogs. California drivers are used to driving in sunny weather on dry streets so the traffic was especially bad. There were seven bumper-to-bumper lanes of slow-moving traffic creeping along with the glare of red taillights reflecting off of the wet freeway surface. This particular rainy evening I was looking especially forward to getting home so that I could take off my work clothes, put on my robe, and stretch out on my couch with a soothing cup of tea. I was coming home from a very hectic Friday, at the end of a very hectic week, as a telephone systems account executive for AT&T.

My exit was coming up within the next half-mile, so I pressed down on my car's accelerator to speed up to change lanes. My car accelerated, then I felt the engine go dead. I pushed on the accelerator again but nothing happened. I looked down at my dashboard to see my red engine warning light illuminate. Immediately, I put on my flashing hazard lights and navigated my way across three lanes of traffic just as my car coasted to a stop on the shoulder of the freeway. I put my car in park and tried to start it four times. Nothing. I tried it a fifth time. *Nothing.* It was dead.

Okay, okay, okay, I thought. *Stay calm.*

I didn't have a cellular phone, AAA Auto Service, an umbrella, a raincoat, or even decent walking shoes. I looked up and down the shoulder of the freeway, straining my eyes for signs of a call box nearby. No sign of one. (A call box is an emergency roadside phone drivers can use to call for assistance if they get stranded on the side of the road.) Since L.A. drivers don't stop to help one another out when someone has car trouble, you have to make your way to a call box to phone for help. Too much fear and mistrust, and everybody seems to have somewhere to go, go, go that is urgent. So if you're stranded on the side of the road, you're on your own.

I definitely felt very much on my own at that moment, and I didn't know what to do. So I closed my eyes, leaned my head forward to rest it against the steering wheel, and began to pray. *Dear God, I need your assistance. . . .* I had been praying for less than three minutes when I was interrupted by someone's tapping on my window. I rolled down my window to find a man standing in the rain outside of my car. He looked surprised. He said, "Oh, I'm sorry. I've made a mistake. I'm a tow truck driver and I saw your car pulled over on the side of the road." I looked in my rearview mirror and could see the silhouette of his tow truck. He continued, "My cousin has a burgundy Ford Taurus just like yours, and I thought it might be her pulled over on the side of the road with car trouble. I can see I've made a mistake. Please excuse me." He started to walk away and then turned back around to ask, "By the way, do you need some help?" I almost shouted my answer, "YES! Yes, I do!"

Could this really be happening? Seven lanes of traffic on one of the worst freeways in the country on a rainy Friday night during rush hour. Thousands of cars in L.A. just like mine, and this brother notices my car on the side of the road and actually pulls over. To top it off, he has a tow truck. *Thank you, God! Thank you, thank you, thank you!* I went on to explain that my car wouldn't start and I needed to get it towed to my mechanic's shop in Inglewood. "No problem," he said. "I'm glad to help out."

My "angel" proceeded to maneuver his tow truck around to the front of my car and hook it up with chains as I waited inside the cab of his truck. When he got in the truck, I explained the location of my mechanic's shop and asked how much the towing fee would be since it was more than the standard five miles. He said he would give me a 50 percent discount and only charge me $40. *Thank you, God.* My other problems were that I didn't have my checkbook, $40 cash on me, or a way home from my mechanic's shop, which by now was closed. My "angel" volunteered to take me by an ATM machine after dropping my car off, and then take me on home. *Thank you, God. Thank you. Thank you. Thank you.*

Not for one moment did it occur to me to be anxious or worried. After all, I was getting into a stranger's vehicle, with only a little money in my pocket and my car in tow. Instead, I was inexplicably calm. Fifty minutes later, after dropping off my car at the repair shop and swinging me by an ATM machine, I walked into my apartment, one very grateful woman. Divine order was at work and my prayers had been answered.

God is moving and working in our lives in visible and invisible ways, whether we are aware of it or not, whether we believe it or not. Know that God has your best interests at heart—*always*. Sometimes we don't recognize God's fingerprints or footprints in a situation until after the fact, but they are always there. Other times, we are so busy hanging our heads in despair or defeat that we don't see or recognize the divine agents She has sent into our lives as the answer to our prayers.

You are in good hands.

Learn to allow divine order to work in your life.

41. *Ride through the funk*

You're in a funk when you get stuck in a rut or at a low point for two to eight weeks. A funk is not the same as a depression because it is a temporary spiritual or emotional state versus a long-term mental, chemical, or psychological one. You can usually pull out of a funk on your own without professional help. When you are in a funk, you are still able to function, you are still able to carry out your regular routine. On the outside, your behavior is usually not too noticeably different.

A funk can be brought on by several causes: the need to make a major shift or change in your life; the need to do some serious soul searching; the need to reach resolve on an important decision or issue; turning a certain age; or starting something, ending something, or needing to complete something. Sometimes a funk swoops down on you after your spiritual energy has been depleted by the convergence of several challenging circumstances all at once and you need to "check out" for a few weeks to recover yourself. A funk is your spirit's way of taking some down time.

If you lift your feet and ride out the funk, it should pass within a few weeks and last for no more than two months. However, if you resist it, fight it, or keep trying to operate as if it is "business as usual," it will drag on much longer than necessary. I believe going into a funk is our spirit's way of going underground to recover, sort things out, restabilize or rejuvenate itself. Yes, a funk can serve an important purpose. A funk can also be your spirit's way of taking a break to process significant changes going on in your life.

Lifting your feet and riding through a funk can actually prevent you from slipping into a depression.

How do you know if you are in a funk? It could be a sudden need to spend more time alone, having low energy and low motivation, feeling internally restless, being scattered and unfocused in your thinking, feeling the urge to withdraw from others and be alone, or having no desire to be in contact or in communication with family members or close friends for several weeks. When you are in a funk you may want to stay in bed or stay close to home. You may not want to go to work or speak to or see certain people for a period of time. And you definitely aren't interested in fulfilling any heavy responsibilities when you are in a funk.

A funk can be a blessing or a curse, depending on how you choose to move through it. A funk can be your spirit's way of cocooning and regathering its energy. Being in a funk is an opportunity to get clarity, regain your spiritual and emotional energy, and/or make key decisions you may have been putting off. A funk can swoop down on you when you've been in deep denial, operating without integrity for a long time, not being true to yourself, or you've recently suffered a big personal defeat. A funk is an opportunity to start putting things in perspective and pulling yourself back together.

I could sense that my girlfriend and business associate Alisa was in a funk. I had left several messages for her on both her office voice mail and her home phone over a period of two weeks, with no response. This was definitely out of character for Alisa, especially since we were working on a project together. After leaving my fourth message for her, I stopped to get a "read" on her energy. I could actually sense her energy field across our separation. It felt weak, but calm. I thought to myself, *I bet she's going through a funk.*

Two weeks later, Alisa "resurfaced" and finally returned my call. We made plans to get together at her house for a lunch meeting to discuss the project we were co-developing. At our lunch meeting, what is usually time devoted to a brief fifteen-minute check-in and update at the start of the meeting on what's been happening in our lives turned into an hour and a half. The business project got tabled all together. As I listened, Alisa shared what she'd been going through over the past month. Sure enough, she described what I call being in a funk.

She had been doing a serious assessment of her training and consulting business, thinking deeply about what was and what wasn't working, and about what really brought her joy in her business. She looked up one day and realized that she wasn't enjoying her work anymore. She'd been accepting projects that were lucrative though the nature and content of the work felt "heavy" to her. She had been slowly drifting away from the types of projects that brought her joy and accepting projects based solely upon the dollar amount. She'd been drifting away from her center and she wanted to get back on track. While she was in this down time, she'd also been reevaluating the types of clients, contracts, and projects she'd been taking on over the past year and had decided that she needed to make some changes. She was propelled, head first, into a funk as a result of her inner conflict and suffering spirit. Her "funk time" had been about coming to these realizations as well as getting clear on how she could change direction in her business, refocus, and get back on course. By the time her funk had run its course, four weeks had gone by.

Her biggest concern was that I might be upset with her for not being in communication, not returning phone calls, and for delaying the progress on our business project. She was hoping that our friendship was not damaged. She mentioned that one of her friends had gotten really bent out of shape and upset because Alisa had not returned her phone calls, and she knew Alisa was not out of town.

I let her know that I wasn't upset. I understood. I knew the deal. I'd been there before. As I described the characteristics of being in a funk to Alisa, she exclaimed, "Yes, that's exactly what I was going through! That's exactly what happened to me!" Then she asked, *"But how did you know?"* I explained, "Well, for one, I could sense it. And for two, I've been there myself and I recognized the signs."

Another girlfriend, Crystal, found herself in a funk when parts of her world seemed to be crumbling around her, all at the same time. Her sixteen-year-old son was having serious academic challenges in school and had taken it upon himself to decide he didn't want to go to school anymore; her younger son was talking back and expressing lots of anger toward her at home; she was working long hours at a job with people who got on her nerves; her ex-husband had missed his last month's child support payment; her car had just died, and she didn't have enough money to get it fixed. The combined effect of these multiple challenges was too much. A funk descended on her for five weeks while she sorted out, evaluated, processed, and decided what she needed to do. When she emerged from her funk, she was stronger, focused, and had clarity about what she needed to do and the courses of action she needed to take.

At one time or another in your life, you will probably go through a funk. For me, one seems to come around every few years. You can either dig in your heels and resist it every step of the way, or sit back, relax, and *enjoy the trip*. Remind yourself: *This too shall pass.*

Remember, a funk is temporary. And useful.

42. *Call your spirit back*

Q: *How do you know if you have spiritual energy that needs to be "called back" or retrieved?*

A: *You have feelings of anger, hurt, jealousy, resentment, guilt, or pain about someone or something that was or is in your life.*

I think one of the reasons we feel tired and worn out so often is that we are involved with and engaged in activities, relationships, jobs, and interactions that deplete our spiritual energy instead of renewing and replenishing it. We are involved with and engaged in activities, relationships, jobs, and interactions that don't bring us joy.

Why is joy so important to your well-being? *Because joy renews your spirit.* And your spirit is your Life Force. So when you are constantly tired, this can be a sign that there is not enough joy and, thus, not enough renewal integrated into and present in the content and substance of your life. To recover your spiritual energy and reenergize and renew your Life Force, you literally have to *retrieve* your spirit from places it's been left or entrapped. You have to retrieve your spirit from negative and unhealed memories and experiences, and relationships from your past, so that you can make use of this precious spiritual energy in the present.

So you have to go back and retrieve your spiritual energy, just as you would rare, precious jewels you had unknowingly dropped on the sidewalk. You have to call your spirit back from these entanglements, particularly those that are in your past. As Susan L. Taylor shared in her November 1999 "In the Spirit" column in *Essence* magazine, "no one can take your peace or power unless you surrender it." Calling your spirit back means reclaiming the energy you've invested in staying angry, upset, or pissed off with someone or something. Calling your spirit back is about reclaiming the peace and power you've surrendered.

If thinking about certain individuals, situations, or circumstances triggers feelings of anxiety, anger, shame, embarrassment, sadness, or resentment in you, it is because some portion of your spirit is still engaged and energetically entangled in the past. The more situations and relationships you have in your life in which your spirit is still entangled, the less spiritual energy you have available to you, right now, in present time, for creating and living the life you desire and deserve. Your spirit is entangled if these individuals, situations, or circumstances command too much precious time, energy, or attention.

You can begin the process of calling your spirit back by acknowledging the unfinished emotional business you have in your life, and by acknowledging the situations in your life that are still incomplete for you. Sometimes we need to bring closure to situations that have been dragging on and on. Sometimes we need to let it go, disengage, and then redirect our emotional energy elsewhere. Sometimes it's a matter of acknowledging that we still have an internal emotional charge—that it's not really a bygone, that it's not really over and done with. Sometimes it's a matter of forgiving someone whom we feel did us wrong or disrespected us.

Do any of the following scenarios apply to you? If so, you need to call your spirit back.

CALLING YOUR SPIRIT BACK

- Do you have a friendship that ended suddenly, or the two of you had a "falling out"?
- Do you have a past or present boss, or co-worker, with whom you are upset or holding a grudge?
- Do you have individuals in your life who really get on your last nerve, or whom you think of and get a bad taste in your mouth?

- Do you have a past love relationship that ended abruptly, unexpectedly, or against your wishes?
- Do you have a child or a particular family member who really tests you or "gets under your skin"?
- Is there an unfavorable situation from your past where you still feel responsible, still have guilt about the outcome, or wish things would have turned out differently?
- Do you have a particular decision made or course of action taken for which you still have regret?

Calling your spirit back is part of the emotional and spiritual healing process. Calling your spirit back is a spiritual recovery mission. When you recognize that you need to call your spirit back, you are acknowledging that you have *allowed* someone or something to *hold claim* to part of your spirit. Metaphorically, your energy becomes entangled with that of other individuals like an energetic umbilical cord that needs to be cut. The more situations or individuals who are holding claim to your spirit, the more claims there are on your power. The more others are holding claims on your spirit, the more control they have over you and your emotional states, and the less inner power you have available to you. Without your spiritual energy, you cannot bring about change in your life; you do not have fuel for manifesting your dreams or realizing your goals. Without your spiritual energy, your spirit suffers from malnutrition. When you call your spirit back, you cut these umbilical cords.

So how do you begin to call your spirit back? First, you acknowledge the individuals or situations with whom you still have your energy negatively entangled. When you acknowledge, you establish a place to *choose from*. When you acknowledge, you elevate your awareness to a place that enables you to become more conscious instead of unconscious to the effect someone or something may be having on you. When you acknowledge, you tell the truth about what is so. Then you can choose to allow love, compassion, mercy, grace, and forgiveness to replace the unhealthy feelings and negative emotions. You can choose to let go. You can choose to withdraw your attention from the individual or the situation and redirect it elsewhere. You let go by making a conscious decision to do so.

If you find yourself resistant to letting go instead of willing, take a closer look and ask, "If I maintain my current emotions and attitudes about this person or this situation, what do I get to be *right* about?" If I maintain my current emotions and attitudes about this person, what is the payoff I am getting from it? If you are unwilling to let go, realize that you perceive yourself as getting mileage out of keeping things as they are, *at some level*, otherwise you'd be willing to forgive—you'd be willing to heal the memory and the emotions.

No one can do your "spirit retrieval" work for you. This is internal-self work. As the grips on "pieces" of your spirit are released, and returned to you, you will experience an inflow of energy and vitality. As you call your spirit back, you will feel yourself "inner-gizing" as the energy literally returns to your body like a dead circuit that's just been turned back on.

Free your spirit and your power will follow.

43. Get grounded. Find your center

Your *center* is both a physical and a spiritual location. Your center is literally in the center of your body, located in the area of your lower abdomen—the area of your uterus and your womb. Your womb is the physical and spiritual seat of your feminine power. This area is also called your solar plexus, or your gut. When you feel nervous, anxious, worried, or fearful, you may put your hand over your center. When you have butterflies in your stomach, this is actually your center sending you messages. Have you heard the expressions "I feel like my stomach is doing flips," or "My stomach is tied up in knots"? Actually, it's your feminine power center, about 1 to 2 inches below your navel, broadcasting signals to you.

To the degree that you are grounded and centered, you're less susceptible to being flustered, swayed, and influenced by outside forces, particularly negative outside forces. To the degree that you are grounded and centered, you stay calm in the midst of life's storms. Fewer things get on your nerves, irritate, or frustrate you. You have fewer "hot buttons" to be pushed. You are not as defensive because you are internally centered versus externally centered.

We see the signs all around of people being off-center and "ungrounded"— a customer, a neighbor, a child, a teenager, a boss, a co-worker who "goes off"; the increase in road rage and killing rampages, people feeling more and more stressed out and overwhelmed. These are all signs of being off-center. When you are too off-center and ungrounded, your spirit can start to literally leave your body. You can have an out-of-body experience. Not an out-of-body experience where your soul leaves your body like a near-death experience, but an out-of-body experience where your spirit is in the earliest stages of starting to check out. Have you ever had a time in your life where you felt "not yourself," off, or "out of it"? Then you were probably having a mild out-of-body experience.

Jamie, a sisterfriend who moved to the East Coast a couple of years ago, was having an out-of-body experience and didn't know it. She thought she was losing her mind. Actually, she was losing her spirit. She felt like she was on the verge of a nervous breakdown. One of the ways the body tries to cope with too much leakage of the spirit is by having what we call a "breakdown." A breakdown isn't necessarily bad, though, because it can lead to a breakthrough or force you to take a long overdue break.

Jamie called me one evening and shared the trials and tribulations she had been experiencing with her boyfriend, her job, her parents, her relatives, and her daughter. As a single parent, she felt like it was all too much. She felt like she didn't have anywhere to turn for a reprieve. She described herself as feeling stretched to her limit, like a rubber band that was about to snap. She had been feeling on edge, off-balance, distracted, unfocused, agitated, and restless for a couple of months. She was having a hard time concentrating and she was agonizing over simple decisions. She felt like she was "losing it." She also mentioned that she hadn't felt herself lately. When she finished describing her "symptoms," I replied, "Girl, it sounds like you're having an out-of-body experience." She said, "*What?!* What do you mean, *out-of-body?*" I replied, "It sounds like you've been giving so much to others that you've almost given yourself away. There's not much of Jamie left. Your spirit has gotten so depleted these last few months from giving, giving, giving, and helping others solve their problems and predicaments that your spirit has taken a little vacation from your body until it feels safe to come back in. You need to get recentered and regrounded. You need to call your spirit back." She asked, "Well, how in the hell do I do that?" I shared with her some techniques for calling her spirit back into her body, and thus recentering and regrounding herself.

Techniques for Recentering and Regrounding Yourself

JOY

Do something that *brings you joy*. To experience joy, your spirit has to be present in your body. The experience of joy calls your spirit back into your body.

DEEP BREATHING

Sit comfortably in a chair or a pillow on the floor. Relax your neck, shoulders, stomach, and legs. Press your finger against your right nostril and inhale through your left nostril to the count of three. Then press your finger over your left nostril and exhale through your right nostril. Repeat this slowly five times.

Another deep breathing technique is to inhale through your nose to the count of three and exhale through your mouth to the count of five. As you exhale through your mouth, let your shoulders down, purse your lips, and make noise as you blow the air out through your mouth. Repeat this process three times.

GET IN TOUCH WITH THE GROUND

For a week, be in contact with the ground or the floor as much as possible. Instead of sitting at your table to eat, try eating a meal while sitting on the floor with your back propped against the couch or a sturdy chair for support. At lunch, opt for carry-out, and take a blanket to the park if the weather allows. Sit down or stretch out. Take a long bath (which requires you to sit closer to the ground instead of standing straight up in the shower).

VISUALIZATION (CONSCIOUSLY CREATING AN IMAGE IN YOUR MIND)

Sit on the floor with your legs stretched out in front of you. Take three deep cleansing breaths, inhaling through your nose and exhaling through your mouth. Visualize a warm, wide golden beam of light entering your body through the top of your head and beaming down through your body, and passing into the ground. Imagine the beam running down through your body and penetrating deep into the center of the Earth. In your mind, broaden the beam. Make it pulsate and glow brighter. Feel the beam warming up the insides of your body. Feel the beam anchoring you to the Earth and reaching deep into the Earth's center.

As you consistently practice these regrounding and recentering techniques, you should start to notice a shift in how you feel. Clarity, decisiveness, focus, and vitality should start to return to you.

Never lose your "centerpeace."

44. Let go

Hanging on tightly takes a lot of energy. We act as if hanging on increases the likelihood of what we want coming to pass. Maybe it's that we confuse "letting go" with "giving up." Giving up is throwing in the towel, becoming resigned, being indifferent, saying you're not going to play anymore. "Letting go" is loosening your tight-fisted grip on having things turn out one specific way, giving Possibility some air to breathe, and lessening your intense emotional investment and attachment to things having to happen according to what you think is right or best. Letting go is about cutting the towline that you've been using to drag around emotional baggage, doubt, pessimism, and negative energy. Another sign that you need to let go is that you are giving something a lot of negative attention in the form of worry, concern, or fear. So why is letting go a big deal for most of us? Because we are control freaks. We want to dominate, control, and micromanage things almost to death. That's the only way many of us know how to make things happen or get things done. We believe that we have to have our hands directly in it and on it for things to turn out like we think they should. We believe "if you want it done right, you've got to do it yourself."

This mind-set can easily lead to your contracting a bad case of the Strong Black Woman (SBW) Syndrome. When you have the SBW Syndrome, you feel compelled to handle it all yourself or keep doing it yourself. When you have the SBW Syndrome, you paint yourself into a corner where you don't feel you have many options, and you start to resent others for not taking more initiative or lending you a helping hand. Truth be told, we train others quite well in how to treat us. When we dishonor our energy and time, guess what? Others do, too. If you insist on doing it all yourself, others will usually let you.

Since our perceptions are a function of our beliefs, we unconsciously go out seeking evidence to make ourselves right—we tend to notice only that which is in agreement with the beliefs we hold. So when you have the SBW Syndrome, you find yourself having experiences where people disappoint you or fall short of your expectations. Then you treat the disappointment as further evidence that you can only rely on yourself, setting a vicious cycle in motion. The line between having high expectations and imposing heavy, stifling demands on others can get very blurred. When you have the SBW Syndrome, you can become relentless or too driven. You then end up not only exerting unnecessary pressure on yourself, but also applying the same types of pressure to others, especially in your love relationships. You end up lowering your expectations to the point where you have a pessimistic outlook on life or lose your faith in others to follow through or come through. You can look up and feel like a lone wolf. But remember, it's probably because you've been acting and behaving like a lone wolf.

I think we also tend to confuse "letting go" with "not having." We get very attached, invested, and locked on to "the way," the one right way or *the* right answer, and we suffocate or eliminate other possibilities. We believe "if I let go, I won't get what I want." Actually, whether you're obsessively attached to getting what you want or not, what is going to be is still going to be, in spite of you. So *exxxxxhale.* Sistahs, we need to learn to exhale, let go, and keep exhaling.

While I was writing the manuscript for my first book, *Sacred Pampering Principles,* one of my dreams was to have my book featured in *Essence* magazine the month of its national release. After the manuscript was completed and approved, I submitted a copy directly to Susan L. Taylor in November 1996, along with my media kit. A month and a half after receiving my packet, *Essence* called my publicist to inform her that they were interested in running an excerpt from my new book in their February issue—the same month as the book's release. *Wow, an excerpt would be great! Much better than a book review,* I thought. They told my publicist they planned to have a definite decision within the next month.

I was beside myself with anticipation and excitement. Every day for the next month, I woke up wondering if this would be the day we'd get the phone call confirming it was a go. This would be the realization of one of my dreams—for my new book to get some serious press in *Essence* magazine. It was on my mind day and night. I thought, *they* have to say *yes. They must say yes. I need them to say yes.* I woke up one morning two weeks later and caught myself. Here I was telling others in my keynotes and seminars to let go, not be attached, and give it to God, and here I was being a hypocrite—doing exactly what I was telling others *not* to do.

So I decided that I would go on a walk early the next morning to the park two blocks away from my house with the express purpose of letting go of my attachment to the outcome about the *Essence* excerpt. I needed to get on the swings. I knew swinging would help me to let go. When I got to the park, I squeezed my butt into one of the swing seats, pushed off, and started pumping my legs until I was swinging nice and high. With each cycle of swinging back and forth, down and back up, I would whisper to myself, *Let it go. It is out of my hands now. I've done my part. Now let it go, let it go, let it go.* With each swing, I was unwrapping my attention and energy from around the outcome that I was so fixated on.

I said this to myself twenty times that morning as I swung back and forth. By the twentieth time, I could actually feel the internal release. I could feel the internal tension and tightness that comes with being very attached to an outcome dissolving. I felt myself arrive at a place internally where I was going to truly be okay with the outcome, whichever way it went. With the help of the rhythm of the swinging, and my let-it-go mantra, I was able to get to a place within myself where I was truly at peace.

When you truly let go, you are not trying to *talk yourself* into it being okay. You are not trying to convince yourself that it will be okay so that if things don't turn out you won't be disappointed. By the time the swing coasted to a stop, I was at this place. I had let go. I hopped off the swing and walked back home, feeling lighter, relieved, and at peace.

The following week my publicist received the much-awaited phone call. *Essence* wanted to run a full, two-page excerpt from my book, with a copy of the book cover in the article and a subtitle on the magazine cover, too! This was far better than I had imagined. Having my book mentioned in a paragraph or two was all I had been hoping and wishing for.

Learning to let go sets your spirit free. When your joy is not contingent or dependent upon a specific outcome, no one or no thing can dictate or control your joy. The reins are in your hands. You're able to experience joy on the journey, as well as in the outcome, whatever it may be.

Learn to let go, trust, and know that everything is gonna be all right.

45. *Evolve, release, or complete it*

Life is a collection of relationships— relationships with our children, siblings, parents, co-workers, employers, spouses, friends, pastors, bodies, money, friends, food, material objects, and so on. One of the ways to experience more of the sacred power in your life is to learn when to E, R, or C a relationship—when to *evolve, release,* or *complete* it. But what we tend to do is H: *hang on, and hang on very tightly.* One of the keys to experiencing more joy and power in your relationships is knowing *when* to make the necessary shifts and *what* shifts to make.

Something needs to shift in your relationship with your job if you dread getting up to go to work. Something needs to shift in your relationship with your religion if you go to church every Sunday because you feel like a "bad Christian" or guilty if you don't. Something needs to shift in an interpersonal relationship if the relationship has become high maintenance. "High maintenance" means the relationship requires lots of emotional energy and care taking. Something needs to shift in a relationship if you find yourself constantly complaining or harshly criticizing that other person. Something needs to shift in the relationship if you feel that the "juice" and intimacy has dried up or if you find yourself frequently exasperated, angry, or yelling at your mate, boyfriend, child(ren), or husband. Any of these can indicate that you need to stop and do some serious relationship reevaluation.

When you don't stop to determine whether you need to *evolve, release,* or *complete* a relationship, the relationship can start to deplete precious spiritual and emotional energy from you. Healthy relationships *recycle* and replenish spiritual energy while unhealthy relationships consume and deplete your spiritual energy.

I had to make the decision to *evolve* a relationship I had with an organization. I had been a successful presenter with a prominent national African-American women's conference for five years. I consistently had standing room only audiences for my seminars and I received excellent ratings on my participant evaluations. My participation as a seminar leader was a win-win situation for both me and the conference. We had a good thing going.

Sometimes the best thing you can do, however, is to evolve a good thing. Grow it. When you make the decision to evolve a relationship, you allow the relationship to *grow* into something else. You allow it to grow or evolve, not because you've gotten angry, frustrated, or pissed off, or because the relationship has gone sour, but because the relationship has fulfilled its purpose at its present level. You have made your contributions to each other, the relationship has come full circle, and it's time to grow the relationship to a new level.

My ultimate goal with this particular conference was to be a keynote speaker, so I knew that continuing to be a seminar presenter year after year had the effect of associating me with seminar sessions only, and not with keynoting. These were two very different leagues, and I needed to posture myself for the keynoting league if to keynote was, in fact, my ultimate goal. My decision to evolve the relationship was necessary if my goal of moving to a higher level—to that of being a keynote at this conference in the future—was ever going to be a reality. So I decided not to return to participate as a seminar presenter for the following year's conference season, after participating as a seminar presenter for five years.

Much to my delight, the following year I received a phone call from the conference's executive producer inviting me to be a featured keynote speaker in all six of the conference cities for the upcoming conference season. Of course, I accepted enthusiastically. This opportunity was a dream come true. And it was also the result of my decision to evolve the relationship.

What we tend to do is sever or break off relationships instead of evolve them. We are quick to end a relationship as a result of something happening that we don't like, don't approve of, or that upsets us. We need to do a much better job of learning how to grow and evolve our relationships. Our track record of abrupt, dishonorable endings is very telling. We get "fired"; we suddenly resign; we divorce or break up, and usually with ill feelings. This way of managing and "doing" relationships leaves a residue of hurt, disappointment, and bitterness. Emotional damage results when we don't E, R, or C our relationships in ways that honor the relationship and honor the connection.

To make my transition with this particular conference, I decided to speak to the executive producer directly as the 1998 conference year drew to a close, to let her know, firsthand, about my decision to no longer be a seminar presenter with the conference. She appreciated my informing her personally, and explained that she understood my decision. After our telephone conversation, I also sent her a thank-you card to express my appreciation for being invited to participate in the conference over the previous five years. Our relationship was able to remain intact even though it was evolving. There were no bad feelings. No funky vibes.

There are times when the situation calls for us to *release* the relationship, not evolve it. We need to relax and release the tightfisted grip we have on the situation. I had the opportunity to practice releasing a situation when my consulting company was a finalist for a sizable training contract with a regional power company. The competition was stiff from the beginning. Only the top diversity training firms in the city were invited to respond to the proposal request, and my company was selected as one of the two finalists.

For this project, I pulled together a powerful team of three other sistah business owners with complementary areas of expertise. The client's final decision was to be made after both companies were interviewed by a selection panel. One week prior to our interview, my team and I had a planning and prep session. We discussed our strategy, the components of our presentation, our answers to anticipated questions, and even what we were going to wear to the interview. I decided that we weren't going to tone ourselves down, or subdue or suppress our energy or enthusiasm one bit. Instead, we were going to go for it—let it rip. Let it flow. And let it flow we did. Fully be our colorful, fabulous selves.

At our appointed interview time, the four of us walked into the executive conference room where the interview was taking place, prepped, primed, and prayed up in our kente cloth; mud cloth; bright reds, purples, and greens; and locked, short, and relaxed hair in full effect. Our presentation was "on," and we were "on." When we walked out of that room, we felt exhilarated and satisfied because we knew we'd given it our best shot.

As we huddled outside of the building, exchanging high-fives and congratulatory hugs for a job well done, I asked each team member if there was anything she would have changed to make our presentation better. Each replied, "No, not one thing." I felt the same way. Then right there on the sidewalk in front of the high rise office building, we joined hands, and I led us in a prayer. "Dear God," I said, "We thank you for blessing our presentation. We thank you for putting the right words in our mouths and the right attitude in our minds and hearts. We declare our presentation perfect and complete. And right now, we release it to you. It is out of our hands. We are at peace with the outcome, no matter what the decision. And so it is."

I think I said this prayer more for myself than for any of the other team members. After the tremendous amounts of time, energy, and preparation that had been invested in this project thus far, this prayer was said so that I could consciously release it—unwrap my concerns, loosen my grip, and release my emotional attachment to the outcome.

Releasing isn't about not giving a damn or acting like you don't care. It is about getting yourself to the point where, whichever way things turn out, you're truly okay with it. You're able to be in an emotional space where you're at peace. Yes, you have a preference for things turning out in your favor, but you're not bummed out or disappointed if the outcome is not in your favor. You're not pacing the floor, wringing your hands, or constantly worried about how things are going to turn out.

When the four of us crossed that street to return to our cars, we crossed the street free of anxiety, concern, or worry. We had turned it over to God. We had released the situation. Nine days later, we received a phone call informing us of the panel's decision. We had won the contract.

There are times when a relationship doesn't need to evolve or be released; sometimes the situation calls for us to *complete* the relationship— bring it to closure. When I decided to stop going to the church I had been attending for several years here in Seattle, it wasn't because I was mad, upset, or pissed off at the pastor, the first lady, or any of the other church members. It was because I was at the point where I was seeking a more spiritual path and a deeper level of spiritual growth in my life. I felt it was time for me to complete the relationship with my church, apply what I had learned, and begin sharing with other women through empowerment seminars. I knew it was time for me to complete the relationship with my church because I felt like an eagle in a cramped shoe box; it was time for me to leave the nest and spread my wings. It was time for me to leave the church in order to *become* the church that Jesus spoke of.

To bring closure and completion means to "bring to an end or to discontinue." A powerful woman seeks to bring closure and completion to her affairs and in her relationships when necessary. Instead of hanging on or allowing things to drag on or drag out, she knows how to bring things to closure, tactfully, elegantly, and honorably.

We don't seem to be too good at reaching closure and completion in the American culture. The way we usually do our endings does violence to the spirit. We tend not to end things *responsibly* and honorably. Our endings are often abrupt, harsh, and emotional because they are the result of built up anger and resentment over time, or a breakdown in communication, connection, or understanding. When you seek closure and completion, you seek to bring things to an end gracefully and thoroughly, with no holes, commas, or question marks. When you end or discontinue something responsibly, there is a period at the end.

When you don't reach closure and completion responsibly, then you haven't really brought it to an end, particularly from an energy standpoint. Some of your spiritual energy is still engaged and entangled. When you have "incomplete" endings, you leave bad feelings, negative emotional charges, regret, disappointment, open emotional wounds, resentment, and unfinished business behind, all of which zap your spirit and drain your power.

So how do you know if you are incomplete with someone or something? *Your body will tell you.* Your body always tells the truth. If you are still feeling wronged by someone, you have unfinished business. If you are still angry with someone or angry about something, you have unfinished business. If you feel tension in your stomach or your head when you think of the person or the situation, you are still incomplete.

There are many ways to achieve completion. Sometimes, it's a matter of communicating face-to-face with the person. Sometimes, it's a matter of calling the person on the phone and having a conversation. Sometimes, it's a matter of writing him or her a letter, sending out a special prayer, forgiving yourself, forgiving him or her, or letting the situation go so that any emotional charge about it is released from your body. When you seek closure and completion, you take responsibility for clearing your own emotional charge. So it's not about blaming the other person. It's about coming clean about the residual feelings you're still having so that your spirit can be freed.

When you're getting restless, bored, no longer feeling challenged, complaining, criticizing constantly, have lost your passion, or feel that a relationship is seriously out of balance, it's probably time to E, R, or C it. When we H, hang on to it, this requires extra energy from us and suppresses the energy of the other. Where do you need to E, R, or C in your relationships?

E, R, or C—begin setting yourself and your relationships free.

46. *Face your fears*

We must think horrible things will happen if we face our fears, otherwise more of us would do it, and do it willingly. By the way most of us behave, we must not realize that when we turn to face our fears, they evaporate. They fizzle. They lose their power and their grip over us. What you deny and avoid becomes more real instead of going away. When you acknowledge and face your fears, you realize that your fears exist in your mind as illusions that have no real power over you, except the power you *assign*. When we turn to face our fears, we discover that our fear is really False Evidence Appearing Real—an illusion manufactured by our egos.

We must remember that we are the authors of our fears, not God. Fear arises out of our own misperceptions. You can't pick up a fear, set it on the table, pet it, or hold it in your hand, because it is an *idea* that exists in your mind. When you *don't* face your fears, you are confirming that the fear's power over you is real.

Fear has a low vibration of energy that closes down, suppresses, contracts, withdraws, clutches, clings, grabs, clenches, and harms, while love, its opposite, has the highest vibration. Love energy allows, accepts, expands, opens up, shares, heals, reveals, soothes, calms, forgives, and nourishes. Which of these energies are you expressing in the various areas of your life?

Fear keeps you in bondage and paralyzes you from taking action because of what you *think* will happen as you compare a *new* situation to a *past* experience. We manufacture in our minds what we *think* is going to happen, using our past experiences as our frame of reference. We try to move forward while anxiously looking back over a shoulder and wonder why we keep running ourselves into walls. Fear feeds on your insecurities and self-doubt—the inner chatter that insists you aren't good enough, smart enough, pretty enough, dark enough, or light enough. In *Divine Daughters*, Rachel Bagby speaks of our "wasting so much time rehearsing strategies for handling adversity that fail to arise." Fear will keep you rehearsing and rehearsing and rehearsing. Fear will keep you in the grip of "analysis paralysis."

I think our big issue with fear as a culture arises from our core beliefs that failure is bad; failure is to be avoided at all costs. We're told failure means you made a mistake, and a mistake is bad. These core beliefs don't make for a very rich and satisfying life. When you operate from these core beliefs, your life becomes an ongoing attempt to avoid anything that remotely looks like failure or a mistake. This yields a culture where people are very uptight, self-conscious, and dissatisfied.

Before I went full time with my own business, it took me a full year to quiet my fears and gather my courage. It didn't matter that I had support and encouragement from friends, the startup money, and a solid base of existing clients. I was still afraid. My inner demons were raging. It took me a full year to *nourish my courage* enough to birth my business full-time. But I had to *keep peeling back the layers of my fears* until I got to the core. As I peeled and peeled, this is what I uncovered.

> *I feared that I didn't have what it took to be successful at training and consulting full time.*

And what was beneath this fear?

> *I feared that if prospective clients found out my age or that I didn't have an advanced degree, they would think I didn't know my stuff.*

And what was beneath this fear?

> *I feared that I was inadequate because I didn't have any formal education in organizational development work.*

And what was beneath this fear?

I feared that I wouldn't be able to generate enough income to help support my family.
And what was beneath this fear?

I feared that I would have to compromise our lifestyle, and maybe lose our home.
And what was beneath this fear?

And at the root of it was . . .
I feared that my natural gifts, talents, abilities, and skills weren't good enough and wouldn't measure up and be worth receiving compensation for. As a result, I wouldn't make enough money for us to continue living where we lived, and our quality of life would suffer severely.

As it has turned out, my gifts, talents, skills, and abilities do measure up; I really do know my stuff; clients willingly paid me for my expertise, and we haven't had to move. At the same time, we've learned to decrease excesses without compromising our quality of life.

Oh, yes. Fear can rob you of your dreams. Erode your confidence. Cast doubt. Drain your energy. Undermine your faith. Keep you from fully contributing your gifts, talents, skills, and abilities to the world. Paralyze you. Keep you in your comfort zone. Keep you doing the familiar and keep you doing the comfortable, though the familiar and the comfortable aren't rewarding or fulfilling anymore. Fear will keep you playing small. Fear will keep you believing that "going for it" means to play it "*unsafe*" or risky. Fear will keep you trapped in a job or line of work that is killing your spirit.

When you are "in fear," you are denying the truth about yourself, and thus the truth about God. When you are "in fear," you have not yet learned to accept your greatness.

Is there a situation in your life where the fear of what *might* happen has you paralyzed? And if something "bad" *did* happen, what would you make it mean? What do you think the consequences would be? Go deeper and peel back the layers by asking yourself what is beneath each level of fear. Don't keep your core fears hidden in the dark. This will make them seem to grow and expand. Bring them out of the dark and expose them to the light. Fears hate being brought to the light of truth because then they are seen for the illusions that they really are.

Fears can be very dangerous because they cause you to concentrate on what you *don't* want. Your fears can keep you looking over your shoulder or waiting for the other shoe to drop. Fear will have you convinced that failure is almost synonymous with death. Fear will convince you that you are not worthy. Fear will hold you hostage in your own life.

At the 1998 session of the annual women's Advance event mentioned earlier, one of the presenters, Asara Tsehai, a healer and wellness teacher from Oakland, California, led us through an exercise to help us name and face our fears. We sat with our legs crossed facing a partner, holding her hands and looking her in the eye. Asara gave us a series of three questions to ask each other:

> Who are you?
> What do you dream of?
> What obstacles are keeping you from fulfilling your dreams?

You had to repeat the first question after your partner shared her answer, until she had exhausted her answers to the question. Then you moved on to the second and third questions, using the same process. Though my partner and I had very different aspirations and dreams, our core fears were the same. The obstacle that first rolled off of both our tongues was *money*. But as we dug deeper, it became apparent that money was not at the root of the matter. It wasn't the real obstacle.

When Asara debriefed the exercise with the group, amazingly all of our responses could be distilled down to the top two core fears: the fear of our natural gifts, talents, and abilities not being good enough; and the fear of failing. Money did not make the list. Even though we were a room of highly capable, gifted, experienced, educated, and talented women, we still had deep-seated issues about our own worth and adequacy.

The key to being able to move beyond your fears is to recognize that they arise out of your distorted perception of Who You Really Are. Yes, you can move on, go on and be powerful, *in spite of them.*

> *For God has not given us a spirit of fear; but of power,*
> *and of love, and of a sound mind.*
> —2 Timothy 1:7

47. *Exile guilt*

> *Guilt is self-punishment for inability to change the past.*
> *Worry is self-punishment for inability to change the future.*
> —Harold M. Bloomfield and
> Robert Kory

I haven't been able to find a single positive purpose that guilt serves in our lives. As women, we especially have a challenge with guilt because we tend to feel guilty when we are doing well, doing something good for ourselves, or honoring our own needs first. *If it is good and healthy for you, it is irrational to feel bad about it.*

I read an article in a metaphysical newspaper in which the writer asserted that there's "good guilt" and "bad guilt." She explained that good guilt arises when you've wronged someone or are aware that you've done something wrong. To me, this isn't good guilt. I believe our bodies have a natural bias for integrity, and this is your body's built-in integrity gauge communicating a violation to your psyche.

As Burt Hotchkiss shares in his exquisite little book *Your Owner's Manual,* "If you've ever felt ashamed, embarrassed, inadequate, or felt for a moment that you didn't like yourself, it comes from the ageless teaching that you are guilty." He explains that we seem to have an *ingrained,* deep-seated belief that we are inherently flawed or not good enough, that "there is something inherently wrong with being human." He suggests this deeply ingrained belief goes way, way back to the Hebrew view of Adam and Eve's Fall from Grace, the expulsion from the Garden of Eden, and the concept of Original Sin. And it is this deep-seated belief that we are flawed, whether you are conscious of it or not, that causes us to feel deserving of punishment.

It is this deep sense of feeling deserving of punishment that attracts crisis and drama and keeps us in a perpetual cycle of hardship and struggle. It is this belief that causes us to feel bad when we take time for ourselves, when we pamper ourselves, or when we practice self-care first. It is this unhealthy belief that allows us to use, abuse, or take ourselves for granted. It is this same belief that has us sabotage ourselves, fear success, or feel bad or uncomfortable when things start to get a little too good.

Sacred pampering is an antidote to feeling guilty because self-love is guilt's arch enemy. Sacred pampering, which is an expression of self-love, has the effect of neutralizing guilt and dissolving it. Sacred pampering is choosing to do what brings you joy, and what nurtures and renews your mind, body, and spirit.

Notice *where* you may be feeling guilty in your life, and choose to let the guilt go. It is not serving you. Apply the following recipe for homemade "anti-guilt salve" to places in your life where you need to dissolve feelings of guilt.

Recipe for Anti-Guilt Salve

1 generous scoop of Sacred Pampering
2 tablespoons of Self-Respect and Self-Love
1 heaping tablespoon of Worthiness

Mix well. Apply generously to affected areas for as long as guilty feelings prevail.

48. Don't complain

*B*eware. Complaining can lead to your contracting diseases such as "victimitis" or "frustrationitis." If you listen to yourself long enough, you'll become convinced that there's nothing you can do to impact the situation or make a difference. You can begin to feel powerless. You'll start to believe that you have no choice, no say-so in the matter. Complaining is disempowering.

In this culture, we've learned that the squeaky wheel gets the oil, so we have become dependent on complaint as a way to get action, bring a change about, or get others to do what we want them to do.

I know a woman who constantly complains—about her kids, boss, co-workers, family members, boyfriend, aches and pains, or debt. She has a permanent scowl on her face, and when she smiles, it looks like it is painful for her. I have compassion for her, though, because she is dealing with her pain in the only way she knows how.

But the danger of complaining is that it creates the illusion that you are actually doing something about the situation. Complaining does not *discharge* and dissolve the negative emotion you may have built up around a situation—it *recharges* your negative emotion. We have a lot to learn from who and what we complain about in our lives. Complaint without constructive action leads to frustration, finger-pointing, and the blame game. The more you complain, the more you convince yourself that the situation is hopeless and unworkable. Or that the other person is just an asshole. When we have been complaining about a situation or the individuals involved in the situation for a long time, it is easy to become convinced that the other party is the problem.

When I moved back home to Washington State after graduating from college and living in Los Angeles for a couple of years, I accepted a position in our family business. After I had been working for three years as regional vice-president of my parents' telecommunications company, I found myself experiencing frustration and conflict with my dad, the president and CEO. I secretly, and not so secretly, started to complain, criticizing his decisions, his leadership style, and his management style. I was so busy complaining, criticizing, and tearing my dad down that I eluded the real reason I was complaining.

A complaint is usually the vehicle you use when you haven't identified your own deeper unmet needs, deeper issues, unfulfilled expectations, or disappointments. Complaint can also be a way to avoid personal responsibility, self-accountability, or taking personal action. For me, I had a deeper issue lurking beneath the surface that I wasn't addressing, and complaining about my dad was my way of keeping my attention focused on him instead of on the real issue. My complaints were a *front* for the personal call to action that I was so slickly avoiding.

While driving to work one morning, it hit me. The lightbulb came on. Right about the time I started to turn up my "complaint volume" at work was also the same time I started giving some serious thought to going full time with the training, consulting, and speaking business I had been doing "on the side" for three years. Having my own full-time business had been a dream of mine since I was a little girl. My complaint volume was turned up and directed at my dad because, as my boss, he was a logical target. Externally, I was hurling complaints because, internally, I was frustrated and fearful. What I *really* wanted (and needed) to be doing was my own business full time, but I was afraid and insecure about my ability to generate enough money to help support my family. So I had craftily repackaged my frustrations with myself, and directed them at my dad in the form of the toxic bullets of complaint I had been shooting at him. The more I procrastinated and let my fears delay my actions, the higher I turned up my complaint volume at work.

My ego was being very slick. Instead of owning up to my own doubts, fears, and insecurities, I was making up ways to project them on to my dad by complaining about what I thought he was or wasn't doing. Actually, I was frustrated with myself for what *I* wasn't doing—not taking action on my business. I was directing my negative energy outward instead of facing the fact that it was time for me to make my move and step on out. I was biding time. And my biding was making me bitter.

It really had nothing to do with my dad. He was acting as an unknowing agitator. Yes, he was the *object* of my complaints, but he was not the source of them. I was experiencing discomfort because I was not honoring my desires and I was procrastinating out of fear. I was trying to pin the blame for my discomfort on my dad, so that I could have a sense—a false sense— of relief. It was this discomfort that became my wake-up call.

I needed to transform the negative energy I was shooting at my dad into positive energy for developing my transition plan—my transition from being employed to being self-employed full time. Five months later, I had resigned from my parents' company, registered my full-time training and consulting business, and acquired some new, full-time clients.

Take a look beneath the complaints in your life to find out what may really be hiding there—what's the real deal?

49. *Suspend judgment*

*D*o not judge others. I remember hearing this admonishment many times as I was growing up, all the while not understanding what it *really* meant. I didn't really get it. It wasn't until just a few years ago that I began to develop a deeper understanding of the effect judgment has on me and on others.

It goes back to our notions of right and wrong. We act like right and wrong are fixed and eternal, though they keep changing as we get older, wiser, more experienced, and more aware. However, we tend to define *wrong* according to what we disagree with, don't know, or think is different from us. And we define *right* according to what we agree with, already know, or are familiar with. So right and wrong are very subjective, and very relative.

I think our tendency to be so judgment prone can be traced back to our childhood, when our parents or parent figures programmed and conditioned us with their notions of right and wrong. In many cases, it suppressed much of our natural curiosity, aliveness, freedom, self-expression, and critical thinking skills. We were judged as "being good" if we did what was in agreement with our parents' version of right, and we were judged as "being bad" if we did what was *not* in agreement with their version of right. We became programmed to avoid being bad or doing the wrong thing, for fear of falling out of favor with Mom or Dad, or not being loved and approved of by Mom or Dad. This formed early patterns of seeking approval and receiving *conditional* love from our parents.

Between the years of 2 and 7, we probably heard some version of "DON'Tshouldn'tSTOPcan'tNO" thousands of times. I think this is how judging ourselves and others becomes second nature to us. We were judged, therefore we judge. However, judgment binds your spirit. *Where judgment exists, unconditional love cannot.* Along with this judgment mentality, we've adopted some false beliefs that keep our judgment mentality in place. Notice where and when your actions and behaviors have supported these erroneous beliefs.

False Belief: Judging people puts you "one up" and them "one down."
Actually: Judging puts you both "one down."

False Belief: Judging has everything to do with the other person nothing to do with you.
Actually: What bugs, bothers, or irritates you about someone else is a mirror that reflects back to you those aspects of yourself that remain unhealed, denied, repressed, or you don't like or accept fully.

False Belief: Judging someone means you care about the person and want him or her to grow and improve.
Actually: Judging someone decreases the possibility of intimacy and authentic connection with him or her. In our minds, the more we judge someone or something, the more the person is "not okay."

False Belief: My judgment of someone else is no reflection of my own level of self-love and self-acceptance.
Actually: You recognize what is "not okay" in someone else because you've judged it as "not okay" in yourself.

False Belief: When I judge others, I am simply recognizing things they need to correct.
Actually: We judge others because we think they are defective or flawed. Otherwise we'd stop thinking they should be any way other than the way they are. We easily recognize what we judge in ourselves as defective and flawed when we see it outside of ourselves.

False Belief: People are inherently flawed, bad, or evil. This is why they make mistakes and do things that are "wrong."
Actually: No one does anything "wrong," given a person's level of self-love, perspective, experiences, awareness, and particular view of the world at a given point in time. This also applies to you.

I recall a powerful "learning" I received about negatively judging someone else last year when I was the mistress of ceremonies and panel moderator for a businesswomen's luncheon featuring five accomplished women. The five panelists and I sat at the VIP table together as we ate lunch. The panel portion of the luncheon was to begin shortly after the final course of the lunch had been served. One of the panelists kept suggesting that it was time for the panel to take the stage, as well as offering unsolicited suggestions to me on what she thought the seating order of the panel should be and how the panel should be moderated. I smiled at her through gritted teeth. After the third time of offering her "suggestions," *girlfriend really began to get on my nerves.* She leaned over once again to suggest that the panel go forward and take their seats on the stage. And I thought to myself, *Miss Thang, you need to chill out. Stop being so anal. Stop trying to run the show.* Before I had escorted the panelists from their lunch table to their seats on stage, I had decided: *I did not like Miss Thang.*

Four months later, I was sitting in Chicago's O'Hare Airport after a speaking engagement, waiting to catch my flight back to Seattle. I glanced up from the book I was reading, and who do I see sitting across from me about eight seats down? Miss Thang! Apparently, she was returning to Seattle on the same flight. Did I go over and say "Hi"? *Heck no.* I quickly remembered how she'd gotten on my *last* nerve at the women's luncheon months earlier. I sat right there and kept reading my book.

As we disembarked from the plane in Seattle, she was walking up the ramp of the jetway a few yards ahead of me. When she emerged through the gate's doorway into the airport, she was greeted by a giggling entourage of four kids and a man. When all four of the kids started jumping up and down, clapping their hands, and shouting "Hi, Mommy!" I figured they were her children. Then she walked up to the man whom I presumed was her husband, and was given a big hug and a warm kiss.

I observed Miss Thang with her family as we walked to the underground tram, and then rode the tram to the baggage claim area. Each of her children looked very loved, attended to, energetic, happy, and healthy. And her husband, who appeared very relaxed and at ease, gazed down at Miss Thang adoringly as he put his arm around her shoulders.

She was clearly the sun in their solar system.

When the tram came to a stop and the door slid open, all four of her kids spilled out of the tram, grabbed her by the hands and arms, started laughing and talking loudly, and began pulling her along as they dashed toward the baggage claim area. Instead of yelling at them, insisting that they quiet down and let go of her arms, or telling them to "Walk, don't run!" she ran along willingly, laughing and giggling with them as her husband sauntered along behind them.

Later on that evening, once I returned home, I reflected on the airport scene with Miss Thang and her family. From my brief experience of her at the women's business luncheon, I had judged her as being uptight and domineering—someone I definitely didn't like. Yet at the airport, I'd seen an uninhibited, carefree, fun-loving woman who was also a wife and the mother of *four* kids. I had slapped negative labels on her at the luncheon, and in so doing, I had put her in a box with all kinds of negative judgments attached. In the airport, I had been exposed to another dimension of her that I would have missed if we hadn't happened to be on the same flight. And wasn't it interesting that I decided to label her behavior at the luncheon domineering and controlling instead of concerned and attentive?

As I thought more deeply about what had irritated me about her, I realized that, at the luncheon, she was acting as a mirror for me. The qualities I noticed the most in her, though she had many, and considered most irritating were reflections of aspects of myself that still needed work. I had judged her as being a pest and too controlling. But how many times had I been too controlling—with my children, with my husband, with friends, or with an event in which I was involved? How many times had I stepped in, in the name of trying to help out, and I came across as controlling and domineering? How many times had I been uptight when what I needed to do was relax, chill out, and trust that things were in capable hands? Many, many times.

The reason I could so readily judge these particular behaviors in her and they could draw my attention in the first place, is that I was denying how real these "undesirable" behaviors still were in me. Miss Thang wasn't the *source* of my irritation, *I* was the source of my irritation. She was simply an *unknowing agitator.* She was just being herself, and in the process, she was reflecting back to me what I couldn't see or didn't want to see in myself. She served as a mirror that provided me with a reflection of what still triggered and activated my hot buttons. And these hot buttons and triggers existed based upon the qualities I had not yet embraced and refined in myself.

We relinquish our compulsion to judge as we learn to observe without labeling right or wrong. We relinquish our compulsion to judge as we heal our own "raw" inner places. *As we learn to relinquish our need to judge others, we give others the space to be who they really are just as we are giving ourselves the space to be who we really are.*

Acceptance eliminates the need to judge.

50. *Give and receive graciously*

s women, giving is familiar to us— it's our comfort zone. We tend to be very comfortable giving, helping, assisting, and supporting. Where we have trouble is in receiving. But you can't have one without the other. Giving and receiving are like yin and yang. Giving makes receiving possible, and receiving makes giving possible.

Learning to balance our ability to give and receive, so that we are able to receive as willingly as we give, is an antidote for the Strong Black Woman (SBW) Syndrome. When you have the SBW Syndrome, you define yourself, validate yourself, and confirm your value by how much you give and do for others. Many of us have thrown things out of balance because the SBW Syndrome establishes a pattern of give-give-give-give-receive in our lives—a pattern of *overgiving* and *underreceiving*. This imbalanced pattern then sets unhealthy dynamics in motion, especially in our close relationships.

Take the following quiz to find out if any of these *overgiving* and *underreceiving* tendencies apply to you. Get out a pen or pencil and check off those that apply to you, *sometimes* or *frequently*.

THE STRONG BLACK WOMAN SYNDROME— SIGNS AND SYMPTOMS

◇ You don't feel you can rely on others and you often end up doing things yourself.

◇ You don't think anyone else can do it right.

◇ You feel that you don't get much help or support.

◇ You often feel overwhelmed or overloaded.

◇ You have a hard time saying no.

◇ If you say no, you feel guilty.

◇ When you say no, you feel compelled to explain why you said no.

◇ You are overweight by thirty pounds or more.

◇ You are frequently tired or worn out.

◇ You get very angry and resentful when people in your life don't "come through" for you or don't do what they said they were going to do.

◇ When someone offers to do something for you, your reply is "No, that's okay."

◇ Someone offers to help you with something that will make things easier on you, and you decline the offer because you don't want it to be "too much trouble for them."

◇ When someone gives you a compliment, you refute or negate the comment out loud or in your head.

◇ When you are at home, you are in a state of perpetual motion and rarely, if ever, sit down just to relax.

If you are not able to give *and* receive graciously, you short-circuit the entire give-receive process. If you are not able to receive graciously, then it affects your ability to truly give graciously. When we are unable to receive graciously, we squash the possibility of reciprocity. Reciprocity, which is based on mutual exchange, is a natural and necessary ingredient of healthy relationships. When we block reciprocity, we have relationships in which we constantly feel disappointed, unfulfilled, frustrated, taken for granted, or like we are the ones doing all of the work.

Learning to receive graciously is our challenge. Being able to receive graciously is an expression of power. It is about allowing others to contribute to you and about being comfortable with it. We actually *in-power* others in our lives when we receive graciously because we are allowing them to give and share of themselves. Others actually become *more* capable and *less* dependent when we allow them to give to us.

We set cycles of dependency in motion when we are always giving, doing, and *overnurturing* others. Overnurturing others means we are doing for others what they can and should be doing for themselves, in the name of trying to be supportive, caring, and helpful. This can suffocate the other person and also take a negative toll on your spirit, whether you realize it or not. Overnurturing can also start to emotionally cripple others because they have come to rely on your emotional strength as a prop and a crutch. Overnurturing can also prevent others from developing their own capacity to care for themselves.

As I explained in *Sacred Pampering Principles*, when we get trapped in a cycle of giving-giving-giving, "over time we start to become resentful because we don't feel we're getting the support we need. We start to feel others are not pulling their share of the load. We always seem to be the ones doing the initiating and generating. But we often don't realize that we've been instrumental in creating the very situation that has us so frustrated."

We must also look at *how* and *why* we are giving our time, attention, energy, help, talents, skills, or money. Is it out of obligation? Out of feeling we'll lose favor with someone? Out of trying to buy someone's love or friendship? Are we giving to generate a feeling of importance or validation, or to convince ourselves or others that we are needed? Examine your core motivations.

In 2 Corinthians, the Bible advises us to give "not grudgingly," but cheerfully, bountifully and with a light heart. By the same token, we must learn to receive cheerfully, bountifully, and with a light heart.

A powerful woman gives and receives graciously.

51. *Ask and you shall receive*

One of the prerequisites of asking is being clear on what you need, and, more important, being clear on the *essence* of what you are asking for.

Two months before our third baby was born, my sister, one of my baby shower planners, called me to find out what special requests I might have for my shower. I had already given this some thought. In addition to receiving the traditional baby shower gifts, I asked her to coordinate a "meal squad" for me. My "meal squad" would free me up from having to cook once the baby arrived, at least for those crucial first weeks. I wanted friends at the shower who were interested to sign up to prepare either lunch or dinner on specific days of the week and then deliver the meal to our house. This way, I could focus on our new baby and not have to be concerned with cooking for my family. At the shower, friends who volunteered to be on the meal squad filled enough meal slots so that I didn't have to cook for a full month from the arrival date of our new baby. *Ask and you shall receive.*

In the three months following the birth of our third child, Kenzie, my husband and I had to work our "asking muscles" like never before. As it turns out, my husband, Joe, ruptured the Achilles' tendon of his left ankle in a basketball game the night before Kenzie was born. Consequently, we ran smack into an unexpected financial blow. I wasn't generating income since I was taking three months of maternity leave from my training, consulting, and speaking business, and we had planned on his income plus our modest savings to sustain us during this time.

The financial hammer fell when Joe's employer declined his unemployment insurance—that meant *no income for ten weeks* while he was home recuperating from his ankle surgery. We had enough savings to only cover our basic living expenses for about a month. As the end of the month neared, I started praying more intently, affirming my trust in a solution, asking for divine guidance, and rebuking feelings of anxiety and thoughts of worry and concern when they tried to creep in. As the month drew to an end, we had almost completely depleted our savings reserve.

The following week, we received a phone call from our good friends Anthony and Marshelle. Kenzie was almost a month old now, and they were calling to check in on our new arrival and the rest of the family. I explained that we were all happy and healthy—doing great. But I also disclosed our financial challenge—not for sympathy or to complain, but to let them know what was up. Without missing a beat, Anthony asked, "What do you need? How can we help?" I paused to think for a moment, then replied, "We need grocery staples, and funds to cover our next month's rent." Anthony said, "No problem. If it's okay with you, Marshelle and I would like to send out a letter to some of your close friends, requesting small financial gifts to help you out. The letter will be from our family to theirs, and it will be tasteful. All I'll need is a list of names and addresses from you within the next three to four days. Is that cool with you?" he asked. I exclaimed, "Yes, Anthony. It's cool, very, very cool. Thank you!"

As I hung up the phone, I could have felt uncomfortable or ashamed because "our business was going to be out on the street." Folks were going to know we were in a financial pinch, and that we needed their help. Instead, I felt good because I was telling the truth about our situation, and we were allowing ourselves to graciously receive with a cheerful heart.

Anthony and Marshelle sent out the request letter five days later. Over the course of that following week, we started receiving financial gifts in the mail. What could have been a stressful, depressing time became an exciting time. Each day Joe and I looked forward to checking the mail as we anticipated another financial blessing. Envelopes were arriving with checks, and with $10's, $20's, $50's, and $100's in them, along with cards wishing us well, congratulating us on the new baby, and letting us know we were loved and supported. This thoughtful gesture from Anthony and Marshelle generated $850 in financial gifts from family and friends. To top it off, Anthony and Marshelle brought over three bags of groceries and a case of diapers for us. I thanked God for sending agents and angels to assist us. *Ask and you shall receive.*

When you get clear on the *essence* of what it is you want, you increase the possible forms and ways in which it can come to you. What we often do is lock in on the form *we* want the fulfillment of our request to take. We remain closed and tight instead of opening up our hearts and minds to the possibilities. This is why we sometimes do not recognize the answer to our prayers or the fulfillment of a desire, at first. If you look closer, however, you'll notice God delivers in accordance with the *essence* of your desires. When you are attached to the "how," you stifle the process, and you limit the forms your blessings can take.

Through this financially fragile time in our lives, I learned that asking and receiving also involves knowing what you really need, being able to articulate it, and then being able to receive it—graciously and gratefully.

52. *Is it a fit or a force?*

*I*f you're having to push, pull, tug, and struggle too much to make something happen or take place in your life, it's a force. This applies to job opportunities, people connections, love relationships, friendships, projects, interactions, plans, and goals. If the process feels too heavy and effort-full, and it's depleting your spiritual energy, it's a force. If you've exhausted all of your strategies and tactics, and still haven't been able to produce or manifest your desired result, you've probably been forcing it.

Many of us feel resistance and interpret it as a prompt to rise to the challenge, or to be even more persistent and dogged. We must remember, though—when something is meant to be, it shall. If it is not meant to be, it won't. *This especially applies in our love relationships.*

In January 1999, I attempted to make contact with the president of a successful subsidiary of a large company in Chicago. The parent company, but not the subsidiary, was already one of my clients. I initiated contact with the president via e-mail, with the goal of scheduling a telephone conversation to discuss the possibility of doing some business with her company. After playing a few rounds of telephone tag and leaving several phone messages for one another to no avail, I decided to send a few more e-mail messages, in an attempt to agree on a time to talk. We played telephone tag back and forth for *two* months, and we still weren't able to connect in person on the phone. I had never tried to reach someone for this long and not make contact. I started thinking about how to get more tenacious and *make* the connection happen. Then I stopped myself.

Our synchronicity at this particular time was apparently off, and it was not our time to connect. Yet I was going to ignore the signs and barrel right on through anyway. *I was going to force it.* What I needed to do was give it a rest and back off. So I put her file away and decided to try again in another couple of months.

Less than one week later, the president of the subsidiary called on a Wednesday morning and connected with me on the phone. She was as shocked as I was to finally make live contact. Our connection occurred three months after my initial e-mail contact. When I stopped trying to force it, I created the *space* for the connection to happen.

Where we most often fall into this "forcing it" mode is in our love relationships. We meet a guy whom we really dig, and all of a sudden he becomes a candidate for being *the one*. We make up our minds that he is *it*, lock on our "potential husband" radar, and then the "forcing it" energy kicks in. Uh oh. So instead of allowing him to *generate and demonstrate* interest, we take off in hot pursuit.

Our "forcing it" energy in relationships can show up as calling him too much, trying to do too much for him too early on in the relationship, or trying to pull him in toward you—all which have the opposite effect of what you want. Forcing it energy actually causes a man to want to move *away* from you instead of toward you. *If there is mutual interest, you both should generate the energy to move toward one another.* We tend to start forcing it when we realize that we like the guy a lot and we aren't quite sure where we stand with him; we start to become concerned that it may not work out, or if we're trying to dominate or control the situation.

You've probably been on the receiving end of someone's trying to force a position or an opinion on you. It doesn't feel very good. It feels "heavy," like you are being smothered or suffocated. When we try to force something, it creates the very opposite effect of what we want. Forcing causes "it" to want to move away from us to be free of the gravitational pull of our *force* field.

Sometimes when an opportunity to grow or stretch presents itself, fear arises to cloud our thinking and decision making. Fearful thoughts can trick us into thinking that the opportunity or situation isn't a fit when it could very well be. This happened to me when I received a request for a diversity training proposal from a top regional company that was due six days after I was to give birth to our third child. I received the proposal three and a half weeks before it was due. Over the ensuing two weeks, I waffled, flipping back and forth between responding to the proposal request and not responding because my due date was so close. In my mind, I didn't see how it could all work, making final preparations for our new baby that was on the way while trying to get a proposal done. I interpreted these circumstances to mean I would be forcing the process, and thus, it wasn't meant to be. After several discussions, the sisterfriend business owner I was going to partner with for the potential project pointed out that I was thinking in terms of limitation instead of possibility. She was right. She explained how it could all work, without stress and strain.

One week before my due date, with an offer from this same colleague to take the lead in getting the proposal completed, I finally made the decision to respond to the proposal. We completed that proposal the week following Kenzie's birth, in the midst of breastfeeding, burping, and diaper changes, but we got it submitted. And we were awarded the contract.

I almost eliminated us from being in the running, though. To me, my circumstances seemed too daunting—working on a proposal right after birthing a baby! Fortunately, with the help of my friend, I was able to recognize that it was a fit after all.

Learn to recognize a fit.

53. *Choice vs. reaction*

How many of the choices you've made in your life have really been *your* choices? Probably not as many as you may think. When I did my first "choices inventory" ten years ago, I could only come up with one at the time that was truly mine—picking my first apartment. It was the first choice I'd made in my recent memory for which I didn't ask for advice, input, opinions, or feedback from a single soul.

As I reflect on the many, many choices I've said that *I've* made in my life, it is surprising to me how the majority were really *multiples* choices—the clothes I bought (the sales clerk's or a friend's input), the car I bought (the salesperson's pitch), the college I decided to attend (high school counselor's, teacher's, and parents' input), where I accepted my first job after college, and the list goes on.

Certainly there are times and places in our lives for *multiples* choices, but when *most* of our choices fall into this category, we need to take notice. Otherwise, you can look up one day and realize that the life you're living is not your own. You can look up and realize that your life is not fulfilling, deeply satisfying, or joyful because you've been living your life through other people's opinions and choices for you. You look up and have a life that is a reflection of other folks' "shoulds," agendas, or motivations. You can look up and be out of touch with Who You Are and what it is you really want for your life. If you're not careful your life can become the vehicle for the unfulfilled dreams and aspirations of others who didn't actualize them in their own lives.

At a sacred pampering seminar I led in Ohio last year for a group of female administrators and professors on a university campus, we had a stimulating dialogue about choice versus reaction. We discussed the distinction between authentic personal choices, and courses of action that live out of others' unfulfilled aspirations and expectations.

One of the women present, Tara, who was a dean at the university, had an epiphany, an "Ah Ha!" as other women shared scenarios from their lives. She explained that her mother grew up in the Deep South, in a generation in which your identity as a woman was through your husband—you were *Mrs.* Willie Johnson or *Mrs.* Charles Smith. The man was the breadwinner, so he had control of the money and most of the decisions made in the household.

While Tara was growing up, her mother had insisted that she "be her own person, do her own thing, don't let a man or kids hold you down, have your own career and your own money." Her mother would say, "I don't want you to have to live in the shadow of a man like I did." As a result, Tara followed her mother's dictates to a tee. She was now 40 years old, unmarried, dean of a prestigious university, without children, and financially independent. Her life was the antithesis of her mother's. The only problem was that she desired to have a marriage partner, and she wanted to have children. In her mind, she had lost a lot of precious time. By her mother's standards, she was successful. By her own standards, she was successful— and very lonely and unhappy.

Tara shared that she was just now realizing, as she sat in the seminar, that she was angry. She felt like she'd been cut with a double-edged sword. She had been a good, obedient daughter. She had become successful, pursued a career, remain unmarried, and made her own money. But she felt like she had to make a trade-off as she recalled her mother's urgings as she was growing up. Now when she attended family events, her older female relatives would repeatedly ask her why she didn't have a husband. They would make comments or ask questions, insinuating that something was wrong with her because she was 40 years old and without a husband, she explained.

As we brought the discussion to a close, Tara realized that much of her anger was because she had done exactly as her mother had told her, but she still wasn't at peace. She recognized that the actions and decisions she had made in her life related to career, marriage, and children were not based upon her choices. Instead, she had been living out her mother's unfulfilled dreams and expectations. In her mother's mind, she was giving Tara advice so that Tara's life wouldn't turn out like hers. But her advice to Tara was largely based on the pain, anger, and unhealed issues from her own life.

At another out-of-town workshop I facilitated, we had a discussion about authentic personal choice versus those "choices" that we make that are really the result of reacting to something from our past. Frances shared that she had been a straight-A student in high school, had graduated at the top of her law school class, and was now a successful lawyer. In the workshop, as she reflected on her childhood, she recognized that her drive to be number one was not a choice, it was a reaction. "Wow," she said, "I can see it all so clearly now. There were two kids in our family, my sister and me. As a little girl, when my mother, sister, and I would go places together, people would assume that my sister was my mother's child and I was a friend, because my mom and sister were both light-skinned and I was brown-skinned. They would assume that I was a friend or a relative since I was darker. So I think the way I compensated for feeling a little marginalized and outcast was carving out my own place by being the very, very smart daughter—top student, top graduate, top lawyer, top, top, top in everything I did."

Frances stumbled upon a very powerful realization. She was starting to become conscious of the mental program she'd been operating from for most of her life. Her reaction to feeling excluded as a little girl was to become the "star daughter" and the family's superachiever. What she thought had been a choice, had been a reaction to feelings of pain and hurt. Now that she was conscious of her core motivation, she was in a place where she could begin to disengage the beliefs that were perpetuating this behavior. She could *choose* to be excellent and do well, instead of being driven to always be number one, at all costs. And the cost had been great— she felt under great pressure and stressed out most of her life. As a result of the emotions she had kept penned up over the years, she had developed a bad temper and was angry much of the time. She could now begin her path to healing as she started to sort out her choices from her reactions.

Sacred power is about authentically choosing and recognizing Who You Are, not as a form of compensation for feeling unworthy, not as a reaction to pain or hurt, but as an expression of your true self. Letting your choices be an expression of Who You Really Are liberates your spirit and frees your sacred power.

54. Change it

If someone were to ask what's up with you, would your answer be "the same old, same old" or "just working"? If so, you could be in need of an infusion of new energy, some change. When you're feeling sluggish, bored, stagnant, or depleted, personal change can be a great jump start.

Whether you are single, married, or divorced; whether you have grandchildren, four children, or no children; whether you are on a very tight budget, or have lots of discretionary income to work with, you can make a change. It is easy to become a creature of habit, and even easier to keep doing the same old thing, the same way, even when it's no longer working for you. It is easy to conclude that your hands are tied, or there is nothing you can do about your situation. Actually there is more you can do about it than you may realize. You can change your mind or your attitude or your appearance or your perspective or your environment. This is what Ca'Thea decided to do.

One of my sisterfriends, Ca'Thea, was ready for a change in her life. She started going to church, got saved, and wanted to distance herself from her old life of smoking, drinking, and promiscuity. She wanted to wipe the slate clean, forge healthier relationships, and "spring clean" her life of her old runnin' buddies. Ca'Thea's change: she moved to a new neighborhood, got an unlisted number, and gave out her new number only to friends she wanted to keep in her life.

Yvette liked the social service agency she worked for, but she was tired of her desk job. She wanted more variety, schedule flexibility, and face-to-face client interaction. Yvette's change: she applied for a lateral move to a position in the field working face-to-face with clients, and she got it.

Eva had worn the same hairstyle for the past ten years and wanted to spice up her look a little. Eva also had a small two-room apartment that she felt needed a facelift. She kept delaying efforts to beautify her little apartment because her money was always tight. Her change: she put some auburn highlights in her hair, moved some of her furniture around to create the feeling of more space, bought two plants, and invested in an inexpensive bright lemon yellow couch cover to liven up her place.

Vanessa had lived in the same city for twelve years and was starting to get stir-crazy. She felt like it was time for a different environment and a faster pace. She had no kids and no husband to consider. Vanessa's change: she dusted off her résumé, started job interviewing for out-of-state positions, and relocated to a new city with her new job.

When my travel schedule started getting very busy in 1997, I wanted a hairstyle that was simple and easy to maintain when I was on the road. My change: I cut my relaxed hair into a simple, low-maintenance short style about an inch long that requires no curling iron or heat.

Change may be as simple as wearing a different style or color of clothes or adding a piece of jewelry, trying a different lipstick color, taking a new route to work, taking a brown bag lunch to work instead of eating out every day, trying out a new restaurant instead of the ones you always go to, listening to a different kind of music, checking out a movie that you normally would say is not your style, trying a new recipe, getting up a few minutes earlier in the morning so that you have time for a cup of tea or coffee before dashing out the door, trying a new nail polish color, buying a new bedspread, adding a plant to your home, or even changing the outgoing message on your voice mail or answering machine.

When you make a change in your life, it usually indicates a change in your consciousness. Decide to become more *change-responsive* in your life. As Eric Butterworth reminds us in his book *Discover the Power Within You,* it is easy to be,

Involved in an experience of limitation, resisting it, talking about it, feeling sorry for yourself in it, but perhaps subtly enjoying it. But when you finally make up your mind that you have "had it" and determine that you are going to rise to a new level of consciousness, a remarkable thing happens. When you turn to God, God turns to you. Suddenly, you have the whole universe on your side in your effort toward change.

Learn to make change your friend.

55. *Claim your gremlins*

Our gremlins are the parts of ourselves that we consider to be ugly, weak, bad, or undesirable. We've been told to play to our strengths, focus on the positives, play down our weaknesses, put our best foot forward. But these philosophies can also lead to being a very lopsided person.

In one of my monthly Wisdom Circle sessions with my mentor, Miss Maxine, she gave me a homework assignment to make out a list of what I perceived to be my strengths and what I perceived to be my weaknesses. At our next session, she took me through a process that, in essence, required me to own my gremlins instead of avoid them. The exercise demonstrated to me how my weaknesses are not fixed and neither are my strengths. Your strengths can become weaknesses and your weaknesses can become your strengths, depending upon the context of the situations you're in.

Miss Maxine asked me to read off my list of strengths from my homework assignment: decisive, magnetic, motivating, compassionate, a leader; and then my list of weaknesses: impatient, selfish, judgmental, picky. As we went through each one by one, she posed a question that revealed how each strength could be transformed into a weakness and each weakness could be transformed into a strength. "Your strengths and weaknesses are not fixed realities," she explained. "Life is made up of paradoxes, and so are we." She went on to explain how each could be transformed, depending on how it was framed, the context, and the dynamics of the situation. Go ahead and make out your own strengths and weaknesses list, and develop your own set of transforming questions. I guarantee you will receive insight into your distinct qualities and the unique combination of paradoxes that are part of you.

Below is part of my strengths and weaknesses list with the transforming questions Miss Maxine posed.

STRENGTH	TRANSFORMING QUESTIONS
DECISIVE	Are there times when to *not decide* is best for the situation? Are there times when what is best is to let go and allow the most fitting course of action to emerge or be revealed? In cases like these, being decisive can be a weakness.
MAGNETIC	Could being magnetic also increase your likelihood of being a target? When you are magnetic, you can attract positive attention as well as negative attention. In which case, being magnetic could be a weakness.
MOTIVATING	Can others start to rely on you to be their motivation? Are there times when you could be providing motivation for people when they should be finding motivation within? In which case, being motivating could be a weakness.
COMPASSIONATE	Are there times when your compassion could turn you into a "bleeding heart" or cause you to be too accommodating of others? Can compassion make you too soft or weaken your stand? Are there times when compassion could prevent you from making hard decisions? In which case, compassion could become a weakness.
A LEADER	Are you also able to be a good follower? Are you able to submit to the leadership of someone else? If not, being a leader could become a weakness.

WEAKNESSES	TRANSFORMING QUESTIONS
IMPATIENCE	Is being impatient a useful quality for someone who is a change agent, a catalyst, or committed to other people's empowerment and growth? Are you impatient with people's mediocrity or laziness? In which case, impatience could become a strength.

WEAKNESSES	TRANSFORMING QUESTIONS
SELFISH	Are you selfish with your energy in a way that you honor yourself? Are you selfish with your energy in a way that gives others no space to use or abuse you? In which case, being selfish is a strength.
JUDGMENTAL	Can being judgmental mean that you have a critical eye or well-developed discernment and assessment abilities? In which case, being judgmental could be a strength.
PICKY	Does picky mean that you have a low tolerance for mediocrity? Does being picky mean that you are selective, have high standards, or are used to excellence? If so, being picky could be a strength.

We continued through the rest of my list with Miss Maxine raising counter-perspectives. She explained, "Being free is about being able to embrace the contradictions that make you up, not necessarily getting rid of or suppressing any aspects of yourself. Learn to transform them. Trying to get rid of a quality you've decided is a weakness doesn't work because it focuses more attention and energy on that which you want to get rid of. It's negative self-judgment. Trying to rid yourself of your so-called weaknesses only entrenches them that much more deeply. Include them in who you are. Accept them. Integrate them into Who You Are. Instead of describing yourself as only a motivator, learn to embrace the paradox and describe yourself as an impatient motivator. Instead of describing yourself as a leader, you can describe yourself as a picky leader. You are compassionate *and* picky *and* a leader *and* a motivator—all at once. All of these qualities are aspects of who you are. Don't fight them. "The point of this exercise," Miss Maxine continued, "is for you to learn *not* to try to cover up, avoid, or ignore your so-called weaknesses, but to bring them forth and set them out on the table. Take a good look at them, put your arms around them, embrace them. You don't want to overidentify with either your strengths or your weaknesses because they are only *aspects* of what makes you You. They are not the *essence* of what makes you You. I want you to learn to make room for your weaknesses as well as your strengths. Claim your gremlins."

So in this session, I learned to start owning *all* parts of me. I learned to start recognizing how my strengths *and* weaknesses could be useful. I didn't have to reject or minimize any part of myself because it was labeled a weakness. Both comprised my unique qualities. Miss Maxine closed by adding, "Remember, you want to bring forth the gifts in your character that support you in your life's work and in creating positive relationships and connections with others. The key is learning to discern when and where you need to emphasize certain gifts, because they all can be useful."

This particular Wisdom Circle session touched some very deep places in me. In the process of doing this "claiming my gremlins" exercise, I was freeing myself up, giving myself permission for a fuller range of self-expression, giving myself more possibilities for being, and developing a greater understanding of how to access all parts of myself.

I walked away from that session claiming not only my gremlins but also more of my sacred power.

56. *That which you are seeking is also seeking you*

Some of the most powerful life-changing books I've read are unassuming and understated. No flashy covers. No expensive point-of-sale displays or reviews in the *New York Times*. Most often the life-changing books I find are squeezed into an unlikely spot high upon a top shelf or way down low on a bottom shelf. They are rarely found at eye level where most people are looking. The book that this chapter's sacred power principle is based on was found in one of these such places. I don't even remember which bookstore I found it in, but I am glad I did.

Do you ever stop to think about what it is that *causes* you to question, ponder, seek, look, strive, change, grow, evolve, or want to get better? What is it inside of you that *causes* you to have feelings of dissatisfaction, restlessness, or loneliness? This special little book, *That Which You Are Seeking Is Causing You to Seek*, written by an author who recognizes herself simply as Cheri, raises these same types of questions and provides some answers. I'd like to share some of them with you. Based upon the narrative at the beginning of the book, Cheri practices Zen Buddhism.

In the foreword to the book, Cheri writes "Life startles us because we keep falling asleep." This reminded me of a passage I read in *Conversations with God: Book Two*, where God explains "Life is not a school, and your purpose here . . . is to re-member." Hmmm, so maybe waking up was about remembering. In *Conversations with God: Book One*, God states, "You are, have always been, and will always be, a divine part of the divine whole. . . . That is why the act . . . of returning to God is called remembrance. . . . Your job here on Earth, therefore, is . . . to re-member Who You Are. And to remember who everyone else is." And it is this desire to reconnect and remember that causes us to seek.

I interpreted these passages to mean that the process of "waking up" is remembering Who and Whose You Really Are. "Waking up" is the process of recognizing that you are already connected to the Source of the universe, that you are already divine and perfect *as you are*. "Waking up" is about seeing yourself for Who You Really Are—brilliant, powerful, loving, and creative. "Waking up" is letting go of who you are not.

Waking up and remembering requires that we interrupt the illusions, assumptions, and conditionings that we've bought into, lock, stock, and barrel. Waking up and remembering requires that we do the uncommon and really start to *think critically* and "outside the box" of conditioned, programmed thinking instead of running on "autopilot," like most folks. It is time to wake up, stop hitting the snooze button in our lives, and start recovering from generations of "spiritual amnesia."

The following ideas, which are based upon concepts found in *That Which You Are Seeking Is Also Seeking You*, jolted me when I read them. They helped me realize the depth of the insanity that many of us are living in. (My definition of insanity is continuing to do what is *not* working and what is causing you to suffer.)

Take one statement per day, and chew on it slowly. Think deeply about it. Reflect, ponder, and meditate upon it. Assess your life for evidence of where your thoughts, actions, words, and behavior have supported the statement. These statements reveal the distortions in our believing and thinking that keep us from waking up. As we start to break the chains of misperception and illusion, we begin to reconnect with our Source and remember.

- By burying, hiding, denying, and then refusing to look, we fool ourselves into believing that we've gotten rid of something when really all we've done is closed our eyes.

- When we stop resisting what is, when we stop clinging to our beliefs and assumptions about how things should be, we are letting go, we are opening ourselves to the present moment.
- We would rather be right than happy.
- Pain is not suffering. Suffering is our reaction to pain. Defensiveness, greed, anger, denial, repression, rejection, and fear are all, at their source, reactions to pain.
- Everything that is the way I want it to be is good. Things that aren't the way I want them to be are bad. (Then we develop judgments to support our notions of "good" and "bad.")
- As we start to replace the insanity in our lives with clarity and truth, we begin to find what we've been looking for.
- What would happen if I . . .

    let go of all my defenses?
    lived in the present?
    let myself off the hook?
    put all my energy into enjoying my life?
    stopped believing the things I tell myself?
    loved myself unconditionally?

What would happen? YOU'D WAKE UP.

Seek and ye shall find.

57. *You can love from a distance*

O ne of my favorite authors, Susan L. Taylor, said it in a nutshell: "Not everyone is healthy enough to have a front-row seat in our lives." You know what I'm talkin' about—some folks who are in the front row of our lives need to be in the balcony. *Can I get a witness?!*

In one of my seminars, I explained that some folks are riding in first class in our lives and they need to be in coach. Then a sister in the audience chimed in, "Girl, there are folks riding in first class in my life that need to be on stand-by!" To love others, we don't have to put others front and center in our lives. Our ability to love is more expansive than that. Yet, we keep investing major T.E.A. (time, energy, and attention) on people in our lives (and this includes family members and relatives) who don't want to or who are not capable of reciprocating.

We've been told, taught, and conditioned, through the words, behaviors, and actions of older women in our lives, our mamas in particular, that to love someone, the person has to be center stage, our "main attraction" and get all of our prime T.E.A. When we keep giving people front-row seats in our lives who don't appreciate it, abuse the position, take advantage of it, or don't know how to reciprocate, it starts to create resentment in us. As a result, we start to lower our expectations of others, expect to give a lot and receive a little, get resigned, or come to the conclusion that love is about constant sacrifice of self, or being a martyr. *Not so.*

One evening I was watching the Discovery Channel with my husband, and it was featuring the lions of south-central Africa. The narrator was explaining how female lions behave and interact in a lion pride. When one of the lionesses gets mildly sick or injured, all of the other lionesses come to her aid, helping her out with her lion cubs and sharing the food they've hunted. But if one of the lionesses gets really sick, this all changes. When the sickness of one lioness is serious enough that it starts to hinder the pride or take too much energy to help and assist her, the other lionesses will start to move away from her. They start to love her from a distance, so to speak. She is on her own to keep up, heal, and become healthy, then she is re-embraced by the pride once again.

I found this very fascinating. This behavior demonstrated that a lioness that becomes too sick is treated as a liability to the pride. It is clear that lions value being well, healthy contributing members of the pride over being sick and weak. In my mind, this behavior makes a lot of sense. We have a lot to learn from other animals, since we are ones ourselves. In this culture, being sick gets us a lot of attention and energy from others in our lives. What would happen if we made a shift in what we value—from giving attention to what is sick or unhealthy to giving attention to what is strong, healthy, and well? I guarantee that we'd have fewer and fewer people get sick.

Sisterfriend and motivational speaker and author Jewel Diamond Taylor advises us to "spend major time with major people in our lives," and "spend minor time with minor people." There are people in our lives who we need to move away from until they can become healthier, people in our lives who we need to learn to love from a distance. Otherwise, they can start to drain us, try to project their smallness on us, suppress our joy, or deplete our spirit. This is when they need a new seat assignment in our lives, one farther back from the front.

Loving from a distance is not about being arrogant, selfish, or stuckup. It's not about punishing someone else. It's about being smart, honoring your energy, honoring your boundaries, and taking a stand for your well-being and for more reciprocity in your relationships. This is a healthy, *natural*, and empowering way to be in relationships.

Loving from a distance doesn't have to be cruel or about cutting folks off, as much as it is about doing a serious evaluation: with *whom* are you investing precious T.E.A. (time, energy, and attention)? Is your T.E.A. invested in relationships that have stagnated, fulfilled their purpose, or reached their maturity? Often we stay deeply invested in these types of relationships because this is all we know, it's comfortable, we feel obligated, or we don't really know how to establish and build new friendships, and make and sustain new connections.

Do you have the same fixed set of close friends year after year? Is any new relationship energy being added? When you meet someone new who seems interesting to you or is of like mind, do you know how to initiate, cultivate, and then grow a new friendship? Often we fill our front-row seats with nothing but stale, stagnant, or old relationships. Loving from a distance means managing your time and energy differently. You might need to make out a new seating chart, leaving some front-row seats available for some new relationships.

For years, I watched an aunt continue to pour her precious T.E.A. into her adult son, bailing him out of tight situations, making excuses for him when he didn't show up or come through, covering up for his drug problem, and going out of her way to help him time after time without appreciation or thanks from him. She was a mama trying to save her son.

As a mother, I know she was doing it out of love. She so badly wanted to see him get himself together. Problem was, *she* was more committed to his getting himself together than *he* was. The more she tried to save him, the more irresponsible he became. In her efforts to help him the only way she knew how, she was actually weakening him. Her "rescuer" reaction actually established a cycle of co-dependence. He was losing power and becoming less capable and responsible, and more dependent on his mother's inner strength. And she was giving her power away by continuing to make energy investments in her son that weren't yielding positive returns. She was also losing power by thinking and acting as if she could get it together *for* him.

On my most recent visit to my aunt's, I saw a different woman. She had stopped *allowing* herself to get entangled in her son's life; feeling his life would fall apart if she wasn't there holding it together for him. She stopped allowing her mental, emotional, and spiritual energy to be consumed by his circumstances. She stopped being at his beck and call, dropping everything to come to his aid. She stopped forgoing her own needs and plans to help him out of yet another jam. She didn't love him any less or stop wanting the best for him. She decided to start loving him from a distance and supporting him from a distance until he learned the lessons he needed to learn, and gained the insights he needed to gain that would enable him to get well, heal, and move forward. She started loving him from a distance until it was safe for her to love him up close again.

She had to learn to stop judging his choices and the path he was choosing. She began to recognize that he was being who he was based upon his level of awareness, knowledge, and understanding. As she learned to take care of herself, protect her space and her energy, she was modeling healthy self-care while also giving her son the space he needed to learn to take care of himself.

It is actually unfair of us to expect others, especially our loved ones, to be where we want them to be instead of where they are. We have to decide how *we* are going to respond to them and what *our* posture is going to be instead of trying to make them into something they are not, based upon our own internal pictures and expectations. This is an exercise in mutual frustration—frustration for the other person and for you. What's powerful is for us to recognize our "response-ability," our ability to respond to who they are and where they are in the present.

When we decide that we need to start loving someone from a distance, we don't have to cut the person out of our lives. To love from a distance means we give them less of our energy and attention, at least for now. It may mean not calling them first on the phone, being less available, or initiating fewer contacts and get-togethers. The purpose of loving from a distance is to disengage some of your energy so that it can be directed elsewhere. This is what my aunt decided to do. And in the process, she became a different woman. She even looked different. She stopped giving herself away. Once she started loving her son from a distance, giving him space to live his life the way he was choosing to live it, and keeping more of her energy to herself, her son slowly started to make positive changes. By withdrawing some of her energy, she was giving him the opportunity to build up his own emotional energy. As a result, she had more energy; released a few pounds of extra weight; smiled more; complained less; had more clarity and focus; and looked more peaceful and radiant. She had stopped giving her energy and power away.

58. *Turning points*

One day in the mail I received an unassuming little booklet-style magazine called *The Lioness*. As I was sitting at my kitchen table sorting out the junk mail, I stacked this booklet on top of the junk mail pile, got up to take the junk mail outside to the Dumpster, and at the last minute, decided to retrieve this little booklet and thumb through it first. I was surprised to find that the pages of *The Lioness* were filled with wonderful stories, lessons, words of wisdom, and practical self-help information. I had judged this little book by its cover, and almost thrown it away. Thank goodness I didn't.

After reading a particular passage in one of the issues, I thought I'd take a chance and try to contact the editor and publisher of *The Lioness*, Reverend Victoria Lee Owens. I made contact with her and asked if it was okay to share some excerpts from one of her entries, entitled "Turning Points." She graciously obliged.

Turning points are those pivotal moments in your life when you have an insight, realization, or revelation that changes how you see yourself, others, or the world. Turning points occur when you are given a new perspective, new clarity, or new resolve. A turning point can set change in motion in your thinking, your beliefs, and your behavior. Turning points affect your consciousness and send you off in a new direction, a clearer direction, or down a slightly different path, toward recovery, toward healing, toward love, toward your sacred power. Remember: *it's never too late to turn.*

Reverend Victoria recommends that you summarize *in writing* what you feel about yourself as you slowly read each of the following twenty-five "turning point" passages. "The question," Reverend Victoria reminds us, "is not whether you NEED or WANT to change, but are you WILLING to change?"

TURNING POINTS by Reverend Victoria Lee Owens

1. If you have pain, you deserve to heal.
2. If you have anger or guilt from the past, you deserve to heal.
3. You have the opportunity to turn now.
4. You deserve to begin rebuilding your life in a new direction.
5. Recovery isn't changing who you are. It is letting go of who you are not.
6. If you are protecting yourself from past pain in ways that are causing you even more pain in the present, you deserve to heal.
7. The pain you feel is not only from the past but also from the past-driven present.
8. You are not your pain.
9. Your pain is your responsibility.
10. What you do about your pain is a choice you make.
11. To say "I did not learn this very basic skill and I need to know how" is a turning point.
12. By recognizing you are in the process of recovery, you are beginning to shine your own light.
13. You are not "in control."
14. It is in the acceptance of all that was and is that your spirit becomes whole.
15. I do not depend on others in order to accept myself.
16. When people leave (abandon) me, it is not a judgment of my worth.
17. Intimacy is about being close. Intimacy is trusting another with whom you are without fear of rejection.

18. A turning point will come when you can identify a safe way to share the secret.
19. The awareness that now you can choose to be free from the secret is a turning point.
20. The awareness that we have adopted a protective role to survive is a turning point.
21. The awareness that we no longer need that role to survive is a turning point.
22. The turning point in your relationships is the awareness that your growth is not about getting other people to change.
23. You were powerless in the past, but you are not powerless in the present.
24. God is always present in your heart. Look within.
25. Learning to love yourself does not mean you love others less. Instead, it frees you to love them more!

Now, read all twenty-five passages *again,* this time *out loud.*

Amen! Want to subscribe to *The Lioness?* If so, you can visit The Lioness Web site at www.ezbsnet.com/Vleeowens, or e-mail Reverend Victoria at Vlee-owens@aol.com

It's never too late to turn.

59. *Life cycles and seasons*

*O*ne of the reasons that life occurs as hard and effort-full for many of us is that we fail to recognize that life has continuous cycles and seasons. It is not just a fixed, linear path that has ups and downs, peaks and valleys along the way. Life is a series of cycles, subcycles, and seasons, ongoing transitions and transformations.

We can still hear and see evidence of the beliefs we brought with us across the Atlantic Ocean and the Caribbean Sea from the Motherland of Africa on the ships carrying our kidnapped ancestors. In our community, we still talk about dying as "going home," or making a transition, not as an ending. This speaks to our cultural belief in the circle of life. If we look closely, we find overwhelming and obvious evidence that life is not linear and one dimensional. It is a constantly unfolding, ebbing, flowing, evolving process that is more like a circle or a spiral.

Just as we have the seasons of spring, summer, fall, and winter in nature, these seasons also play out metaphorically in our lives. When we are in the season of spring in our lives, we are seeding and planting new ideas. We are birthing, incubating creativity, initiating, beginning, cultivating, and planning for forward motion and action. Summer represents fruition and coming into fullness and ripeness. It is arriving at the apex or the zenith. It is the cycle reaching its maturity. Fall represents release, letting go, a falling away, harvesting, clearing out, shedding the old, recycling, and converting the by-products of summer into compost and fertilizer. Winter represents transformation, reflection, retreat, rest, contemplation, quiet preparation, and recovery. In nature, it may appear that winter is a barren time of coldness and death. Actually, much is going on beneath the surface. Winter is the soil's time to replenish nutrients in the soil that were utilized in the spring and the summer seasons. For us, too, winter is a time of restoration.

When we encounter periods in our lives that are challenging, and it's hard to see the light at the end of the tunnel, we must remember: seasons pass. We must remind ourselves, *This is but a season. And this, too, shall pass.* We must learn to recognize the seasons in our own lives. Every season serves a purpose. Each season brings unique insights and "learnings."

We can also be going through several seasons in our lives at the same time. As I sit here propped up against my backrest in my bed writing this chapter, I am in many seasons at once. I am in spring, giving birth to this book. At the same time, I am entering my fifth year of my training and consulting business, where I am making a transition from the last stages of spring into early summer. In my marriage, Joe and I are entering our eighth year, and to me it feels like we've moved through all four seasons at one level, and now we are at a higher level, entering into another season of spring.

Sometimes things don't manifest or come to pass in our lives, not because we didn't do all of the right things but because it is not the right time, it is not the right season, or it is not the right "soil" or conditions for that particular seed to take root and grow. So we must be patient and work on our ability to discern the right season. When there is too much effort and struggle trying to *make* it happen, recognize that it may not be the right season. Yes, friendships, marriages, bodies, relationships, and businesses go through seasons, too.

We get out of touch with ourselves and others when we don't acknowledge significant seasons in our lives. We not only can have seasons, cycles, and transitions around coming of certain ages like 16, 18, 21, 30, 40, 50, or 100 but also around certain events or experiences such as beginning a marriage, ending a marriage, having a baby, starting a business, completing a relationship, closing a business, leaving a job or position, recovering from a serious illness, starting to menstruate, going through menopause, releasing weight, completing a certain level in school, getting saved, recovering from an addiction, or relocating—all of these can move you into or out of a season. They can mark a key transition for you. The point is to develop your ability to discern and be in tune with the seasons in your life. This helps you move through them with ease, grace, fluidity, and knowing, instead of resisting or kicking and screaming the entire way.

Ecclesiastes, Chapter 3 of the Bible, tells us,

> *To every thing there is a season*
> *And a time to every purpose under the heavens.*
> *A time to be born, and a time to die;*
> *A time to plant, and a time to pluck up*
> *That which is planted;*
> *A time to kill, and a time to heal;*
> *A time to break down, and a time to build up;*
> *A time to weep, and a time to laugh;*
> *A time to mourn, and a time to dance;*
> *A time to cast away stones, and a time to gather stones together;*
> *A time to embrace, and a time to refrain from embracing;*
> *A time to get, and a time to lose;*
> *A time to keep and a time to cast away;*

A time to rend, and a time to sew;
A time to keep silent, and a time to speak;
A time to love, and a time to hate;
A time of war, and a time of peace.

To everything there is a season.

60. *Become a spiritual gardener*

A spiritual gardener understands there are cycles and seasons in her life, not just linear time lines and deadlines. A spiritual gardener takes her understanding of the cycles and seasons mentioned in the previous principle and uses it to actualize her desires and aspirations. The seeds the spiritual gardener plants can be projects, ideas, friendships, or love relationships. In life, she understands that spiritual gardening is an ongoing process of growing and manifesting that involves cultivation (preparing and fertilizing the soil), seed planting, nurturing, growth, bearing fruit, death or harvest, transformation and rebirth. Spiritual gardening is based upon a circle or a spiral. If her seeds are not germinating and reaching maturity, she recognizes that it may be because her seeds are not receiving enough water, light, attention, or air. Are you keeping your seedlings free of the weeds of jealousy, self-doubt, judgment, contempt, and toxic thoughts and words in your life? Or are your seeds being choked? When you understand how the Spiritual Gardening Cycle applies to your life, you increase your ability to "bear fruit" and manifest the life you desire and deserve.

The spiritual gardener recognizes that she and God are gardening partners. The spiritual gardener recognizes that faith, love, self-reflection, patience, and discernment are her most important fertilizers. She looks for the right conditions for planting so that her seeds will flourish. The spiritual gardener knows how to go with the flow. When you take on the mind-set, attitude, and outlook of a spiritual gardener, keep the four following considerations in mind.

THE SPIRITUAL GARDENING CYCLE

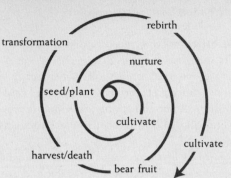

Is it the Right Seed?	Seeds can come in the form of projects, ideas, friendships, love relationships, business or job opportunities, etc. Is the "seed" a desire of *your* heart? Does it reflect *your* truth?
Is it the Right Season?	You know there is a specific planting season for every seed. Are you trying to plant a spring seed in the winter season?
Is it the Right Soil?	Is the "soil" you are planting in best for the type of seed you are planting? Has your soil been cultivated and prepared for your seed(s)? Is it properly fertilized? Do you have the necessary mind-set, resources, tools? Are you planting your seed where it is most likely to flourish? *Where* you plant your seed(s) is very important.
Is it the Right Timing?	*When* you plant your seed(s) is very important. Do the conditions support the healthy germination and growth of your seed? Is it too soon? Is it too late? Does it feel like you're having to work too hard to get your seed to grow?

As a spiritual gardener, you work on understanding and applying the Eight Principles of Spiritual Gardening to your life.

1. If you are not reaping the size, quantity, or quality of "fruit" in the form of results, outcomes, or goals that you'd like, you must better prepare, cultivate, and fertilize your soil. Remember, manure is "waste," but it makes for great fertilizer. A masterful gardener can take waste and transform it into something that supports growth. You recognize that the quality of your soil determines the quality of the "fruit" you bear.

2. Faith and patience are necessary in spiritual gardening because all growth is not above ground. God works in visible and nonvisible ways.

3. You have to understand that God has placed the "blueprint" for success within the seed. It is up to you to activate it.

4. You understand that you will always be given other opportunities to plant. There are no mistakes, only "learnings" with spiritual gardening.

5. Death is part of the spiritual gardening process. When something comes to an end, it is transformed and the process continues. In the mind of the spiritual gardener, death is not inherently bad or negative. It is part of the process. It can signify a rebirth or set the stage for a powerful new beginning.

6. When the seed, season, soil, timing, and conditions are "right," the seed takes root, pushes up through the ground, and bears fruit.

7. The spiritual gardener is able to take manure and use it as fertilizer. You know that all that smells and looks bad can be used for good if you know how to transform it.

8. The spiritual gardener knows that even if all of the conditions are right, the unexpected can still occur and wipe out what you've grown. You are not in control ultimately. You also know that you can begin again. This, too, is part of the process.

As I mentioned earlier in this book, I wasn't able to appear on the TV talk show *The View* because of scheduling conflicts, though we tried to make it work three times. At first, I was one bummed-out sistah. The seed was right—I was going to be discussing my book *Sacred Pampering Principles;* the soil was right—*The View* was witty, progressive, and popular among thirty-something and forty-something aged women, the target market of my book; and the season was right—in this case, it literally was Christmas season, which I hoped would translate into increased book sales. The timing, however, was off. *The View* and I were not able to get in sync at that time. In the context of spiritual gardening, I could see that it was not my time for being on the show. One of the factors, right timing, was not in place.

On another occasion, a state agency contacted my company about doing some diversity training for its employees. The agency's written request described what they were looking for: a highly interactive, engaging, and thought-provoking diversity training session. This sounded just like the type of diversity training we provide. But when I called the agency to get clarification on the expectations of the training, I discovered that what they *really* wanted was a low-key informational session that would not make people uncomfortable or challenge them. Though our chances of winning the contract were high since the agency had contacted only four other companies about this training opportunity, we decided to decline the opportunity. It wasn't the right soil for the type of diversity training we provided.

As we become more skilled at spiritual gardening, we learn to recognize when all of the factors are aligned for manifestation to occur.

How does your garden grow?

61. *What the world needs now*

What the world, more specifically America, needs now is rituals—rituals for reconnecting, remembering, and returning to our true selves. In his book *Ritual: Power, Healing and Community,* author Malidoma Somé explains that it is probably impossible to live a sane life without ritual. Ritual is a process or a ceremony that represents and strengthens your connection to the larger whole, to Spirit, to the Creator. If you are not connected and in touch with Spirit, you become *disconnected* from life. When you are disconnected, you lose sight of Who You Are and Why You're Here.

Rituals are important for staying centered and grounded. Rituals help you keep things in balance, in context, and in perspective. Rituals are intended to help us transcend the physical realm and access the power of the spirit realm. So a ritual is not a routine, a habit, or a tradition. It is a spiritual process that has the effect of anchoring and stabilizing you. Rituals can help you through times of change, transition, rites of passage, or cycles and seasons in your daily life. Rituals help you live your life more sanely, more rooted, more conscious, more aware, and more connected to your Source.

In his book *Ritual*, Malidoma Somé, who is from the small village of Dano in Burkina Faso, West Africa, recaps a moment when he is in his village attempting to explain to his village elders the American notion of speed and time, and why Americans "rush" so much. One of the elders asks, "Where do these white people run to every morning?" Malidoma replies, "To their workplaces, of course." The elder then inquires, "Why do they have to run to something that is not running away from them?" In the context of this West African culture, speed was considered more of a movement *away* from something. This village elder noticed that in our "modern" American society, the idea of speed and motion seemed to be a distraction. As Somé goes on to explain, in the mind of his elders, our constant motion represented,

> Moving away from something that we do not want to look at or moving away from something that others do not want us to look at. . . . When you slow down, you begin to discover that there is a silent awareness of what it is that you do not want to look at. . . . This speed is a way to prevent ourselves from having to deal with something we do not want to face. To be able to face our fears, we must remember how to perform ritual. To remember how to perform ritual, we must slow down.

Rituals usually have an opening and a closing, a clear purpose, and often make use of a ritual object. Some of the rituals you may have already experienced in your life are baptism, saying grace before a meal, or the vows at a marriage ceremony. There are as many rituals as there are situations in life. So let your creativity out and trust yourself to begin creating more rituals in your life. Let your inner knowing guide you.

A powerful woman understands the importance of rituals and integrates them in her life. Rituals can be a means of beginning, ending, cleansing, releasing, purifying, blessing, healing, bringing clarity, grounding, centering, reconciling, protecting, and formalizing, to name a few. Below are descriptions of simple rituals I've created and integrated into my life that have made a huge difference. Feel free to use them and modify them for yourself.

NAME OF RITUAL	DESCRIPTION	PURPOSE
Pampering Bath Ritual	Taken twice a month. A 30-minute spiritual and therapeutic bath. I add fruit-scented bath bubbles, Dead Sea salts, and essential oils; stretch out with my head resting against my bath pillow; burn my favorite incense; and listen to my most soothing jazz tunes.	To unwind, wash away negative energy, relax, hold still, turn inward, reflect, contemplate, pray, sit my butt down (literally) for 30 minutes, and thank God for my blessings.
Wish Box Ritual	Once a month, I sit down in front of my altar in my bedroom and write out what I want to *come to pass* in my life over the course of the following month—my manifestation list. Once I write out my list, which covers all areas of my life, I fold it up and write a date on the outside that is 30 days ahead. I place my wish list in my special fabric-covered wish box, and open it up 30 days later. I rejoice in the things that came to pass, and for those that don't, I decide whether to carry them over to my next month's list, or to release them.	To plant "seeds" each month that help me to direct my energy. To bring greater clarity and focus to the manifestation process. To have appreciation for my ability to create certain outcomes in my life.

NAME OF RITUAL	DESCRIPTION	PURPOSE
Thanksgiving Ritual	Instead of holding hands, saying grace, and then eating Thanksgiving dinner, as had been the practice in our family since I was a little girl, I wanted us to focus more attention on giving thanks. Now, before sitting down to enjoy the meal and saying grace, we turn the lights down and pass a single lit white candle around the table. When you receive the candle, it is your turn to share something for which you are grateful and thankful, and then pass the candle on to the next person.	To remind us that Thanksgiving isn't just about eating Mama's jammin' cooking, but about being grateful and thankful. An opportunity to pause for the cause and articulate some of your blessings to others.
Valentine's Day Love Letter Ritual	Every Valentine's Day since we've been married, my husband and I write Valentine's love letters to each other. We read the love letters out loud to each other at Valentine's Day dinner.	Remind us of our love for each other. Keep our love fresh. Provide an opportunity to express deep, touching thoughts and feelings we have for one another.
Altar Ritual (nightly)	I have a personal altar in my bedroom that is a little two-tiered white shelf covered with a piece of African fabric. On my altar, I have candles, rocks I brought back from my trip to Egypt, crystals, special photos, affirmations, my Bible, a journal, and two black ceramic angels.	My altar is my special place for my nightly devotion time. This ritual brings closure to my day and strengthens my connection to Spirit. Each night before going to bed, I light a candle, pray and/or meditate, read a passage from one of the inspirational poetry or affirmation books that sits on my altar, and write in my journal. My altar is my sacred space, and my altar ritual is my sacred time.

NAME OF RITUAL	DESCRIPTION	PURPOSE
Welcome to the World Celebration	Instead of only having a baby shower, which is before the baby is born and is usually for women only, I decided to create an experience that would be for friends and family to celebrate with us after each of our babies was born. The Welcome to the World Celebration, which takes place when the baby is two to four weeks old, is a family potluck event where guests bring gifts for the new baby. After we eat and before the gifts are opened, we gather everyone together and join hands in a circle to share words of wisdom and encouragement. We close the "village circle" with a prayer from the grandparents.	Gives family and friends a chance to see the new baby and celebrate a new life. Supports the African proverb that says, "It takes a whole village to raise a child." Recognizes those who we see as part of our village.

Make rituals an integral part of your Life.

62. Create intimacy with sisterfriends

I'm convinced that, as African-American women, much of our emotional and spiritual healing is going to come through developing intimate connections with one another where we feel safe, understood, and can speak our truth without judgment.

One of my wise women sistahfriends defines intimacy as "in-to-me-I-see" because intimacy allows us to see the "real self" within ourselves and the "real self" in another. Intimacy emerges from a feeling or experience of connectedness. Intimacy emerges when the space calls for being authentic. Intimacy develops when we drop our masks, our armor, and the various personas and roles we put on, and we *allow* another to see into us. Intimacy exists when my real self and your real self are communicating without pretense, when we speak our truth and extend mutual trust, nonjudgment, acceptance, and love.

When Rachel Bagby, author of *Divine Daughters*, shares her experience of attending a life-changing workshop called "Black and Female: I Know the Reality," she describes the gathering as "simple and ancient." What took place, she explains, is "We told one another the stories we dare not tell anyone else . . . in witnessing one another, in listening and receiving and giving love to the depths of our beings . . . we were called into full feeling."

Developing intimate connections with other sisters replenishes my spirit, grounds me, and energizes me like nothing else can. It calls me into "full feeling." Some would say that intimacy requires being vulnerable. Maybe not. More than being vulnerable, it requires being *real*. In our effort to avoid being vulnerable, we compromise our realness. Being real shouldn't be painful—it should be liberating. When we gather with other sistahs in the spirit of nonjudgment, authenticity, acceptance, love, and truth telling, *healing happens*.

Inviting sisterfriends over to your home instead of meeting out somewhere public, like a restaurant, is one way to create more intimacy. Because your home is a sacred space, sisterfriends can get more relaxed. Once a year I invite my closest girlfriends over to my home for my annual pampering party. My pampering party is my gift to my sisterfriends. One year, we gave each other hand massages; another year we did a feet-washing ritual; and another year we had a winter evening tea sip as we sat on the floor around my fireplace. At the end of each pampering party, I give each sisterfriend a book from my personal library as a small appreciation gift.

Another sisterfriend had a big girl's slumber party once she moved into her new house, complete with sleeping bags, popcorn, flannel pajamas, and telling stories late into the night. Seeing one another without makeup on, in head wraps and head scarves, and with titles, kids, and day jobs aside, allows a realness to emerge that can remain hidden behind the various masks we wear and the many roles we play in our lives.

For my 32nd birthday, I had a potluck and pajama party. To make things a little more daring, I requested that my friends come over to my house *in* their pajamas—no changing clothes once they arrived. So when my sisterfriends arrived, they were already loosened up and in a party mood. Being in your pajamas can have that effect on you. Sitting on the floor or on oversized pillows on the floor can also increase intimacy. Sitting on the floor literally grounds you and gives you an increased feeling of connected-ness to the others who are present

I used to be part of a small women's leadership development group that met once a month. Instead of always sitting in chairs, we'd often sit on the floor around a coffee table, sipping herbal tea and coffee, and nibbling on bagels, cream cheese, and grapes while we discussed women's ways of leading.

Look for ways to create more intimacy with sisterfriends. Eliminate third-party distractions such as the TV so that the focus is on the heart-to-heart connection. As we learn to create intimacy with other women, we also learn how to create more intimacy with ourselves.

63. *Find your power pack*

When I was in high school I was on the varsity track team, and one of the events I competed in was the 200-meter run. At track practice, in prep-aration for upcoming track meets, the coach would have us run "ladders," or sets of 200-meter runs, one after another, to condition our bodies. To run ladders, the coach would match us up in packs according to how fast we could run the 200. He wanted us to run with other girls who clocked in at about the same time for the 200. The rationale behind running our ladders in packs was so that you could both be paced by the others in your ladder running group. If you were placed with a ladder pack that ran a lot faster than you, you'd be struggling to keep up, and it could negatively affect your time. If you ran with a ladder pack that was a lot slower than you, you'd be in danger of getting lax, having no motivation for improving your time; not push yourself to shave a few tenths of a second off of your time; and keep clocking in at the same or a slower time. So finding your pack, your "running buddies," became the key to your continued growth and improvement.

The same dynamic applies in our lives. Find your pack, your power pack—a group of positive, like-minded progressive sisterfriends on the grow who match or *slightly* exceed your present level of spiritual awareness, growth, and consciousness. Often, we have only one pack, often it's very small, we've outgrown it, or it's consisted of the same friends year after year. If you have the same faces in your pack year after year, it may be time to expand your circle or develop some additional packs in your life.

Don't get upset with your "old" pack because you think they are lagging or not able to "run as fast" as you. These are simply signs that you're outgrowing them. Having a power pack isn't about having to always get together in a group or hang out as a group. You may get together individually, in small clusters, or as an entire group once in a while. Your power pack is the sisterfriends you've consciously identified as being in your pack. Your power pack should evolve and grow as you do.

And you certainly don't have to be limited to one power pack—you may have several. I usually have three power packs at a time. And over the course of the past ten years, my core pack has changed three times. When you start to run with a different pack, it's not about kickin' anyone to the curb; it's about learning how to "make new friends and keep the old" as my Girl Scout campfire song used to say, "one is silver and the other gold."

> *Finding your power pack*
> *brings many good things,*
> *like growth, extra lift,*
> *and wind beneath your wings.*

64. *Pray and meditate*

⌐⌐⌐⌐⌐   *I* think of prayer as sending divine communication and meditation as receiving it. Another way to say it is: Prayer is speaking to God and meditation is listening to God.

A Course in Miracles defines *prayer* as a "means of communication of the created with the Creator." When we pray, we acknowledge our Higher Self, our Source, and our connection to the Creator, the Prime Mover, the Supreme Being, Allah, Jehovah. To pray is to demonstrate a belief in a picture that is bigger than you. To pray is to demonstrate that there is something beyond what you can hear, taste, touch, and smell at work in the world. To pray is to draw upon more than your human strength and ability, and to more fully access the power of God in you and around you. To pray is to recognize that you have the ability to direct your consciousness and to effect change with your words, your interactions, and your thoughts. Many of us have only scratched the surface of prayer as a force that effects change, affects outcomes, and affects our minds, bodies, and spirits.

For years, the only kind of praying I knew how to do was asking God for help or guidance when I was in a bind or got into a jam. I grew up in churches where the preacher instructed us to "call on Jesus, lay our burdens on the Lord," and pray for forgiveness of our sins. This led me to believe, from a very young age, that prayer was for the purpose of pleading, imploring, begging, and turning to God when you were in a crisis, at the end of your rope, or in a state of desperation and you didn't know where else to turn. I didn't realize, at that time, that prayer served many powerful purposes, and asking was only one of them.

As I have continued to grow spiritually, I've come into a better understanding of the various purposes and forms of prayer. As a result, my prayer life has grown and deepened. Understanding that there are distinct types of prayer has helped me to use prayer more purposefully in my life. *Prayer changes things; prayer changes people.* Here is a list of some of the various types of prayer, so that you can more fully tap into the power of prayer in your life.

TYPES OF PRAYER	PURPOSE
Prayers of Affirmation	Calls forth a desired outcome or new reality; is spoken in the present tense as if it is already done.
Prayers of Healing and Restoration	To erase or reprogram the core emotional patterns, mental thoughts, and beliefs that gave rise to the physical disease
Prayers of Meditation	To focus upon a few meaningful words or phrases and then contemplate them deeply.
Prayers of Forgiveness	To release the mental or emotional grip or charge you have on a person or a situation. To consciously release the anger, resentment, hatred, disappointment, or frustration you may be harboring toward someone.
Prayers of Thanksgiving	To demonstrate gratitude for learnings, healing, answers, awareness, clarity, blessings, resources, provision, manifestation, guidance, etc.
Prayers of Invocation	To invite the spirit of God or the ancestors to come into a place. Often done at the beginning of a church service or a ceremony.
Prayers of Praise	To rejoice or glorify.
Prayers of Supplication	To request. To make an earnest appeal for the supply of something (material or nonmaterial; i.e., transportation, financial resources, humility, patience, courage, understanding, protection, etc.).
Prayers of Benediction	To bring completion or closure to a ritual, event, or ceremony.
Prayers of Surrender	To surrender the ego or the compulsion to dominate or control; relinquish control or attachment to how a specific outcome is achieved. Yield to the will of God.

Meditation is also an essential part of divine communication. Without balancing prayer with meditation, you can become spiritually lopsided. Meditation is the complement to prayer, as yin is to yang and male is to female. There are many forms of meditation, just as there are many forms of prayer, but the purpose remains the same: to think deeply and quietly, to ponder, to contemplate.

This is easier said than done though, with the always-on-the-go lifestyles of perpetual motion that we've created for ourselves. Life doesn't require that we bang our heads into a wall even once, not to mention multiple times. If meditation were more of a reality in our lives, we wouldn't have to run into a wall before we finally got the message. Meditation helps you learn to pay attention. We wouldn't miss the signs that say "Wall Ahead."

Meditation is also a process of listening to and receiving the answers to many of our questions. If meditation were more of a reality in our lives, we wouldn't miss the answers that were waiting to be heard. We wouldn't be so busy living our lives on automatic pilot. When you're on autopilot, it's easy to feel like "life is doing you"—you're reacting, you're defending, you're *at effect* instead of *at cause*. No need to call the 1-900 psychic hotline. You have an inner psychic you can access without having to pay $3.99 a minute.

The title of my first book, *Sacred Pampering Principles*, came to me ten years ago as a result of specifically meditating upon the book title. I had come up with several titles, but none of them resonated with me. Then one morning, I decided to turn it over to my Higher Self. I asked, "God, what is it that you would have me name this book?" Later that night, as I was doing my evening meditation, three words came to me—*sacred pampering principles*. My first reaction was, *What?! What kind of title is that?!* I had the nerve to ask God for an answer and then argue back. Fortunately, my hard-headedness was short-lived. *Okay, God, I hope you know what you're doing*, I thought. Of course, She did. It proved to be the perfect title for my book.

On another occasion, my girlfriend Juanita had an 84-year-old grandmother in Virginia who had taken very ill and was in the intensive care unit at a local hospital. Juanita's grandmother was the matriarch of the family, so all six of her adult children and a host of grandkids flew in from around the country to keep an around-the-clock vigil at her hospital bedside. Before Juanita flew back to Virginia to join her aunts and uncles at her grandmother's bedside, she asked me to pray for her grandmother Violet's recovery. A couple of days later, as I sat in front of my altar praying for Juanita's grandmother, a voice floated into my consciousness and started to speak to me. The voice told me, *"Violet wants to make her transition, but her children are holding on too tightly. They're not giving her the space to choose whether to stay on this plane or to make her transition. They need to let go so that she can rest in peace and her soul can be at ease."* I sat there a moment, stunned. I knew this wasn't my ego or my subconscious speaking to me because the voice wasn't located in my head. I was familiar with the voice of my own inner chatter. This message seemed to be coming up through my solar plexus, my lower stomach area. And the tone and cadence of this voice was different from my own.

I knew I needed to pass this message on to Juanita. After making several phone calls, I was able to track her down at her aunt's house in Virginia. I shared the message with her, exactly as I had received it. She was silent for almost thirty seconds, then she replied with a heavy sigh, "You know, you're right. We all are hanging on so tightly. We don't want her to go. We can't imagine life without Grams. She's been the glue of this family."

Juanita knew that she couldn't be responsible for anyone else's process of letting go, only her own. So she decided to shift her gears, from praying for God to heal her grandmother, to giving her grandmother's spirit the space to choose to stay or go. As a result of our phone conversation, Juanita decided to focus her energies on reaching closure with her grandmother, so that she would be complete if her grandmother's spirit decided to leave her body and make its transition.

Two weeks later, Grams had recovered enough to be discharged from the hospital and she was even allowed to go home. She was recovering slowly, but steadily. The family was so relieved and so grateful that she'd been able to pull through. In their minds, she was "out of the woods." Then one month after being released from the hospital, the unexpected happened: Grams collapsed and died as she was being helped into the car to be driven to church. All of the family members were devastated, except Juanita.

When Grams died, Juanita was at peace. She had given Grams the space to make a choice, and she had taken conscious steps to reach closure with her grandmother. She'd spent time alone with Grams in the hospital room before Grams was released to go home, brushing her hair, stroking her face, massaging her feet, and sharing deep, tender thoughts with Grams that she'd wanted to express to her for years. She was complete. However, to this day, nearly two years later, there are family members who have not yet recovered from Gram's death and have been unable to move forward emotionally. I am so grateful that I was able to receive this message in a meditation. And I am even more grateful that Juanita trusted me enough to heed the message.

Make prayer and meditation an integral part of your life.

65. *Cultivate your intuition*

We *all* have it—a sixth sense. Intuition. It is your inner voice, your Inner Teacher, your Higher Self, the aspect of your being that feels and receives subtle information that your other five senses do not register and cannot detect. This aspect of you has access to the bigger picture, the non-visible realm, and can interpret subtle and unseen forces. It may seem that some of us have intuition and some of us don't. *Not so.* Actually, intuition is just more "awakened" in some of us than in others.

To cultivate means to "prepare, improve, and refine." There's only one way I know of to cultivate your intuition and exercise your intuitive muscles: to listen, practice being obedient to your intuition, and then take action. Just as the muscles of your physical body are toned and strengthened through regular workouts, so are your spiritual muscles. Intuition operates on a different level and uses a different kind of data than our other five senses. Our intuition operates off of *energy data* by tuning us in to energetic vibrations and impressions.

This is why your Inner Voice is able to send you messages that are complete and clear. When you are subconsciously "reading" energy data that is unsettling or discomforting, it registers in your gut. Your gut, or solar plexus, also the location of your womb, is Intuition Grand Central. It is your spiritual message center. A message from your Inner Voice may feel like a very strong urge, suggestion, or idea that seems to just "come to you." We need to stop saying "something told me," and call this "something" what it is—your Intuition prompting you. Instead, say "my intuition told me."

This happened to me one Wednesday afternoon last year as I sat at my desk in my office typing up a consulting proposal. Over the previous week I'd thought a lot about my friend Stephanie Stokes Oliver, editor in chief of *Heart & Soul* magazine, whom I hadn't spoken to in over a year. I had recently received word that Black Entertainment Television (BET) had bought *Heart & Soul* magazine from Rodale Press, so I wanted to be in touch with Stephanie to find out how she was doing and see how the buyout affected her position.

As I sat there at my desk typing, my Inner Voice said *"Call Stephanie now."* I now know, after learning the hard way, that I need to listen and follow instructions when my intuition communicates to me. So I stopped what I was doing and dialed Stephanie's office number. When I reached Stephanie's office in New York, her voice mail message informed me that she was no longer with *Heart & Soul*. At the end of the message, it gave a phone number for the main BET office in Washington, D.C. So I hung up and dialed BET. After encountering an automated menu giving me myriad options, I pressed "0" to speak to the operator. The operator came on the line and I asked her if she had a forwarding number for Stephanie Stokes-Oliver or knew how I could reach her. Unfortunately, the operator had no forwarding information. As I was about to hang up the phone, the operator suggested that I might try someone in the magazine's editorial department. Maybe they could help me. She transferred me to someone whose name I didn't know or recognize, and I encountered yet another voice mail recording.

I was starting to get a little discouraged, so I decided that I would hang up the phone instead of leaving a message. But just as I was about to hang up the phone's receiver, my Inner Voice said, *"Go ahead and leave a message."* I put the phone receiver back to my ear and left a message, asking for assistance getting in contact with Stephanie. I expected to have my call returned in a couple of days, maybe, if at all. Much to my surprise, I received a return phone call fifteen minutes later from the woman whose voice mail I had been transferred to by the BET operator. The woman explained that she had only one solitary phone number for Stephanie that she believed was a home number. I took the number appreciatively and thanked her profusely for her assistance and prompt response.

Since getting in contact with Stephanie was turning out to be much more involved than I had anticipated, I decided that I would wait and try the phone number the next day, after I had finished the proposal project I was in the middle of working on. Again, my Inner Voice told me, *"Call Stephanie now."* After letting out a sigh, I went ahead and dialed the phone number, thinking, if I had the right phone number Stephanie would at least get my message when she got home later that evening. The phone rang three times and was picked up. The voice on the other end said, "Hello, this is Stephanie." I couldn't believe it. I had made live contact, even with the three-hour east coast–west coast time difference. Stephanie was as delighted and surprised to hear my voice on the other end of the phone as I was to hear hers.

It soon became clear why my Inner Voice had been so persistent. It turns out that, after leaving *Heart & Soul* magazine and starting her own communications company, Stephanie had landed a national book deal. She was in the process of completing her book manuscript as we spoke. She explained that she wanted to include a few more original entries in her book before her deadline in three more weeks. She'd been thinking about me because she wanted to include me in her book but had misplaced my business card. She couldn't believe it—here I was calling her.

Now I understood why my Inner Voice had been so persistent. I was supposed to connect with Stephanie before her manuscript deadline had arrived so I could be included in her new book. Stephanie then asked me if I would submit an entry for inclusion in her book. Of course, I accepted enthusiastically. I was able to get it to her in time to meet her deadline. (Read Stephanie's book, *Daily Cornbread: 365 Secrets for a Healthy Mind, Body and Spirit* and check out the June 4 entry.)

Never once has my intuition led me astray. Never once has my Inner Voice been inaccurate or "off." Never once has my intuition failed me, but there have certainly been times when I have failed it—ignored the message, doubted the message, or didn't take action in a timely manner.

It isn't enough to listen to your Inner Voice. You must heed it.

66. *Understand the power of your spoken word*

One afternoon while driving to a client appointment, I popped in an audiotape of a presentation given by my sisterfriend and fellow motivational speaker Dr. Traci Lynn. She had given me the tape to listen to when we saw each other at a recent African-American Women on Tour conference, where we both had been speaking. The title of her presentation was "The Tongue Is a Creative Force." Traci, who is both an evangelist and a successful entrepreneur, kept emphasizing a key idea throughout her presentation, "Understand the power in your tongue. You will have what you *say* you can have." Traci wanted us to know, in no uncertain terms, that the tongue can be a creative force or a destructive force, depending on how you use it. "When you speak, you express an intention," she explained. "You actually charge the atmosphere with vibrations and commands that the universe responds to. So be conscious about the directions you give to the universe."

We have greatly underestimated the power of destruction and creation that resides in our spoken words. We've been told "talk is cheap" and "actions speak louder than words." I would modify this statement to read "Your actions speak loudly, and so do your words." Do you realize that when you speak, you create a vibration that travels through the air and charges the atmosphere? Do you realize that the words you speak carry and communicate your intentions? Do you realize that the universe is the perfect listener, the perfect copying machine, delivering your reality according to the instructions you give it, first through your thoughts, then through your words? How many times have you heard yourself say "Oh, I didn't mean that." *Too late*. You can't take it back. The universe already heard you.

You can wreak some serious havoc in your life when you don't recognize and understand the power of your spoken words. Your words are far more than strings of syllables, nouns, verbs, and adjectives. Our words are the ambassadors of our thoughts and beliefs. Our words convey how we see, perceive, interpret, and experience life. Thus they act as a bridge between our inner world and our outer world. When we utter words, they become symbols that allow us to connect, communicate, and express ourselves and our inner reality. The words you use are a function of your awareness, your consciousness, your state of heart, and your state of mind. Don't treat them lightly.

Take notice. What do you say? What words do you use? What message(s) do you communicate to others and the universe when you speak? Every moment, the universe is eavesdropping on your conversation, the ones you are having inside your head as well as the ones going on outside of your head, with other people. The universe waits to find out what you want it to manifest through your thoughts and words. The universe waits to find out what to create and deliver to you, and what experiences to bring to you based upon the instructions you are giving it with your words and thoughts.

For one week, do an audit of the words you use. Notice the words you use in your interactions and conversations with others. Pay close attention to the words you use around the issues, situations, or circumstances that are most challenging for you, whether it be money, your body, love relationships, your parents, a relative, a work situation, or a physical illness. Get conscious about the words you are speaking, using, and exchanging with others. Do they convey possibility? Do they convey esteem of others? Do they convey self-esteem?

Over the past few years, I have made a conscious effort to change my language and my vocabulary. This change has come about as I've learned more and more about the power of my words, and as I have learned to be more responsible with them. I've gradually replaced words in my vocabulary that were feeding into and supporting struggle, hardship, lack, and limitation with words that empower choice, possibility, triumph, joy, ease, and manifestation. As you grow in spiritual awareness, your words should reflect your growth. Some of the changes I've made in my vocabulary are:

FROM	TO
I'm broke	My cash flow is low
	I am temporarily out of cash
	My money is circulating
	That is not in my budget right now
I'm stressed out	I'm feeling pressed
I'm busy	I'm making things happen
Problems	Challenges
I'm sick	My body is telling me I need to rest
I'm on a diet	I'm making conscious eating choices
Weight loss	Weight release
If . . .	When . . .
I should/I have to . . .	I choose to . . .
Speaking of the devil . . .	Speaking of an angel . . .

FROM	TO
I love him to death	I love him to life
I'll be damned . . .	I'll be blessed . . .
Maybe/I'll try/Probably not	No, I decline. No, I'll pass
God, damn it	God, bless it

Treat what comes out of your mouth as an affirmation. To affirm means to "make firm" or to confirm. Keep in mind that *words spoken with intention and conviction call forth a reality that is in agreement.* What are you affirming with your words? What instructions are you giving to the universe? An affirmation takes root if it is said often enough or with enough conviction, feeling, and intention.

Affirmations are powerful because they program your subconscious mind much like a software programmer programs a computer. Guard your words carefully, and be wary of the words others direct at you or use in your presence. There are times when I make a statement that is negative or disempowering, and I will say "Cancel, cancel" out loud to myself. There are times when someone describes a negative experience they've had and then will make a comment to me like, "You know how black folks are . . ." or "You know how brothers are . . ." I will rebuke their comment with "I hear what you're saying, but *that is not my reality.*" This response lets them know that I have a different reality; I am not in agreement with the summary of their experience, but I can still hear what they are saying. Our words are serious business.

There are times I have to rebuke or correct certain statements or comments others make to me to keep me from absorbing the negative energy of what was said. You cannot let others put things on you, especially their negative experiences. You bring thoughts and emotions into your consciousness not only when you send out or speak words but also when you hear and receive words. Yes, our words are very serious business.

A powerful woman understands the power of her spoken word
and speaks carefully and deliberately.

67. *Insperience it*

One afternoon, my husband and I stopped to browse in one of Seattle's most popular metaphysical bookstores. On the bottom shelf of a bookcase, stuck in an unlikely place, among the scented soaps and candles, I noticed a bright gold half-sized book entitled *Your Owner's Manual* by Burt Hotchkiss. As I was flipping through its pages, a statement caught my eye. Near the bottom of one of the pages it said, "It's not yours until you express it, give it away, or teach it. The true purpose for teaching (sharing) anything is to reinforce it in your own mind." This statement seemed to resonate with a passage I had read in *A Course in Miracles* that explained the fundamental law of sharing: *give what you value in order to keep it in your mind.* And both of these passages were echoed in the words I heard my friend Phillip Aaron share at his Success Seminar a few weeks earlier: *to see and feel yourself having and experiencing something you desire draws it to you.*

At first these notions were mind-blowing to me because they flew in the face of how I thought manifestation worked. I thought if you wanted something, you affirmed it repeatedly, named it and claimed it, and spoke it as if it were already so. And this brought it forth, eventually. I had results to prove that this approach worked.

But what I was gathering from these passages was something deeper. Yes, using affirmations alone can produce results over time. My usual approach to manifesting what I desired was an *outside-in* approach instead of *inside-out.* What these passages revealed was a path to manifestation that was less traveled—a path that was more powerful, produced results more quickly, and took far less effort. Both Burt and Phillip were suggesting a path that worked from the inside-out, a path that combined affirmations with another powerful spiritual treatment.

The most powerful path to manifesting your goals and desires is to first create the *inner* experience, the *insperience* of having what you desire. *To insperience* means you create the image and feeling *internally* first, so that you are *holding the vibration* that will attract the *experience.* As you create the insperience in your body, you also must align your language to support what you want to manifest—you affirm and confirm with your words.

We've been told to "fake it until we make it," meaning *act as if*. Yes, this is true if you want to work from the outside-in. Working from the outside-in is when you try to change your behavior in order to affect your consciousness. Yes, acting as if and behaving as if *eventually* affects your consciousness, but *insperiencing* it affects your consciousness first, which is more powerful. *Create the insperience of having what it is you desire, and you will attract the experience that matches.* By learning to apply this inside-out approach to my life, I have produced some powerful results.

I didn't know it at the time, but this was the process I used to win my high school state discus championship my senior year of high school. In my junior year I had competed in the state track championships in the discus, but had placed fifteenth. At the end of the track season, I set a goal for myself. In my senior year I wanted to place in the top three so that I could stand on the awards podium in the middle of the stadium's field and have a medal placed around my neck.

When track season began the following spring, I went into preparation. During my junior year, I had treated track like more of a social opportunity. But in my senior year, I was a different Debrena at track practice. I asked myself, what does being state discus champion *feel* like? How would I think, move, speak, and act? What are the emotions, sensations, and feelings that I would *insperience* as state discus champion?

I'd been running track since my freshman year, and Tuesdays had always been weight training. In previous years, it was typical for me to cut my weight training workout a little short by fudging on my repetitions, doing four sets instead of five, keeping the weights set at the same weight week after week instead of increasing them incrementally. Or I would spend a lot of time chatting with other teammates in the weight room who weren't taking their weight training too seriously, either.

This track season was different, however. I was on a mission. In weight training, I completed all of my repetitions and steadily increased my weight load. Each week, I started reading the high school prep section of the newspaper to find out the distances other girls were throwing the discus at rival high schools around the state. I was especially keeping an eye on Chris Larson, a 6'1", 250-pound senior girl at the high school across town who was the reigning state discus champion *and* javelin champion. Chris Larson had a reputation that preceded her. In addition to being a tour de force in track, Chris was also a linebacker on her high school's football team! Chris had even received national coverage in *USA Today* because she had placed high at the national Junior Olympics track meet. Each time I had come up against Chris Larson in the regular season, I had placed second to her.

I progressed through the regular track season and then through districts. I then qualified to participate in the state meet in the discus competiton. The state meet was now less than two weeks away. I kicked into high gear and went into serious preparation. Every night for the next fourteen days, ten minutes before getting in the bed, I would create an inner vision of myself throwing the discus 135 feet with a perfect approach, perfect form, and a perfect release. I ran that inner vision through my mind, complete with the *insperience* of it, every night. This was the distance that I had determined I needed to throw to earn myself a spot on the awards podium. Every night for fourteen days, I ran that inner image through my mind in slow motion, and in full color and sound, being sure to include every detail—how I felt as I approached the throwing ring, how I was breathing, how I was walking and holding my body, how my muscles felt, how the discus felt in my hand, how I executed my spin, how I placed my feet, how I extended my throwing arm, how I turned and opened my hips to get the most torque. I also took four index cards and wrote 135 feet in big bold numbers on each one. Beneath "135 FEET," on the index card I wrote this affirmation: *I deliver my approach flawlessly and powerfully. I release the discus with my hips open and my throwing arm fully extended.* I taped the index cards at eye level around the house—in my bedroom, on the refrigerator, on the bathroom mirror, and on the back door so that it was the last thing I saw before I left the house to go to school each morning.

Each night I replayed my inner vision and insperienced it until I felt that my throw was completely "on." I allowed this feeling of being "on" to flow throughout my body. In my mind, I saw my discus sailing out to the 135-foot mark and stirring up a small cloud of white marker chalk as it landed. I also created the feeling of elation I would insperience from placing in the top three. At track practice, the effects of my insperience process were showing. I had increased my distance *twenty feet* over my regular season personal best in those fourteen days of insperience treatment.

The day of the state meet arrived. When I reported to the discus staging area with the other twenty girls, I walked, moved, stretched out, and warmed up like a discus champion. Once the warm-up period was over and the competition began, I was friendly and cordial, but instead of clustering with the other girls and laughing and chatting between throws, I stayed to myself. I was whispering my index card affirmation to myself and re-creating the feeling in my body of a making a 135-foot throw. I was re-creating the feelings of joy and deep satisfaction I felt as my name was announced over the main loudspeaker as one of the top place finishers.

Going into the third round, I was in fifth place, two places away from a slot that would earn me a place on the awards podium. The best throw so far was 127 feet. I had one throw left. I was one of the final four left to make her third throw. I entered the throwing ring and delivered my throw. My throw felt good, very good. It felt "on." I watched the discus sail through the air and hit the ground, stirring up a small white cloud of chalk dust as it landed. The line judge shouted back 135 feet 7 inches to the discus official. I was now in first place with three girls left to throw! And one of them was Chris Larson. The next two girls completed their final throws. *Whew*—my throw was still the farthest. Then Chris entered the ring in all of her 6'1", 250-pound glory to take her third throw. Her final throw was 129 feet.

I had won first place!

My mom ran toward me from the spectator bleachers in the discus area and my discus coach ran toward me from the sidelines shouting "Debrena, you did it! You did it!" A flood of emotion welled up and surged through my body as the magnitude of what I'd just accomplished hit me, bringing tears to my eyes that were soon running down my cheeks.

I had done it.

Twenty minutes later, as I was stepping up to the first place spot on the awards podium, I heard the announcer blast my name over the loudspeaker. I bent over for the judge to hang the gold medal around my neck. My preparation and my insperience treatment had worked!

For you it may be attracting a soul mate, attaining a slimmer body or the perfect profession, more self-discipline, more patience, more peace, more prosperity, or being on time. Regardless of what it is you want to manifest in your life, the same process applies. Write down the desired outcome you seek to manifest. Develop supporting affirmations Be clear and be specific. Create the inner vision and the insperience of having it.

The key to manifesting powerfully:
In-vision it → insperience it → experience it.

68. *Be the architect of your life*

> *"Can't nothing make your life work*
> *if you ain't the architect."*
>
> —Terry McMillan

*O*ne of my spiritual mentors once told me that spirit communicates in the language of symbols, images, and pictures. You must be able to not only *speak* with authority in your life but also be able to create, as I talked about earlier, an *inner vision* of what you desire and *insperience the feeling* of having it. Then you will be able to bring it forth and manifest it. If you can do this, you hold the keys to becoming the architect of your life.

A great exercise for creating an outer *visual* affirmation (external picture) is using visual tools such as a Treasure Map. A Treasure Map combines visual affirmations with written affirmations. A Treasure Map, which operates like a personal blueprint of your dreams and desires, helps you focus your thoughts and feelings on what you desire in specific areas of your life. It is an "outpicturing" of your inner vision.

To create a Treasure Map, cut out words, phrases, pictures, images, and colorful scenes from sources such as magazines and newspapers and glue them onto a large piece of cardboard, a piece of typing paper, heavy construction paper, or into a scrapbook. You should use color pictures, words, phrases, and scenes instead of black and white ones because color has a greater effect on your subconscious. You can create a Treasure Map for a job, business, or career; for finances; for healthy love relationships; for friendships; for health; or spiritual growth, for example. Your Treasure Map is accompanied by statements that describe, in the present tense, the reality you want to manifest.

If you want to make a transition to a different line of work, career, or profession, you can create a Treasure Map to support you in attracting your perfect work. If you value creative expression, laughter, casual work attire, and interacting face-to-face with customers, you will want to cut out pictures, words, scenes, and images that convey this. Next to the images, you may write an affirmation such as *I am guided to my perfect work*. If you are seeking more joy, peace, and relaxation in your life, you will want to cut out pictures and images that convey this. Next to these images, you may write an affirmation such as *Peace is real in my life* or *Daily prayer and meditation feed my spirit*.

So that the images and affirmations on her Treasure Map would remain in the forefront of her mind, my sister decided to convert half of an entire wall in her apartment into what she calls her Dream Wall. For each key area of her life, she has created a mini-Treasure Map: (1) love relationships and friendships, (2) body and fitness, (3) finances and money, (4) leisure and hobbies, (5) spiritual growth and development, and (6) home environment and living space. So she now has six large pieces of construction paper mounted on her wall and covered with colorful Treasure Map images and affirmations for each of her six areas.

If you don't already have a personal Treasure Map, I suggest you create one. My Treasure Map is on several pages inside a three-ring notebook I keep on the bottom shelf of my altar in my bedroom. I review my Treasure Map once a month. As a suggestion for sharing the Treasure Map experience with other women, you may call together some sisterfriends for a Treasure Map–making party. Have each bring old magazines, scissors, glue, and her favorite tape or CD, and you provide the space and the refreshments. After everyone has completed her Map, each of you takes a turn and shares your Treasure Map with the others.

Bringing things forth in our lives with spoken affirmations alone works, but it usually takes a lot of energy, effort, and repetition. A powerful woman combines: (1) spoken affirmations with written and visual affirmations (i.e., Treasure Map), and (2) inner visioning with creating the inner feeling, the insperience. When you bring these "ingredients" together, you have the recipe for being the architect of your life, for being its designer, sculptor, and molder.

Being Architect of Your Life:
Spoken words + written affirmations + visual affirmations + inner vision
(in-vision) + inner feeling (insperience) → → → *desired experiences*
and outcomes

Every architect needs a blueprint. Every woman on the path to discovering her joy and power needs a blueprint. Let your Treasure Map become the blueprint for creating the life you desire and deserve.

69. *Master manifestation*

We already have manifestation mastered—every one of us. *We've been manifesting all over the place.* But we are often oblivious to how we've been doing it. Some of us have been manifesting drama, crisis, and chaos. Some of us have manifested relationships and situations that continuously bring us strife. Some of us have manifested a reality that consists of struggle, hardship, and being a victim.

Whatever types of results you are producing in your life, whether good, bad, or ugly, you are using a process to generate them. *Become conscious of this process* and you will be able to create the life you desire and deserve in all areas of your existence. In *The Dynamic Laws of Prosperity*, Catherine Ponder tells us, "desire is God tapping at the door of your mind, trying to give you greater good." *God always gives you all the joy and good you can stand.*

If you understand how the process of manifestation works, you can strive to more accurately and effectively manifest your desired outcomes and increase your ability to produce the desires of your heart. Manifestation is the process of bringing things from the invisible plane to the visible plane. In order to increase your ability to manifest good in your life, keep the following eight ideas in mind.

1. Your core, deep-seated beliefs make up your Manifestation Command Center. Your thoughts are a function of your core beliefs.
2. Your core beliefs establish the boundaries of what you believe to be possible or impossible, hard or effortless.
3. Your beliefs and thoughts determine the feelings you have. Your thoughts give rise to feelings.
4. Your perceptions and experiences are always consistent with your beliefs.

5. What is in agreement with your beliefs, we label "right," and what is in disagreement with your beliefs, we label "wrong."
6. Your thoughts have form, substance, and vibrations. Your thoughts are real. Your thoughts are magnetic.
7. Your attention and focus determine which of your thoughts will be most magnetic.
8. Whatever you focus on most is what you get.

The manifestation process operates in accordance with spiritual law, so being ignorant of it does not mean you avoid its effects. If I were to write the manifestation process like a formula, it would read:

The Manifestation Process

WHAT YOU BELIEVE (Your core beliefs and core assumptions about reality) → Gives rise to WHAT YOU THINK (your thoughts and forms of thought) → Which gives rise to WHAT YOU FEEL AND PERCEIVE (your feelings and interpretations) → Which gives rise to WHAT YOU SAY (Your inner reality is converted into word vibrations) → Which gives rise to WHAT YOU DO (Which charges the universe, and is further concretized into actions and behaviors over time) → Which gives rise to WHAT YOU CREATE, ATTRACT, AND EXPERIENCE (results, "your reality," manifestation of an outcome).

If you are not creating the results you desire, *work backwards* through this process, starting with your end result and working *back* to your core beliefs. Get clear on the parts of the process that are *out of alignment* with your desired outcome.

My girlfriend Antoinette discovered that every time she got close to achieving an important goal or experiencing significant success in her life, a drama or crisis would arise. What she didn't realize was that she was afraid of success. She kept subconsciously sabotaging herself every time she got close. She had core beliefs about success that were undermining her efforts to move to a higher level in her life. Growing up, she had been indoctrinated with negative comments and messages about success being bad and undesirable, something that only greedy people desired.

As a little girl, penny-pinching, being very frugal, and being "ordinary" were very important values in Antoinette's household. When she dreamed big or shared her goals and aspirations, she was shot down with negative comments from her mom, that discouraged her from trying to be "extra-ordinary." She was told that she was trying to be "better than everyone else." To aspire to be successful was looked upon with scorn and contempt in her household.

When Antoinette worked backwards through the manifestation process, she was able to uncover the core beliefs that were beneath her fear of success. She was able to see how and where they originated and to understand how they were preventing her from manifesting desired outcomes and results in her life.

Antoinette had a breakthrough in her ability to manifest what, for her, was consistent with success, when she was able to break the grip of her core beliefs about success that had a vise-like hold on her. She has now redefined success for herself as having two happy and healthy daughters, being in a line of work that she loves, having her business generate enough income so that she doesn't have to struggle to make ends meet, and having friends in her life who love and support her. Antoinette now declares herself a successful woman, without guilt and without the internal tug-of-war that was previously preventing her from manifesting success in her life.

Are you clear on the essence of what it is you desire? Do you know where your blocks are? Are you able to *in-vision* yourself having it? Being it? One day I came across a poem that beautifully describes the power of your mind and the essence of the manifestation process. Read it through *twice*, slowly, substituting she for he, her for his, and woman for man.

> *Mind is the Master Power*
> *that molds and makes*
> *And man is mind*
> *and forevermore he takes*
> *his tools of thought*
> *and shaping what he wills—*
> *brings forth a thousand joys,*
> *a thousand ills.*
> *He thinks in secret*
> *and it comes to pass*
> *Environment is but his looking glass.*

—Author unknown

70. Redefine success

No wonder more of us don't consider ourselves to be successful. Webster's dictionary tells us that *success* is the "gaining of fame" or "the achieving of something you desire or attempt." When a culture has presented you with images of success that equate with making a certain amount of money, gaining a certain status, reaching a certain level of education, or having certain types of material things, this sets you up to be in *constant pursuit* of these "certain things." In this kind of setting, few will feel as if they've actually "arrived." Within this context, I can understand why so few of us feel comfortable considering ourselves successful. We've been programmed to believe that success is "over there," so we don't consider "over here," where we are, to be successful.

One way to empower yourself is to redefine or reframe your concepts of success as Antoinette did. Success is one of those concepts that we certainly need to redefine. To me, success now means many things:

Having rich, fulfilling, nourishing friendships.
Wanting what I have.
Having a livelihood that brings me joy.
Receiving compensation for contributing and sharing my gifts, talents, and abilities.
Being involved in a line of work that energizes me.
Having the content and substance of my life bring me joy, peace, and pleasure.
Being able to do things that nourish my soul and feed my spirit.
Being tuned in to God.
Being ecstatically married.
Being clear on my ministry, mission, and purpose.
Having happy, healthy, self-expressed children.
Recognizing that the grass is green on my side, and knowing how to keep it that way.

Affirmation for the Week: I AM SUCCESSFUL!

71. Rewrite the script

Our scripts are the collection of dominant, prevailing, or subconscious beliefs we are born to. Our scripts shape our actions and behaviors, what we think is right or wrong, or acceptable or unacceptable. Cultures have scripts. Families have scripts. And thus, as individuals, we have scripts that we inherit or absorb unconsciously. Scripts can limit us or liberate us.

We inherit scripts not just through the comments and words we hear but also through what we *observe* and the images we *absorb*. The good news is that once you recognize and become conscious of the scripts from which you've been operating, you can choose to rewrite the scripts that haven't been working for you. After all, you are the ultimate scriptwriter of your life.

Last year I was leading a sacred pampering seminar with a group of female professors and administrators at Ohio University in Athens, Ohio. As we were discussing the societal and cultural beliefs that prevent us from having lives of ease and grace, I asked the women to share the scripts they had inherited that were limiting their ability to experience more joy, peace, and pleasure in their lives. Here are some of the scripts they identified:

"You can't have your cake and eat it, too."
"A good woman takes care of everyone else and tries to make them happy."
"Save the good stuff for special occasions."
"A good woman keeps her house clean—all the time."
"You have to be all things to all people."
"A woman's work is never done."
"You're not complete until you're married."
"Something must be wrong with you if you're almost 40 and don't have a husband."
"You have to choose between career and family. You can't have both."
"Life is a struggle."
"Life is hard, and then you die."
"Business before pleasure."

"Good things come to those who wait."

"Nice girls don't . . ."

"Boys can do that, but not you, you're a girl."

"A woman should always be busy, or look busy."

"Taking time for yourself is selfish and lazy."

"Others first."

"To give is more blessed than to receive."

"Anything that even remotely looks like selfishness is not good, and is downright sinful."

"There is no rest for the weary."

"Delay gratification."

"Patience is a virtue."

"Suffering, struggle, effort, and pain are par for life's course."

"You can't have it all. You've got to make sacrifices."

"If you want it done right, you've got to do it yourself."

_____ (add your own)

_____ (add your own)

Do any of these sound familiar? I've noticed that each generation has its own particular set of scripts. What scripts have you unknowingly absorbed that have been limiting your power or suppressing your joy? Add your own in the space provided. How do these scripts translate into what you think is right, wrong, acceptable, unacceptable, possible, impossible? How have these scripts suppressed your brilliance, self-expression, creativity, freedom, and capacity for experiencing ease, grace, love, peace, and pleasure in your life? We tend to think that these are seemingly harmless comments and messages that we hear, but don't absorb. They go in one ear and out the other, right? Wrong. We don't realize the extent to which we've actually *internalized* these comments and phrases; we've cemented them deep in our psyches, where they harden into the bedrock of our personal belief system.

The limiting scripts we inherit are often the by-products of unhealed patterns and issues that are passed down to us, primarily through the female *line in our families.* Yes, media has a huge impact on our minds, too, but our *initial* scripts are received within the home from close family members, particularly from our mamas. In many cases, these scripts have functioned as a generational curse. Instead of being healed, challenged, or rewritten, they are perpetuated. We think it is *us* making choices and decisions, and really it's our scripts being played out. So that we get better, not bitter, we must remember that Mama could only pass on what had been passed on to her. Mama did the best she could with what she inherited and absorbed from her mama and the other important women in her life.

A little ritual you can do to begin rewriting your own scripts is to cut or tear out twenty strips of blank paper. On each of the first ten strips of paper, write a limiting script that you've inherited, been affected by, or absorbed. Write the script as a statement. See the previous examples for help. For each of these ten scripts, write a new script using "I" statements. For example, one of my limiting scripts was "I can't have it all without sacrifices and trade-offs." I rewrote this script to read, "I can have it all with ease and grace."

Once you have written your ten new scripts, tear up the old scripts in itty, bitty little pieces and burn them in your fireplace or flush them down your toilet. When doing a ritual that involves releasing the old and bringing in the new, as this one does, you want to be sure to physically remove the physical or symbolic representations of the old. This is also a great ritual to do with a group of enlightened sisterfriends.

You are the ultimate scriptwriter in your life.

72. *See your life as an unfolding story*

Life is without meaning.
You bring meaning to it.

—Joseph Campbell

When you step back and view your life as an unfolding story, you begin to have a clearer picture of the plots, characters, scripts, and "learnings" that have come with it. Being able to see your life as an unfolding story can be very empowering because it helps you keep things in perspective and see events, situations, and circumstances in your life as parts of your story.

When I speak of *story* in this context, I do not mean a falsehood or a tall tale. I mean story as in the chronicle of a journey, your journey. The beauty of a story is that it doesn't contain labels of "good" things and "bad" things that happen. A story is a narrative of a series of events and experiences, *all* of which are useful and relevant.

Looking at your life as an unfolding story can help you appreciate the twists, turns, challenges, peaks, and valleys that have been a part of your journey thus far. One day I had lunch with a friend who recently learned to start viewing her life as a story. She had been going to a therapist to help her deal with some serious unresolved issues from her childhood. One method her therapist used was to have her *reframe* her life as a story so that she could more readily recognize the meaning and the value of its events and occurrences. This empowered her to look at her life through a new lens, a lens through which she could see that even the ugly parts had value. Up until this point, she had seen her life as a string of hurts, disappointments, "raw deals," and misfortunes. She had been so focused on the ugly parts that she had forgotten there were also some pretty parts. What she considered to be the ugly parts so overshadowed and dominated her memories that she had perceived herself as a victim. And her "victimitis" came through in her language and her relationships. Reviewing her life as an unfolding story moved her out of the victim's seat into that of the author of her story.

I invite you to *reframe your life as a story*—a precious, unfolding story that no one else has ever lived. What a privilege to be who you are. Each of us is living a unique and distinct story, one that no one else has *ever* lived. What an honor to be given a life to live.

When we don't keep our lives in perspective, life can seem to be a hassle, hard, difficult, or worthless, but not a privilege. Like most us, you have probably assigned a negative charge or negative memory to your life's ugly parts. In a story, there are no ugly parts, only events, happenings, and occurrences. Reframing your life as a story empowers you to face, explore, and embrace all parts of your story.

The power in seeing your life as an unfolding story is in the opportunity to acknowledge the "chapters" that you've already written and lived—and then the chapters yet to be written. You may have past chapters in your life that are full of pain or disappointment, or you are not proud of the way you acted or the decisions that you made. That's okay. You are the author of your story, so you get to decide if the chapters you have yet to "write" and live will have the same plot, characters, and drama. You hold the pen. The pen is in your hands. So you have the power and the permission to rewrite the parts of the story that didn't work for you in previous "chapters" of your life, to write new chapters, or to decide upon a different ending.

A great exercise for reframing your life is to uncover the themes your life has presented. Get out a piece of paper and a pen. In your mind, scroll back *ten* years. On the paper, write the years down the left side of the paper, starting with the year ten years ago. Leave writing space for entries between each year. For each year, describe key events and happenings in your life, and then on the right side of the paper, develop your personal themes for that year of your life. This will create a time line that will help you more clearly see the path, "learnings," events, and stepping stones that have shaped who you are. Here's what I came up with when I did this Life Themes exercise.

LIFE THEMES EXERCISE

YEAR	HAPPENINGS	THEMES
1989	I felt like I'd hit the glass ceiling at AT&T as an account executive; participated in a personal effectiveness course that was very transformational; had been living in Los Angeles for a couple of years after graduating from college. Had experienced a lot of the L.A. life.	Reevaluation Restlessness Completion of a cycle
1990	Moved to Seattle (new place, new city); became regional vice-president in my parents' telecommunications company; started on a path of heightened spiritual growth and understand my identity as a woman of African descent. Did lots of reading and spending quiet time alone.	Decisions Transitions New beginnings Spiritual discovery Clarity

YEAR	HAPPENINGS	THEMES
1991	Wrote first self-published version of *Sacred Pampering Principles;* established Seattle Chapter of the Enlightened Women's Circle; new boyfriend; many new friendships.	New connections Settling in Getting acquainted
1992	Broke up with boyfriend; met my future husband; took a trip to Egypt as an educational and spiritual vacation.	Passages Pilgrimage Insights
1993	Got married; had first baby; did a lot of self-reflecting and emotional healing and forgiveness work; reevaluated several close friendships; second version of *Sacred Pampering Principles* published by a small, local publishing house.	Partnership Motherhood Reflection Introspection Healing and "housecleaning"
1994	Took a personal retreat to Sedona, Arizona; had second baby; decided to leave family business and start own training and consulting company full time; first year as presenter with African-American Women on Tour conference; started speaking more and leading more seminars.	Seeding plans and dreams Bold moves Acts of faith Nurturing and cultivating my soul Launching and initiating
1995	My business is off to a great start; was approached by top African-American literary agent in the country to pursue national book contract for *Sacred Pampering Principles;* landed national book deal; first year doing the African-American Women's Advance. Event is a stellar success.	New beginnings Seeds starting to bear fruit Creativity Ripening and fruition
1996	Took seven-day cruise to Caribbean with husband; released 20 pounds of weight; business continues to do better and better.	Reaping bountifully Harvest time

YEAR	HAPPENINGS	THEMES
1997	National release of *Sacred Pampering Principles* in hardback; in *Essence* magazine with 2-page excerpt of book; national book tour; travel; meeting many new people.	New horizons National connections Expansion Evolution
1998	Third baby born; cut hair short; in *Essence* four times; land my company's biggest contract; leadership; move to new level in speaking career; financial lessons and breakthroughs.	New levels New awareness Actualizing my desired life
1999	Land second national book deal; focus on my body—releasing weight; cleansing; change eating habits; focus on health and exercise; internal preparation; start Wisdom Circle.	Powering up Preparation Cleansing Releasing Maturing

As I reflect on the themes of the last ten years of my life, I can see the progression. I can see the growth; I can see the "learnings." I can see how each year's events propelled me to the next level or stage in my life. I see the triumphs and the challenges, and I can appreciate *all* of my experiences. What themes and insights did your ten-year reflection reveal?

Cherish your story.

73. *Balance yourself*

How well do you know you? How well do you know your gifts, talents, skills, and abilities (GTSAs)? I'm not talking about skills only, which are usually taught or learned through training or formal education. I'm talking about the gifts, talents, and abilities that have been *naturally* cultivated and developed in you over the course of your life journey.

When I speak of balance, I'm not speaking in terms of balancing business and pleasure, work and play, career and family, or personal and professional. I'm speaking of balancing core aspects of your own psyche—*the leader, healer, visionary, and teacher within.*

Though one of these core models or archetypes tends to be dominant in our lives, balancing ourselves means that we are able to readily call on any one of these aspects of ourselves as a situation or circumstance dictates. In her book *The Four-Fold Way,* Angeles Arrien points out the importance of balancing yourself. She points out how indigenous cultures consider optimum health to exist when there is a balance of leading, healing, visioning, and teaching in our lives.

Do you know which of these archetypes, or core models, is underexpressed or overexpressed in your life? Review the four archetypes and the description of their guiding principles to discover aspects of yourself that you need to bring into fuller expression in your life.

ARCHETYPE	GUIDING PRINCIPLES
Leader	Alignment between words and actions
	Flexible, willing, open
	Gives honor and respect to others
	Has clear personal boundaries
	Self-disciplined
	Takes personal responsibility
Healer	Pays attention
	Is open-hearted, clear-hearted, full-hearted, and strong-hearted
	Is able to equally give and receive
	Is able to connect with others
	Understands the healing power of love
Visionary	Tells the truth
	Communicates with no blame or judgment
	Capacity to magnetize and galvanize
	Is real and authentic
	Transcends polarities and paradoxes
	Honors intuitions and insights

Teacher	Has wisdom
	Teaches trust
	Is not attached to outcomes
	Has clarity and discernment
	Comfortable with uncertainty

I can see that there are aspects of *each* of these archetypes that I need to bring into fuller expression within my self. Balancing my leader archetype requires my working on being more self-disciplined. This applies to being disciplined with my eating choices, eating habits, and exercise. Balancing my healer archetype requires that I be more open-hearted and full-hearted. Balancing my visionary archetype requires that I work on communicating without blame or judgment. And balancing my teacher archetype requires that I work on not being attached to outcomes.

The goal in balancing yourself is to balance the expressions of each of these aspects within you so that you are able to call on whichever aspect is needed in a given situation or circumstance in your life. Often we justify our imbalances by saying, "This is just the way I am." Not necessarily so. Yes, our life experiences shape our personality and way of being, but we can choose to change. We can choose to develop aspects of ourselves that enable us to be more balanced.

A powerful woman strives to balance herself.

74. *Recognize your gifts, talents, skills, and abilities*

*I*sn't it amazing? There's only one of you in all the world. There has never been another you, and there will never be another you. You are a unique combination of gifts, talents, skills, and abilities (GTSAs) that make you distinct from any other human being who has ever walked the planet!

You will be able to fully contribute your gifts, talents, and abilities to the world after you first recognize what they are. The first step to uncovering your divine purpose is being able to acknowledge your personal GTSAs. They give you deeper insight into your self. And the more you express your true self in the course of your everyday life, the more you will experience fulfillment, deep satisfaction, and authentic success.

Become better acquainted with your GTSAs. Get out your pen and read through the descriptive verbs in each of the following rows. Circle the items you are most passionate about doing or that you are drawn to, even if you have never done them. You might learn something new about yourself. Our natural gifts, talents, and abilities usually fall into three primary categories: a preference for dealing with people, a preference for dealing with things, or a preference for dealing with data, information, or ideas. Each category has twenty-one items listed. Count up the number of items circled in each category. Did one category have more items circled than the others?

> **Dealing with PEOPLE:** working with individuals, working with groups, leading, communicating person to person, training, initiating, visioning, entertaining, instructing, teaching, consulting, listening, advising, coordinating, healing, negotiating, referring, persuading, influencing, selling, motivating
>
> **Dealing with THINGS:** using your hands, agility, speed, strength, sewing, cooking, drawing, painting, producing, making, constructing, cleaning, repairing, inventing, operating, driving, assembling, shaping, cutting, growing, sculpting
>
> **Dealing with DATA/IDEAS:** gathering, researching, organizing, analyzing, synthesizing, designing, planning, tracking, compiling, prioritizing, deciding, recommending, computing, developing, filing, calculating, comparing, sorting, categorizing, summarizing, selecting

These are not exhaustive lists, but they are a start. Take the words you've circled to help you build your GTSA Profile. Your GTSA Profile is a summary of what is most motivating to you, what you're most passionate about, what seems to come naturally to you, and what types of activities and interactions engage and stimulate you the most. Here's my expanded GTSA Profile.

> **Debrena's Gifts-Talents-Skills-Abilities Profile**
>
> *leading, initiating, motivating, transforming, visioning, converting vision into action, communicating with people in person, over the phone or in groups, clarifying, observing, synthesizing, summarizing, coaching, listening, enterprising, consulting, training, persuading, influencing, interacting, imagining, designing, distinguishing, problem solving, questioning, inquiring, dialoguing, facilitating, generating, creating, developing.*

Now develop your own expanded GTSA Profile.

> (Your name here) ———————————————————'s GTSA Profile
>
> ———————————, ———————————, ———————————,
>
> ———————————, ———————————, ———————————,
>
> ———————————, ———————————, ———————————,

Before going into business for myself full time, I developed my GTSA Profile. I discovered that what brings me the most joy is communicating and interacting with people. My GTSA Profile became a road map for steering me to clients and projects that would be most stimulating and rewarding for me. I also used my profile to decide how I would diversify my business. It has been a process, but I have now arrived at a place where my livelihood allows me to fully express my natural gifts, talents, skills, and abilities. The activities that constitute my business consist of what motivates me the most, and what brings me the most joy and passion: training and consulting, presenting keynote speeches, leading empowerment seminars, workshops and retreats, and authoring books.

Are you making full use of your GTSAs in your profession or line of work? Are there hobbies you've put on the back burner that need to be resurrected? Do you need to make changes or adjustments in your activities or involvements?

A couple of months ago, I had dinner with a 25-year-old sisterfriend, Tina, who had just completed her master's degree in English at the University of Washington. She asked that I keep my ears open for any job opportunities I could direct her to. After we ate dinner, she presented me with what was the equivalent of her GTSA Profile. Instead of a traditional résumé, where you list your past job responsibilities and tasks performed, Tina gave me a summary that communicated her natural gifts, talents, skills, abilities, and passions, not just her work experience.

Tina handed me a piece of paper on which she had typed a description of her gifts, talents, and passions. She wrote: "passionate planner, passionate organizer, detail oriented, effective at managing multiple tasks, effective at following through on multiple tasks, embraces new ideas, takes initiative in problem solving, serves as a valuable liaison, serves as a valuable mediator." The next section of her "profile" communicated her gifts, talents, skills, and abilities. She wrote: "planning, organizing, managing, following through, developing, instructing, tutoring, facilitating, researching, editing, evaluating, advising, and coordinating." More of her essence was communicated in this profile. A traditional résumé wouldn't have conveyed her passions, gifts, and talents because résumés are biased toward your educational background, past work experience, and taught skills. Tina's approach was particularly useful because she was not looking to go into a line of work directly related to her master's degree and education track.

Three weeks later, I was meeting with a new client, and she shared that she was looking to fill a position in her event-planning business. She described the type of person she envisioned for the position and the qualities she was seeking. As she spoke, a light came on in my head. She was describing Tina. My client was using many of the same words Tina had used in the profile she'd given me a few weeks earlier. I said to my client, "I think I have the perfect person for you," and I proceeded to give her Tina's phone number. The following week, I received a phone call from a very excited Tina. My client had interviewed her and hired her for the event-planning position. Consequently, Tina excelled in the position and was offered a promotion after only one month.

Tina made my job very easy because she was in touch with herself and her natural gifts, talents, skills, abilities, and passions. She was not allowing herself to be limited or boxed in by her English degree or her past work experience.

Recognizing your GTSAs means that you have to "name them and claim them." You have to uncover and acknowledge your natural gifts, talents, abilities, and passions; what brings you joy; and what motivates and engages you most. Recognizing your GTSAs is also part of the self-discovery process. Embedded in your GTSAs are the nuggets of your life purpose.

Know thyself. The final frontier is not outer space, it's inner space.

75. *Know your ministry*

Whether you go to church or not, whether you have a college degree or a high school diploma, *you have a ministry. Ministry* means "the act of serving." When you approach something with an attitude and posture of service, you are ministering. What you do with a commitment to excellence, thoroughness, and helping to better others is your ministry. And many of us have more than one ministry.

The lady who provides day care for my daughters does so with enthusiasm, excellence, a cheerful heart, and attentiveness. She doesn't just baby-sit—her ministry is providing loving care and home-cooked meals in a safe, nurturing, home-style environment for children. Appropriately, her business name is Home Away from Home Daycare.

Another sisterfriend is involved part time in a network marketing company. She decided to focus exclusively on promoting wellness and body-care products—the vitamins, weight management, and makeup lines. She is able to put her extensive health and fitness background to use by ministering to the minds, bodies, and spirits of her clients through the products and knowledge that she offers.

Another girlfriend, Marlena, converted a room in the basement of her mother's house into a pampering room where she specializes in doing evening manicures and pedicures for women who can't take time off during their workday for an appointment, or those who have busy Saturdays. When you step into Marlena's little pampering room, she has soothing jazz playing and scented candles burning, and she offers you herbal tea and butter cookies. Massaging, nurturing, and beautifying the hands and feet of her clients is her ministry.

My good friend Dr. Traci Lynn, speaker, evangelist, author, and self-made millionaire, has an audiotape of one of her speaking presentations. On her audiotape, Traci Lynn declares her ministry as, "Communicating the Good News while motivating those in pursuit of purpose; while encouraging those preparing for destiny; setting the captives free of mental bondage; and helping others get a check-up from the neck up!"

What is your ministry? Have you declared it? Have you written it down? If not, take this opportunity to start developing your *ministry statement*. Write it down on a notecard or on an 8½ × 11-inch piece of paper and post it in your bedroom, office, kitchen, or bathroom. My ministry statement, which is taped to the closet doors in my office, is: *To initiate change and foster transformation using my talents of speaking, writing, consulting, facilitating, and training; and to create and develop transformational gatherings and experiences for women's spiritual growth and personal empowerment.* Revisit your ministry statement and edit it and refine it if necessary. Let it be your guiding light—a reminder to you of the reason you're here on the planet. Your ministry is exactly that—*your* ministry. You get to declare it. Your ministry is an expression of your mission, and one of the avenues through which your purpose fulfills itself.

*Nothing is more powerful than a sistah on a serious mission,
clear about her ministry, making a difference in the world.*

76. Answer your calling

*Many are called,
but few listen.*

—djg

*I*n *Callings*, author Gregg Levoy states, "A call is only a monologue. A return call, a response, creates a dialogue." In other words, our lives are a "process of calls and responses."

In the original sense of the word, religion is based on the Latin word *religio* or *religare*, which means to reconnect with or remember what has been dismembered. I believe that answering your call and discovering your purpose are forms of reconnecting and remembering Who and Whose You Really Are.

Our purpose leaves footprints and fingerprints right under our noses, but often we're too distracted, too tired, or too busy to take notice. You don't have to look far to find our purpose. You just have to look within. Get out a pen or pencil and write in your answers to the following questions. Ask yourself,

What are the clues my life has been giving me about my purpose?

_____

What am I passionate about? _____

_____

What am I doing when I feel most alive and engaged? _____

_____

What am I doing when I feel my energy growing and expanding?

_____

What am I doing when I feel my energy shrinking or being depleted? _____

_____

When do I feel most energized, alert, and awake? _____

_____

What am I doing when time seems to fly? _____

_____

When do I feel most centered and clear? _____

_____

Look back over your responses. Are there any patterns you notice in your responses? If so, what are they? What insights did you gain about yourself?

PATTERNS AND INSIGHTS

_____

_____

Your responses to these questions can begin to direct you to when and where you are most "on" and "in the flow." You are "in the flow" when you are "on purpose," doing what brings you joy, doing what engages your natural gifts and talents, and what enables you to feel that you are making a difference. This is your calling. Answering your "call" connects you to your purpose and, thus, to what brings you joy. *Reconnect with what brings you joy. Therein lies the key to tapping your sacred power.*

When I answered the above questions for myself, I noticed a pattern in my responses. What emerged was what I call my 5Cs. I was most engaged, "on," and "in the flow" when I was:

- *Communing* and connecting with family and friends at gatherings and events
- *Consulting* with clients
- *Creating* transformational events, experiences, and rituals for women
- *Crafting* and presenting transformational messages through the spoken word (public speaking) and through the written word (authoring books and articles)
- *Communicating* with others through enlightened dialogue and conscious conversation

When I examine my life, I can see how I have gradually shaped, sculpted, and molded my life to where the content and substance are aligned with my 5Cs—through my consulting business, through my public speaking, through my books, seminars, and workshops, and the annual women's Advance I produce. My GTSAs served as the building blocks, and my calling is what allows me to express and contribute these GTSAs in a meaningful way. What I refer to as my 5Cs are avenues of self-expression, avenues through which my divine purpose expresses itself.

I believe that life is a process of discovering and uncovering your calling. Your purpose does not have to be limited to one form of expression. Are you answering your call?

It's time to answer your call.
It's time. It's time. It's your time.

77. *Free your creative genius*

Genius—Creative power and natural talent.

When sistergirl Madame C. J. Walker became the first female self-made millionaire in America through masterminding a unique marketing strategy to sell her hair care products, she created the prototype for what we now call multilevel marketing or network marketing. You GO, girl! Did you know that it was a sister who pioneered multilevel marketing? Madame C. J. Walker was tapping into her genius.

It's creative genius my daughter Adera taps into when she turns an empty toilet tissue tube into a telescope, a microphone, or cellular phone. It's creative genius that my girlfriend Linda Coleman-Willis, who is also a professional public speaker, draws on to speak passionately and eloquently to hundreds of people without use of a script or notes. It's creative genius my sisterfriend Danae draws on when she hears a song once and is able to play it "by ear" on the piano. It's creative genius my sisterfriend Eloise draws on when I show her the sketch of my wedding dress I've drawn on a napkin and she is able to create a pattern for it out of newsprint. It's creative genius that enabled my sisterfriend Melanie to stretch $15 to feed her four kids for almost an entire week; or a sisterfriend to think of a creative alternative to a purchased baby shower gift, giving a healthy basket of assorted fresh fruit to the mother-to-be at a time when her funds were running low.

It is this same creative genius that dwells in you. God has deposited creative power and natural talent in all of us, not just some of us. Your creative genius may be found in your problem solving; the way you cook; how you can take fabric scraps and turn them into a quilt or a dress for a doll; your eye for decorating on a budget; your eye for fashion; your organization skills; your multitasking skills; or how you can take a $25 dress and make it look like a $125 dress with the right accessories.

Get to know your creative genius and let her come out to play.

78. *Appreciate your spiritual gifts*

My friend Reverend Victoria Lee Owens, writer, editor, and publisher, has done it again. She has dropped some serious science on me in the pages of her little magazine, *The Lioness*. It was just too good to keep to myself, so I asked her if it was okay to share another one of her insightful pieces with you called "Psalms of the Twelve Gifts of Spirituality." And of course, she, in all of her graciousness, said yes.

Reverend Victoria acknowledges both the masculine and feminine aspects of God in her writing, so *notice how it feels* to read about God using the feminine references of "Goddess" and "She."

Psalms of the Twelve Gifts of Spirituality
by Reverend Victoria Lee Owens

The Goddess is my Source
I need want for no thing.

She maketh me gain "a reason to be" through personal empowerment.

She leadeth me to "consistency," listening with an open mind
as I replenish my storehouse of beliefs.

She restoreth me to "health and wealth" through self-awareness
of what is best for me.

She teaches me "love and happiness" through being gentle
with myself and more tolerant of those about me.

She giveth me "golden opportunities" to honor myself,
to be generous with others and grateful for all, great or small.

She teaches me through my "perfect mate,"
sometimes unknown and unseen by me,
to accept the things I've chosen to change,
patience to wait for change in other things
and when to use wisdom to know the difference.

Yes, though "self-realization" may be slow in coming,
I am guided to know that it will come
when the time is right.

She encourages me to find "financial security"
and protects me in the presence of mine enemies—fear, anxiety, and self-pity,
reminding me that poor is a permanent state of mind
and broke is a temporary state of being.
She admonishes me not to accept either.

She anointest me with "spirituality" soothingly
with recognition that "I am always restored in beauty"
and all things work together for my total good,
though negativity would seek to confuse my consciousness.

She preparest a table before me in the presence of "family unity"
nourishing all who abide there
insuring me that I am never alone.

My cup runneth over with the joy of "oneness with all life"
so that serenity follows me all the days and nights of my life.

Verily, because of my "high consciousness,"
I shall dwell in the warm, nurturing womb
of the magnificent goddess forever

And so it is!!

Thank you again, Reverend Victoria!

79. *Strengthen your gratitude muscles*

*B*eing grateful helps you keep things in perspective. Being grateful helps to remind you that blessings come in all shapes, sizes, and packages that may be invisible to you at first, but become visible over time. Being grateful helps you to become conscious of your many blessings.

In general, the American culture is an ungrateful culture—we've gotten spoiled by technology, too many creature comforts, and living lives of waste and excess, all of which greatly weaken our Gratitude Muscles and cause them to go limp. We start to take things for granted and feel entitled to certain treatment and material comforts. It's time to shift to becoming a culture of gratitude.

You can strengthen your Gratitude Muscles by being more grateful and finding ways to express your gratitude. One way I've strengthened my Gratitude Muscles is by sending handwritten thank-you cards and notes. I adopted this practice in 1995 when I started my training and consulting company—sending clients thank-you cards; sending prospective clients a thank-you note after an initial meeting; sending colleagues a thank-you note for a lead, referral, helpful suggestion, or valuable connection.

This practice of conscious gratefulness has flowed over into my personal life. Often it's a thank-you or an "I appreciate you" phone call or voice mail message left for a friend. Other times, it may be a thank-you via e-mail or a postcard sent in the mail.

My sisterfriend Sharon decided to express her gratitude to her closest friends by hosting a Fifty and Fabulous party for her 50th birthday. She sent out handmade invitations, prepared a delicious home-cooked meal, and gave each of her girlfriends a personalized handmade gift. Each friend was absolutely delighted to be treated like the guest of honor by Sharon, at *her* birthday party.

I sent a thank-you card to a business client who agreed to expedite an invoice payment for me, ensuring that it was processed and paid in seven days instead of the customary thirty days. After receiving my card, she called to tell me that after all the times she had expedited invoice payments for vendors over the years, she had never received a thank-you card. She was very appreciative.

An acquaintance, Gracie, first heard me speak at one of my sacred pampering seminars. As a result, she arranged for me to come and speak to her women's church group. None of the other women in the group knew me or had heard of me, including the first lady of the church, who was the leader of the group. I knew that Gracie was putting her neck on the line and personally vouching for me. I also knew that planning and coordinating this type of seminar for her women's church group was a first for her. So I presented Gracie with a small gift of appreciation and gratitude at the beginning of the seminar in front of all of the women in the group. Gracie was beaming as she came forward to receive her gift.

One day in June of last year, I received an e-mail message that was a reminder to keep things in perspective, and to be grateful—in all things. Think about this:

Should you find it hard to get to sleep tonight; just remember the homeless family who has no bed to lie in.

Should you find yourself stuck in traffic; don't despair. There are people in the world for whom driving is an unheard of privilege.

Should you have a bad day at work; think of the woman who has been out of work for the last three months.

Should you despair over a relationship gone bad; think of the person who has never known what it's like to love and be loved in return.

Should you grieve the passing of another weekend; think of the woman in dire straits, working twelve hours a day, seven days a week, for $15 a month to feed her family.

Should your car break down, leaving you miles away from assistance; think of the paraplegic who would love the opportunity to take that walk.

Should you notice a new gray hair in the mirror; think of the cancer patient in chemo who wished she had hair to examine.

Should you find yourself at a loss and pondering what is life all about? What is my purpose? Be thankful. There are those who didn't live long enough to get the opportunity.

Should you find yourself the victim of other people's bitterness, ignorance, smallness, or insecurities, remember, things could be worse. You could be them!!

Learn to *mine* and extract gratitude and appreciation from the situations and circumstances life brings your way. Be grateful in all things.

80. Listen carefully

*H*earing and listening are not the same. Hearing is a physical ability. Your ears register sounds without your having to think about them. But listening is a conscious act. Listening requires that you pay attention and be present.

In a recent conversation with my aunt, she shared that, as she grew wiser, she was learning to speak less, and listen and observe more. In her younger years, she explained, she did just the opposite—she talked more and listened less.

God gave us *two* ears and *one* mouth so that we could use them proportionately. Part of stepping into your power is developing wisdom and discernment—learning to determine when it is time to listen, when it is time to speak, when it is time to observe. When we learn to listen carefully, we learn to tune in not just to outer voices but also to our own inner voice. Do you know what your inner voice sounds like? Learn to distinguish it from your ego or your inner chatter.

Listening carefully takes practice because it requires being present and paying attention, two things that seem to be scarce in our fast-paced lives. Learn to listen carefully and attentively to others and watch them unfold and blossom like thirsty flowers receiving a good watering. At a symposium I attended not long ago, I was sitting next to a male author at the authors' book signing table after I had finished speaking at my seminar. While we were taking a short break from signing books, he asked me what inspired me to write *Sacred Pampering Principles,* my first book. As I began to answer his question, he took off his glasses and fully turned his shoulders and body toward me. He listened intently without shifting his attention or being distracted by the others who were talking around us and milling about. His way of listening felt very validating, as if what I was saying was the most important thing to him at that particular moment. It was easy for me to be forthcoming and share the deeper insights that inspired the book though this man was a "stranger." I could feel myself opening up and unfolding, though our exchange lasted only a couple of minutes. Even though it was a brief exchange, I felt we had connected.

Learning to listen carefully, attentively, and consciously to others has helped me understand where someone is *coming from,* which I can't pick up on if I am not paying attention to what they are saying and the words they are using. Listening carefully is a simple act but it speaks volumes. When you listen carefully, your actions say to others:

> "What you have to say matters."
> "You are worth listening to."
> "You have something important to say."
> "You deserve my attention."

At the Women's Advance I hold the second weekend of every March, For Sisters Only: Sharing, Healing and Renewal, we devote a few minutes of the day to sitting in silence, so that we can *listen*—to our thoughts, our endless inner chatter, the birds chirping, the trees rustling, to nothing. I have seen many a sistah get very restless as she tries to fight the silence. We need to become comfortable listening both inwardly and outwardly.

In my sacred pampering seminars, learning to listen carefully, attentively, and consciously is essential because participants ask many personal questions related to their lives. I consider this to be a privilege and also an invitation to assist them in their healing. Many times, the *real* question is a deeper one they are not able to articulate so they ask the questions they *can* articulate. By learning to listen carefully, I find out where they are coming from, and by asking a clarifying question or two of my own before I respond, I am able to help participants articulate the deeper question they really want to ask.

I must also listen carefully for the *motivation* that gives rise to a question. In a seminar, a participant's question can arise out of her frustration with a particular situation in her life that she wants to resolve. Her motivation for asking her question may be to help her uncover a perspective that might direct her to a solution. Again, a question can arise out of a woman's frustration with a situation in her life, but the motivation behind the question is to get me to agree with her about who has wronged her or the position she's decided to take. The motivation behind her question may be for me to tell her that she is right. Or a question may arise out of a woman's discomfort with the internal conflict she's experiencing as she struggles to process some of the concepts or principles I'm explaining. She may ask a question as a way to challenge me, which is fine, too, or she can ask a question in an attempt to get clarification or have a better understanding of what I'm sharing. All of these motivations, and more, can be behind what seems like a simple question. If I am not listening carefully, attentively, and consciously I can do a disservice to a participant.

One evening I was having dinner with a girlfriend who was experiencing a lot of frustration in her marriage. I listened attentively as she shared. She felt she and her husband were drifting further and further apart. She felt that their connection was weakening, their closeness was quickly evaporating, and she didn't know what to do to restore it. They had opposite work schedules, very different interests, and he seemed to be shutting down and becoming less and less communicative with her. She was starting to believe that he didn't want to be married to her anymore.

I asked her about comments he made and behavior he displayed. As she responded and I continued to listen, it seemed to me that there was a message he was trying to communicate that she wasn't hearing. What I heard him saying through his comments and behavior was "I'm feeling rejected and not part of your world. I'm drifting away and I don't know how to get back." That is not to say my girlfriend was at fault or that it was on her to save the relationship, but I was listening to a different message than she was. I heard him saying "I *do* want to be in this relationship though I don't know how to make things be different." When I offered my interpretation, my girlfriend listened carefully instead of being defensive, arguing me down, or trying to convince me of how unworkable her situation was.

Often, because we don't agree with what other people are saying, we stop listening. We cut them off, interrupt them, or start to "zone out" on them. It's when we *don't agree* that we have the most to learn and it makes the most sense to listen and be present. Listen because your opinion may be challenged. Listen *because* another perspective or interpretation is being offered. Listen because a *different* perspective or opinion shouldn't be perceived as an automatic threat. Learn to listen carefully, attentively, and consciously and you can change your relationship with your children, with your spouse, girlfriends, parents, siblings, co-workers, boss, employees, significant others, and men in your life.

> *Learn to . . . listen in, listen to, listen from, listen up,*
> *listen intently, listen carefully.*

81. *Leap and the net will appear*

*Until one is committed there is hesitancy,
the chance to draw back. . . . The moment
one definitely commits oneself,
then Providence moves too.*

—W. N. Murray

*M*ost of us want to be sure the net is in place and safety cords tied, tried, and tested before we leap. I know I sure did. We want to control the situation, know what the outcome is going to be, and ensure that we won't encounter any challenges, surprises, discomfort, rough waters, or lose any money along the way—then, *maybe*, we'll leap. Have you noticed that God designed Life with a lot of unknowns? Otherwise, faith wouldn't have a purpose.

The reason we get so paralyzed and fearful about doing things that we consider to be "risky" is that we get confused about *our* responsibility in the matter. Our responsibility is to be ready, have faith and leap. *Our part is to leap and let God take care of the net.* But we get paralyzed because we perceive leaping as risky. Risk is relative, however. What you consider risky is probably very different from what I consider to be risky. We usually consider something risky if we haven't done it before; we know it is going to test or stretch our character or abilities; or we have allowed others to plant seeds of doubt or fear in our minds, often because *they* weren't successful with it or haven't tried it yet.

We also hesitate to leap because we think a failure is final. You can recover from failure. You can survive a failure. "Failure" is having an outcome that you don't want. Failure is not synonymous with death. We try so hard to avoid anything that looks or smells like failure because we don't want to look bad or stupid if things don't turn out.

You will hesitate leaping if you doubt yourself, doubt that the net will appear, want to see the net in place *before* you leap, or doubt God. After all, to doubt yourself *is* to doubt God. You do your part and God *always* does Her part. The catch is that the "mechanism" or trigger that activates the net is your leap. The leap requires faith. We must remember a bit of advice given to a young Native American at the time of his initiation.

> As you go the way of life,
> You will see a great chasm.
> Jump.
> It is not as wide as you think.

Yes, the chasm is there, but it often isn't as wide as we think. We project our own inner fear or unwillingness on to the chasm, and then say that it's the *chasm* or other people that's stopping us. But self-doubt can sure make the chasm seem like the Grand Canyon. Truth is, God never presents you with chasms in your lives that aren't "jumpable" for you. *Never.* God knows our true capability even when we don't.

God is interested in your Highest Good. Jumping the chasm and taking the leap may require you to stretch, grow, temporarily move into your discomfort zone, or give up limiting beliefs you've been holding about yourself. Once you leap and cross over, there's no turning back. You are no longer the same person. And on the "other side," you discover that you are much more capable and brilliant than you realized.

Go ahead. Leap. Your net is waiting.

82. *Make powerful exits*

When actor Jerry Seinfeld made the announcement that he was going to discontinue his popular TV sit-com *Seinfeld*, Hollywood was shocked. Loyal viewers were aghast. *How could he? How dare he!*

This decision didn't make sense to most people. Why stop when the show was at its zenith and receiving top Nielsen ratings for its time slot? How often do you exit when things are going well? When you are feeling good? When there are no circumstances forcing you to exit? Very rarely. I thought it was a brilliant move—to exit powerfully. Jerry Seinfeld made a powerful exit.

Exiting when you are at a zenith makes a powerful statement, considering that we usually exit once our popularity has waned, when we're not producing or performing as we used to, once we've been replaced by someone younger, prettier, or smarter, or once we've gotten pissed off or angry with someone. Exit like most people and you exit when things get rocky, the going gets rough, things don't turn out as you'd hoped, things get ugly, or you get upset or pissed off at someone, something, or the organization. Exiting powerfully is how you maintain your power because you intentionally exit when things are at their peak. Exiting powerfully also creates a legacy. To exit powerfully is to exit when you *choose* to, not when you *have* to.

As I mentioned earlier, I was an active, highly participative charter member of a new nonprofit women's organization, and I decided to exit powerfully after one year of being on its board of directors. My announcement caused great dismay among the other board members. They wanted to know—was I upset? Had the executive director done something wrong? Was I unhappy about something that happened? My answers were no, no, and no. I was choosing to leave because I had made great contributions in my one year of service, and I felt it was time to "shed" this particular involvement. I was complete. I was leaving from a place of fullness, not from a place of disappointment. Exiting powerfully is about leaving from a place of fullness.

Several months before making my resignation announcement, I'd made a suggestion for a new, creative fund-raising event that was approved by the Board. I also agreed to be part of the event program. My last day of service on the Board was a few weeks before the big fund-raising event, but I still agreed to participate in the event program as promised. The event was a tremendous financial success. The attendance exceeded our highest projections, and 85 percent of the revenue was pure profit for the organization. Much to my delight, during the event, my service on the Board was acknowledged, and the event was also acknowledged as my brainchild. I was able to depart from that event and from my service on the Board with a legacy of positive contribution and feelings of deep gratitude and appreciation in my wake. I exited feeling good, powerful, and complete.

When I decided to make my exit from AT&T, I was in the top 2 percent in sales nationally for my division, and I had just received a promotion. My co-workers couldn't understand it, and neither could my regional branch manager. Why would I leave when I was doing so well? After I announced that I was leaving, the regional branch manager called me in to his office and asked what AT&T could do to keep me. My answer was "Nothing." I was choosing to exit and move on *because* of my success at AT&T.

When you choose to exit powerfully, those that remain have a greater appreciation for you. Yes, there are those who may get angry with you because they feel you are abandoning them, or because you have the courage to do what they've secretly wanted to do but haven't. When you exit powerfully, your absence is felt. The memory of your contributions and impact lingers longer. Don't be like most people and wait until you plateau, crash and burn, or start to experience decline, decrease, failure, or loss before you leave. Exit powerfully.

Leave a legacy.

83. *Blessings in disguise*

> *Though a blessing may be hidden,*
> *deep inside a piece of ore,*
> *There's always a diamond*
> *hidden at its core.*
>
> —djg

Blessings don't really come in disguise, it's just that we often don't recognize them when they get here. We don't always recognize their gift wrapping. I surely didn't recognize the gift within the wrapping when my husband ruptured the Achilles' tendon of his left ankle in a basketball game *the night before* our third daughter was born. When I was in the hospital recovery room, my husband was sitting in a recliner next to my bed with crutches in hand and a huge ice pack on his heel. He ended up having surgery and being out of work for ten weeks. He couldn't walk on it; he couldn't drive for three weeks; he couldn't take a shower; and he had to keep his leg constantly elevated for the first three weeks—at the same time as our newborn baby arrived in the world. And we still had two other daughters to attend to.

As mentioned previously, I was on maternity leave from my business for three months after having our third baby, and was not generating any substantial income. On top of it all, my husband's employer declined his unemployment insurance since his ankle was a non-work-related injury. Since we had planned on Joe's working while I was on maternity leave, we had just enough in our savings to cover our upcoming rent and a few basic expenses. No income for almost three months?! Joe injured, virtually incapacitated *and* his unemployment declined?! I surely didn't see "blessing" written on this situation in no kinda way!

Four months later, I was able to look back on this part of our journey and see blessings sprinkled all over the place. Our family and friends rose to the occasion, and loved and supported us right through this trying time. There were diamonds "hidden in the ore" everywhere. When I looked back, I recognized an abundance of blessings.

SOME OF OUR BLESSINGS . . .

- Instead of one week of official paternity leave from work, Joe got nine additional "unofficial" weeks of paternity leave to connect with our new baby (the blessing: bonding time with our new baby)
- Joe had a chance to spend quality time with our new baby during the first weeks of her life (the blessing: quality time and the arrival of a new life)
- We enjoyed long, rich conversations and many good laughs together in the middle of the day (the blessing: communication and laughter)
- Our two older daughters, Kiana and Adera, had both parents home to get them ready for school in the morning and at home when they returned (the blessing: being here for our kids)
- We learned to put pride aside and let others know our financial situation (the blessing: truth-telling and humbling the ego)
- We learned how to articulate our needs and ask others for help and assistance (the blessing: being able to ask and receive graciously)
- We learned how to allow others to give to us (the blessing: "receivership")

- We learned how much we were loved, supported, and appreciated by family and friends (the blessing: knowing that you matter)
- Our family ate dinner together every evening since we didn't have work schedules to juggle or work around (the blessing: family meal time)
- My husband maintained a positive attitude throughout his ankle ordeal. I didn't hear him complain once (the blessing: right disposition and right attitude)
- Joe didn't act like an invalid or sorry for himself. Instead he hobbled around the house with his big plaster cast, on crutches, helping out in any way he could (the blessing: an attitude of service and helpfulness)
- We became more aware of our invisible resources (the blessing: unseen supply)
- We learned to trust in the face of "not knowing" and uncertainty (the blessing: faith)
- We broke the yoke of letting how much money we had or didn't have determine our peace of mind (the blessing: maintaining serenity in the face of challenging financial circumstances)
- Joe didn't get on my nerves (the blessing: tolerance)

It didn't look like much of a blessing when my mom, a twenty-seven-year resident of our hometown and highly respected leader in the community, lost the primary election for a seat in the State House of Representatives. She was clearly the more qualified, experienced, and accomplished candidate. She had a broad base of support, a long track record of producing results, endorsements from key organizations, a large group of active volunteers, and a fund-raising budget that was twice that of her opponent's. Even the preelection polls showed her ahead of her opponent. But when the final results were tallied, she had lost the election by only a few hundred votes.

Four months later, she decided to run once again for her "old faithful" school board position. It was to be her twentieth year serving on the district school board. Much to our shock and disappointment, she lost her school board race for the first time, ever. Losing the legislative seat was one thing, but losing her coveted school board position was another.

I watched my mom go through a range of emotions—deep disappointment at losing a race in which she was the clear choice, anger at not being supported by certain constituents and community members when they were alone in the voting booth marking their ballots, and resentment. But instead of my mom going into a depression, hanging her head in shame, or floundering about as she tried to figure out what she should do next, I saw her get the eye of the tiger.

Once the word of her school board defeat got out, people concluded that she had a lot of free time on her hands. So she started being barraged with phone calls asking her to be on this committee or on that board—things she had done willingly in the past. She responded to each request by asking, up front, if she would receive compensation for her time—a question she had never asked before. If the answer was no, she politely and firmly declined the invitation.

When I asked Mama about this new posture she was taking, she told me that her election defeats helped her recognize how much she had contributed and given to the community over the years. She was now much clearer and more in touch with her value and her worth, and she was no longer willing to give her gifts, talents, skills, and abilities away for free. She had spent years helping, assisting, advising, giving to, and directing others. Now, it was time for her to tend to her own soul, to give back to herself, and to pursue her long-deferred dreams and aspirations.

She told me that she saw her two election defeats as the universe clearing a way for her to do what she really wanted to do and had talked about doing for years—going back to school to get her doctorate in education, and starting her own education consulting business. Once the dust settled, I asked Mama what was next for her. Without hesitation, she replied, "To finally get my Ph.D., to have more fun, to pamper myself, and do for me first for a change, instead of always doing for me last."

Over the next six months, I saw my mother transform. She enrolled in a fast-track doctorate program. I saw her go from not owning a computer, not knowing how to type, and not even knowing how to turn on a computer, to typing proposals and e-mailing documents to colleagues around the country. For the first time in my life, I saw my mom develop close friendships with a group of new sisterfriends she calls the Whoopi Group, friendships that weren't a by-product of serving on a committee or board together.

One afternoon, I called to chat with Mama and she had to cut our conversation short. She didn't want to be late for her golf lesson! The next day, she called me back to inform me that she had finally decided to start her own education consulting business and needed some instructions on how to get her business registered and licensed. Go Thelma!

Of all the important decisions Mama made after her two election defeats, the one that was most meaningful to me was her decision to go on a program that would help her release the 100 pounds of extra weight she had accumulated on her body over the years—helping, giving, tending to everyone else first and herself last. "No more," she said. "No more."

It may seem like our blessings are in disguise, but it's really a matter of being able to extract the diamond buried deep inside the ore—being able to recognize the gift inside the wrapping.

84. Traveling rules for life's journey

ife is a journey and life is a process. When you understand that the purpose of The Journey and The Process is to remember Who You Really Are, it helps you to move through life with less hardship, effort, and struggle. If you are aware of the Eight Traveling Rules for Life's Journey, you'll find yourself experiencing more ease and grace on your journey.

Traveling Rule 1. *You will be assigned a body.* It is the only one you will be given for this lifetime. There are no exchanges or returns. You may love it. You may hate it. Either way, it's yours for the entire trip.

Traveling Rule 2. *Things will happen along the way.* You will label some of the things that happen good luck, blessings, miracles, or coincidences. Some you will label bad luck, misfortune, or that you were dealt a bad hand. You are the labeler. *What* you label these happenings is up to you. What you label these happenings will also determine your response to and your experience of them.

Traveling Rule 3. *On the journey, you will encounter many mirrors.* These mirrors will be in the form of other people. In these mirrors you will see things you adore, admire, and love. In these mirrors you will also see things that irritate, frustrate, and anger you. Remember, you cannot love or hate something about another person unless it *reflects back to you* something you love or hate about yourself.

Traveling Rule 4. *There are no mistakes in life, only "learnings."* What we call mistakes are really undesired outcomes. The journey will present you with opportunities to learn how to generate and manifest *desired* outcomes for yourself.

Traveling Rule 5. *The journey will present you with specific "learnings" until you get it.* The learning opportunity will be presented to you again and again, in various forms, until you get it. Then you can proceed on to the next learning. If you do proceed, it's okay. If you don't proceed, it's still okay. God does not judge you.

Traveling Rule 6. *On the journey, it will appear that the answers lie outside of you.* This is an illusion. The answers to your deepest questions emerge from within. Be still and know.

Traveling Rule 7. *On the journey, the grass will appear to be greener "over there," on the other side.* Know that this is also an illusion. Once your "over there" has become "here," you will find another "over there" that again looks better than "here." The key is to learn to seed, cultivate, and nurture your own patch of grass instead of coveting your neighbor's. You'll notice that when you stop comparing your patch to other people's patches, you'll start experiencing more joy, delight, peace, and pleasure in your life.

Traveling Rule 8. *The direction, quality, and terrain of your journey is set by the choices you make moment to moment, and your responses to what occurs along the way.* You will encounter both peaks and valleys. Neither one is inherently good or bad. How you respond (your *response-ability*) will determine your experience of these peaks and valleys.

85. *Your everyday survival kit*

In addition to remembering the Eight Traveling Rules, you will want to have an Everyday Survival Kit. Keep these eight items in your "life backpack" throughout the journey. They will prove to be invaluable.

- **A stop sign.** To remind you when to stop, look, and listen within; and to be still and know.
- **Honey.** To remind you of your natural sweetness, and the tremendous amount of love you have to give and receive.
- **Piece of wire.** To remind you to be flexible.
- **Bottle of Wite-out.** To remind you that you will make mistakes. It's okay. They can be forgiven or corrected.
- **Needle and thread.** To remind you that it is possible to mend rips and tears in your relationships with the needle of love and the thread of forgiveness.
- **Mirror.** To remind you of the importance of introspection and self-reflection; and to remind you that the woman looking back at you is precious, valuable, and worthy.
- **A jar of Vaseline.** To remind you that you have multiple purposes.
- **Cup.** To remind you to keep emptying your ego so that you can pour love into others and allow others to pour love into you.

Never leave home without them.

86. *Life learnings*

*I*f someone would have told me a little earlier in my life that there is no such thing as a mistake, I sure would have lived my life more fully and more freely—without so much worry and concern about "failing," getting it wrong, looking bad, or making a mistake.

For most of us, our lives are orchestrated and organized in hopes of avoiding three primary types of experiences: pain, not looking good, and getting it wrong or making a mistake. Even with all of the effort we expend to avoid these types of experiences, we have not been spared them. The way we've been living life has sent us headfirst into all of these at some point in our lives instead of away from them.

Thank goodness life keeps presenting us with new opportunities to drop the blinders, wake up, increase our understanding of the truth, and increase our awareness. Pain is often the result of hanging on tightly to what isn't working in order to be right. This way of learning results in a lot of bumps, bruises, and knocks upside the head. Or you can choose to learn by being willing to make mistakes, knowing that mistakes are useful, listening to the gentle nudging of your intuition, and readily admitting when something isn't working, or acknowledging when you are incorrect, mistaken, or wrong. When you choose to approach life in the latter way, you realize that life learnings don't have to equal suffering, abuse, pain, and constant struggle.

When we stop to reflect, we discover that precious learnings are generously sprinkled throughout our lives, often in plain view if we just pay attention. It doesn't have to take us multiple attempts before we get the "learning." We can get it the first time around.

In my short thirty-two years on this planet, my life learnings have been revealed in transformational, life-changing experiences as well as in simple, unassuming activities.

I'VE LEARNED . . .

- I can't change other folks' circumstances for them.
- Self-love has to be "homegrown" first. It's an inside job.

- I can't express love, share it, or give it away to others until I've had an internal experience of it myself.
- Being an example is the greatest teacher.
- My intuition is the voice of my Higher Self directing me toward my Highest Good.
- I don't have to do it alone
- Overnurturing others ultimately weakens them.
- Being a Strong Black Woman is one of many roles I can choose at the necessary time and place. It does not have to be my identity.
- I can *affect* change in others, but I can't do the changing for them. We each have to make the inner decision first.
- Sometimes I outgrow people in my life. And it's okay. They've chosen a different path from mine. The key is not to think that I'm better, more spiritual, or more evolved.
- God loves me unconditionally, and there is nothing I can do to change this—ever.
- I can't be fearful *and* free.
- I can choose to be motivated by either fear or love. God left this choice up to me. And I have the opportunity to keep rechoosing.
- What I see in others and judge as bad is a beacon that directs me to what I have not yet fully accepted in myself.
- Forgiveness is an essential part of the healing process.
- Life is a process of remembering Who and Whose I Really Am.
- I can get offended by what someone says only if I believe there is some truth to it.

One afternoon, my girlfriend forwarded an "author unknown" e-mail to me that captures the wisdom and insight of some of life's most power-full learnings.

People are often unreasonable,
illogical, and self-centered
Forgive them anyway.

If you are kind,
People may accuse you of selfish, ulterior motives
Be kind anyway.

If you are successful,
You will win some false friends and some true enemies
Succeed anyway.

If you are honest and frank,
People may cheat you,
Be honest and frank anyway.

What you spend years building,
Someone could destroy overnight,
Build anyway.

If you find serenity and happiness,
They may be jealous,
Be happy anyway.

The good you do today
People will often forget tomorrow,
Do good anyway.

Give the world the best you have,
And it may never be enough
Give the world the best you've got anyway.

You see, in the final analysis
It is between you and God.
It never was between you and them anyway.

AMEN.

87. Tune in to radio station WGOD

Girrrrl, let me tell you about this radio station I found. Knowing you, you're probably already tuned in, though. But just in case you haven't, I want to share the good news with you. Radio station WGOD is where it's at.

Station WGOD broadcasts around the clock; it has no commercial breaks, you can tune in every day of the year, it has universal coverage, it has the clearest signal you've ever heard, there's always someone there to take your calls, and you never get a busy signal. This station is out of this world!

The station has millions of listeners, but if you're tuned in to station AOG, Always-On-the-Go, or station CRR, Constantly-Rippin'-and-Runnin', you'll miss station WGOD on the dial. This station is unlike any other station I've ever tuned in to. Every day they have fabulous giveaways. Last week alone, they gave away

amazing grace	patience
compassion	understanding
goodness	unshakable faith
love	and forgiveness

Callers can have as much as they want of each, for free! There is no limit, and they never run out!

I'm told the staff at this station is incredible and their work is nothing less than miraculous. The staff says their CEO knows their every need even before they ask. She completely understands their individual needs; answers every request personally; is always fair; doesn't judge or criticize; gives excellent feedback; listens attentively; always has time for them; never rushes them; constantly urges them to express their unique gifts, talents, and abilities; and takes every opportunity to let them know they are loved and appreciated. They constantly get raises, and they receive raises based upon how much they believe they are worth. She is not controlling or dominating. Instead, she grants each staff member free will and the ability to choose.

She gives them constant support and encouragement, and finds ways to remind them of their greatness and magnificence on a daily basis.

Girrrl, let me tell you. If you haven't tuned into station WGOD, I recommend it highly. Check it out and let me know what you think.

Thought for the day: *If you feel far from God, guess who moved?*

88. *Develop your prosperity consciousness*

When I reflect on my efforts to develop a prosperity consciousness, I am amazed at how much of a challenge it has been, particularly when it comes to money. A prosperity consciousness is a mind-set based on the core beliefs of abundance—*there is enough, there is enough to go around, there is plenty*. A prosperity consciousness transcends physical and material resources and recognizes that the resources available to us are also invisible and nonmaterial. And money is but one dimension of prosperity.

As progressive, forward thinking, and "spiritual" as I consider myself to be, I continue to be amazed at the ways a *scarcity mentality* has insidiously crept in and pervaded my beliefs, attitudes, and language about money.

As Americans, we tend to have a lot of *stuff*, and we spend a lot of money, yet we don't think and act abundantly. Many of us have been bombarded with messages of scarcity since we were children. Whether it was in our households, through what we observed or absorbed on TV, or what we were taught in school, scarcity was the fundamental premise. When I took my first economics class in school, I recall the instructor explaining the fundamental premise of capitalism—*there is not enough for everyone, there is not enough to go around, resources are scarce, so we need a system of producing and distributing supply and demand.*

Looking at the average amount of debt we each have (car note, house note, credit card debt, etc.), how many of us live from paycheck to paycheck, how obsessed we are with spending and buying, and how much power we attribute to money, it's clear that we've got some money issues. You can have a lot of money and still have money issues. It's not just a condition of those who are financially poor. Just look at how much of our attention money commands in this culture.

These last couple of years, I've been on a path to transform my consciousness, particularly as it relates to my notions about money. I've been working to break the shackles of my scarcity mentality. When I reflect on some of the language I've used about money, I hear myself say things like "I *need* some more money; that takes money I don't have; or, if only I had the money." None of these statements has been true, though. As I thought more deeply about my beliefs, attitudes, and behavior about money, I realized that *making* money or *having* money has not been my challenge. It has been saving it and growing it in the form of wise investments. I've *made* plenty of money in my lifetime thus far.

Try this exercise to help you get a handle on how much money has passed through your hands in this lifetime. You'll need a piece of paper, a pen or pencil, and a calculator if you want to be really exact. Stop a minute and reflect back to the year you first started earning money, whether it was baby-sitting or a part-time summer job. Write down the year and calculate the amount of before-taxes money you made that year. Then add up the next year's total and the next and so on. Tally up your grand total. When I totaled mine up, it was over $500,000! but I didn't have much to show for it. I had certainly made some decent money in my life up to this point, but the majority of it had been expended. I didn't *need* any more money. Making it was not my problem. Plenty had come my way. But what had I done with it?

Part of the process of shaking loose the beliefs about money that aren't serving you is to first get conscious about them. I've had to examine and rethink beliefs I'd been holding dear for a long time. I'd heard comments, words, phrases, and messages about money since my childhood that I had internalized unconsciously. What are the comments, words, phrases, and messages you remember receiving about money?

I remember hearing, overhearing, or seeing messages that interpreted as . . .

> Money doesn't grow on trees.
> He who has the money makes the rules.
> Money is the root of all evil.

Rich people are arrogant, rude, insensitive, greedy, and selfish.
Money can't buy you love.
If I had the money, I'd . . .
Money is security.
I'm so broke I can't even pay attention.
It's a dog eat dog world out there.
Money talks.
It is easier for a camel to go through the eye of a needle than for a
   rich man to enter into the kingdom of God.

Add your own to the list. When I examined the "diet" of beliefs I had been
fed about money, I could begin to see why I still had issues with it.

With the heavy meaning and many conflicting messages we've received
about money, it's easy to forget that money is no more than paper printed
with green ink. Money has no inherent value, only the meaning and value
we assign to it. And our experiences with money are always consistent with
our core beliefs about money. On the road to transforming my money consciousness, I've had to carefully examine my actions, behaviors, and language about money. *I could see the signs of a scarcity mentality showing up in many
places in my life.*

For starters, I looked at the attitude with which I paid my bills. Instead of
paying my bills with a thankful heart, on time, and in a spirit of gratitude
for the products and/or services I was receiving (electricity, shelter, a phone
line, car), I was paying my bills with a begrudging spirit. I was not demonstrating the cheerful giving and receiving that is a basic reality of a prosperity consciousness. There was lots of other evidence, too.

- When I paid my bills, I paid some of them late though I received my
  services reliably or in advance of being billed for them.
- When I was out of money, I would say "I'm broke," instead of "my
  cash flow is low" or "I am temporarily low on cash."
- I didn't treat money with respect. There were times when I would
  leave money laying out on the counter, bent and folded up in my
  wallet, or "floating" around in my purse.
- I didn't manage my money well, and my money awareness was low.
  I wasn't sure of my bank balance from day to day. I wasn't paying
  myself first, or setting any money aside for an emergency or for my
  future. I wasn't able to account for exactly how much I'd spent in a
  given week.

- I made negative judgments and assumptions about people whom I perceived as having a lot of money. On numerous occasions, I'd spoken of rich people with contempt.
- I was limiting my tithing to money. I didn't realize that it also included sharing the currency of the heart (love), time, and attention.
- I would worry and get anxious when my money was low. My mood would rise and fall with my bank account balance.

Yes, there is still evidence of a scarcity mentality lingering in my life. I am not fully recovered, but I sure have come a long way. There are several books that have been instrumental in helping me begin to transform my scarcity mentality into a prosperity consciousness.

The Dynamics Laws of Prosperity, Catherine Ponder
Creating Money, Sanaya Roman and Duane Packer
The Abundance Book, John Randolph Price
Think and Grow Rich, Napoleon Hill
Think and Grow Rich: A Black Choice, Dennis Kimbro
Prospering Woman, Ruth Voss

This process of mental transformation has included adopting some new definitions into my thinking and believing. These new definitions have also served as affirmations to help me reprogram my scarcity mentality into a prosperity consciousness.

God is the source of my supply.
Poor is an attitude.
I am a rich woman.
I am the child of an unlimited God.
Money is a form of energy.
I live in an abundant universe.
I am enough.
Abundance means experiencing fulfillment, aliveness, and joy, which is always available to me.
I am worthy of financial abundance.
I welcome money to come, stay, and grow in my life.

I have gained valuable insight and "learnings" from the lean times in my life. I've had to come to grips with how much my state of mind and my mood at a given time were tied to money. I now recognize that there are many *things* I can do without, while not compromising quality, joy, satisfaction, or depth in my life. I realize that I wasted a lot of money on things I didn't really like, didn't really need, didn't use or wear more than twice, or that lost their value over time. I realized that I was carrying around conflicting internal messages about being rich though it was something I said I wanted to be. On one hand, I would make derisive comments about rich people, saying they were greedy, arrogant, or selfish, while at the same time desiring to be wealthy myself. This created a schism in my mind and anchored conflicts deep in my psyche that needed to be healed.

My journey continues. My prosperity consciousness is "still under construction," but now I can see the mountaintop. I can feel the difference. I can feel myself thinking differently; I hear myself speaking differently; and I am handling money differently. I've gotten better at saving and investing my money and paying myself first, even if it is $15 per month.

Yet, I still have to keep reinforcing my prosperity consciousness until it is firmly rooted in my mind. And so I remind myself,

> Making, saving, and growing money is a good thing.
> I give myself permission to have what I desire.
> I readily accept prosperity into my life.

You are a prosperous woman.

89. Be power–full

In my first book, *Sacred Pampering Principles,* I introduced the concept of the Strong Black Woman (SBW) Syndrome of constantly giving to, taking care of, nurturing, and doing for others first and self last. The SBW Syndrome has trapped words in our throats that should be spoken, and forced us to believe that our feelings should be pressed way, way down, trampled on, or balled up and tossed into a corner.

The SBW Syndrome has been killing our spirits, zapping our energy, and creating a perception of black women as being *overly* self-sufficient. The SBW Syndrome causes us to demonstrate actions and behaviors that say to others "I have it all handled myself," so much so that others often don't see how to contribute to us. One of the dangers of the SBW Syndrome is that your ability to receive willingly and graciously, and ask for help from others, becomes severely handicapped.

For decades, *strong* has been the prevailing adjective that has been used to describe black women. I'm ready to retire this long-standing, one-dimensional adjective for some new ones, aren't you? How about *receptive, flexible, sensuous, talented, creative, resilient, wise, grounded, centered, energetic, brilliant, graceful, powerful?*

Strong means "difficult to break, durable, forceful, intense." For too long this has been our legacy in America. This legacy has become our identity. The circumstances and conditions we have faced in this country have shaped much of our identity and, subsequently, our reality in this country. In order to combat and endure the treatment we've experienced, we *had* to be strong to survive. Our families and communities depended on it. Now that we have a different reality, are we still acting and behaving as if being strong is our only option? Are remnants of the SBW Syndrome lingering in how we think, act, and interact?

It is time to make the shift from being strong to being powerful. Being powerful is about your ability to create, manifest, and influence. Being powerful is about taking a stance of authority in your life, being self-accountable. I'm talking about the type of power that is *not* a function of a title, position, or how much money you have. This type of power can be lost or taken away. Sacred power has been deposited in each of us and is a natural part of our being. If the title or position is taken away or the money is lost, the power associated with the title, position, or the money goes with it because it is externally based power. This is superficial power. Sacred power is authentic power.

As you make the shift from being strong to being powerful, you learn how to bring things about in your life by flow instead of force, by grace instead of grit, and by surrendering your ego instead of trying to will and assert things into existence. As you apply the sacred power principles to your life, more and more of the truth about your power is revealed to you.

Your Power	Is the force in you that moves and is directed by your thoughts.
Your Power	Is your ability to create and manifest the desires of your heart.
Your Power	Is your capacity to consciously convert thought into action.
Your Power	Is your ability to influence outcomes.
Your Power	Is the source of your ability to shape and direct your spiritual energy and Life Force to manifest things on the physical plane.
Your Power	Is a function of being in partnership with God.
Your Power	Is a natural resource.
Your Power	Emerges more and more as you recognize your divine and sacred self.
Your Power	Is the ability to create the visible from the invisible.
Your Power	Transcends the physical and the material world.
Your Power	Is real.

More Power to You

90. *In-power your children*

One evening, my 6-year-old daughter, Adera, called me into the bathroom. She wanted to have a talk. Apparently, she thought some of the rules in our household were unfair, and she felt compelled to tell me why. As soon as she began, I could have said, "Excuse me! Who do you think you're talking to?! You're the child and I'm the parent, and as long as you live under this roof, you follow my rules!" But I didn't say any of those things—instead I listened carefully. In making any of these statements, my behavior and actions would have demonstrated to Adera: *What you think is not impor-tant; what I think is more important than what you think; since I'm the adult and I'm big-ger, I'm right.*

"First of all," Adera began, "I don't understand why I have to eat all of my dinner *before* I get to have dessert. If I eat all of my dinner, I won't have any room for dessert."

"Hmmm, good point," I said. "What else?" I asked. She glanced up at me hesitantly, surprised that I was taking such an interest in her feedback. She continued, "And why do Kiana and I have to keep *our* room clean all the time, but you and Daddy get to have clothes on your floor and you don't have to keep *your* room clean all the time? You tell Kiana and I not to raise our voices when we talk to you, but you sometimes raise your voice when you get upset with us."

"Hmmm, you're making some good sense. I hear what you're saying," I replied. "Thank you for sharing your thoughts, Adera. I'm really going to do a better job of practicing what I'm trying to teach." "Okay, Mommy!" she replied excitedly. She hadn't expected me to be so responsive to her con-cerns. "That's all I wanted to tell you," she said as she went back to her bed-room to finish playing.

In choosing to listen to Adera in this instance, I was teaching her many things—her opinion matters; Mommy cares about what she thinks; when she is frustrated with a situation, speaking up can make a positive differ-ence; big adult people can listen and learn from little people; and big adult people aren't always right, even if they are your parents. I was also hoping to teach her to speak up and speak out respectfully to authority figures without fear of retribution or negative consequences.

In the African-American culture, we've created a fine line for our children to walk. We've created a fine line between "talking back" or being "smart-mouthed" and being able to express ourself honestly and fully. Being able to speak honestly and openly with me is how Adera will learn to express her-self without being disrespectful in the presence of other authority figures she will encounter in her life—teachers, bosses, and so on. After all, she is a little woman in training.

As parents, we have to be sure that we *demonstrate* and "example" integrity and consistency. Practice what we teach. When we don't, we create inner conflict, tension, and even anger in our children. They can spot a double standard a mile away. And they have a low tolerance for hypocrisy. When they see us saying one thing and doing another, holding them to something that we are not holding ourselves to, we teach them that hypocrisy is acceptable when you're a big person.

On another occasion, my daughter was quick to remind me that I was walking the double-standard path again. My husband and I do not have a lock on our bedroom door, so our daughters know that, in our household, a closed door means you knock first, identify yourself, wait to be acknowledged, and *then* open the door to enter. They know that this especially applies to Mommy and Daddy's bedroom door. They both are very good about adhering to this rule. Well, one Saturday afternoon while they were in their room playing, I opened the door and walked in to put some folded clothes away in their drawers. I forgot to knock first and follow "procedure." "*Mommmeeeeee*," they sing-sang in unison, "you didn't knock first. We didn't say you could come in." I had to catch myself—*these little 4- and 6-year-olds trying to call me out?!* The seconds immediately following their admonishment were critical. I could have responded with one of the typical parental responses: "What do you mean, I didn't knock first? Who do you think you're talking to?! You don't pay the rent here. I can come in this room if I please." or I could choose to in-power them. I chose the latter. First, I apologized, then I back-peddled out of their room, closed the door behind me, and knocked.

If I had decided to come back at them with one of the above comments, I would have communicated through my actions and behavior that adults can do whatever they please, even if it contradicts what they are telling their children. By asking my kids to knock first before they enter our bedroom, I am teaching them to honor our room and respect our private space. Backing out of their room and entering the correct way showed them that I also honored their room and their private space.

Maybe the premises on which we've been parenting aren't in the best interest of our children. Maybe the premises on which most of us have been operating are an extension of how our parents raised us. But these premises, for the most part, do *not* result in empowered, self-expressed, fearless children. As I was growing up, I believed that a parent's responsibility was to teach a child right and wrong. But teaching our kids right and wrong has become an exercise in teaching our kids to do what meets with approval in Mama's or Daddy's eyes, and avoiding what doesn't meet with Mama's or

Daddy's approval. When they do "right," we approve; when they do "wrong," we don't approve.

Hmmmmm.

Instead of nurturing and developing a self-expressed child, this establishes a pattern of *conditional* love, with the child afraid to fully express herself for fear of receiving disapproval from Mom or Dad. Then it makes sense why making a mistake, failing, or messing up would be avoided at all costs. Why? Because a child doesn't want her parent to disapprove of her. This is very painful to a child because disapproval is a form of rejection in a child's mind. Then this child grows up to be an adult—fearful, with issues, with low self-esteem, suppressed, being out of touch with her true self, and trying to avoid mistakes, failure, or looking bad at all costs. Not fully feeling. Not fully living.

Over time, as we continue to demonstrate double standards, treat our children like property, dishonor their inherent wisdom and integrity, discourage their self-discovery and natural curiosity, and constantly pummel them with directives and commands, it suppresses their spirit. They start to build up anger, resentment, and feelings of powerlessness. I don't think we really get to see the fallout and repercussions of this way of parenting until the children get bigger and reach their teenage years. Then we label them crazy and rebellious. Maybe they are finally getting their pent-up frustrations out of their systems.

If we don't like "what the world is coming to," then we must first acknowledge the degree to which we are contributing to how it is. You may not be able to change the world, but you can affect your part of it—the part that goes on inside of your home.

I surely do not have all of the parenting answers. I'm trying to navigate my way through this "divine experiment" just like the next parent. It seems that my three little women, ages 6, 4, and 20 months, are turning out all right, so far. Yeah, they've still got some rough edges, but that's because I still have rough edges. I think my two oldest still act a little too wild in public sometimes, talk too loud, or argue with each other too much. But what I *do* know is that I am committed to "training up" little girls that are self-expressed, energetic, creative, health conscious, critically thinking, confident, and self-loving, so that they become young women and then grown women who are self-expressed, joyful, self-loving, treat their bodies like a temple, speak their mind, understand their power, and are spiritually attuned and grounded.

What I know is that "training up" little girls who will become this type of woman requires operating from a different parenting premise than most of us are operating from. The example that makes the greatest impression on my daughters is the one *I* provide because they see me as the possibility of what they can do and be. What I also know is that I, as their mama, must, must, must realize each quality in *myself* that I want them to realize in *their* lives. *I can't teach what I haven't learned. I can't make real for them what isn't real in me.*

An empowered mother tends to raise empowered children. A fulfilled mother tends to raise fulfilled children. A joy-filled mother tends to raise joy-filled children.

QUESTIONS TO ASK YOURSELF

What am I demonstrating and modeling in my home?
What am I "exampling" through my actions, language, and behaviors in my home?
Am I "training up" in-powered children?

I don't have all of the parenting answers. I'm learning as I go, but I sure knock first on my daughters' bedroom door now, and I keep my room a lot cleaner.

91. *Become good friends with the "RE" sisters*

⟶ Girl, I know this fabulous family of seven sisters whom I want to introduce you to. They're probably unlike any family you've ever met, though, because all seven sisters have the *same* first name and a different last name. I know it seems strange. But you'll understand once you meet them for yourself. My life has been transformed since these sisters have come into my life. But go ahead and meet them for yourself.

THE "RE" SISTERS

Sister 1	RE-Group	Call on her when you need to collect your thoughts, center, recover, or ground yourself.
Sister 2	RE-Evaluate	Call on her when you need to examine your life, decide upon a new course of action, or assess a situation.
Sister 3	RE-Flect	Call on her when you need to meditate, contemplate, or do some introspection and self-reflection.
Sister 4	RE-Lax	Call on her when you need to unwind, exhale, loosen up, and free yourself from strain, stress, or tension.
Sister 5	RE-Treat	Call on her when you need peace and quiet, sacred space, refuge, and a private place for "down time," prayer, or meditation.
Sister 6	RE-Newal	Call on her when you are in need of restoration or rejuvenation of your mind, body, or spirit.
Sister 7	RE-Lease	As an African-American woman, this is the "RE" sister that should become one of your closest friends. Call on her when you start to show signs of the SBW Syndrome; you find yourself overgiving and overnurturing, you feel overwhelmed and overloaded; you have a problem weighing heavily on your mind, you're feeling confined or burdened, or you need to let go and give it to God.

The "RE" sisters are available to you 365 days of the year, around the clock, for as long as you need them. They never tire of your company because they love being in your life. I know my life has changed since I've gotten to know them. Some of the results I've experienced are:

- I no longer have the experience of not having enough time.
- I may sometimes feel pressed, but not stressed.
- I have more energy and vitality.
- I'm releasing weight with less effort and struggle, and without being on a "diet."

- I'm on time more.
- I rip, run, and rush less.
- I have more clarity and focus.
- I'm more grounded and centered.
- I'm learning to love my body and "love my cells."
- I'm able to find joy in simple things and deep gratification in simple pleasures.
- I'm a more careful, attentive, and conscious listener.
- I seek out time alone rather than avoid it.
- My sex life has gotten even better.
- I move and exercise more—willingly.
- I belly laugh more.
- I pray and meditate more.
- I honor my personal boundaries.
- I sleep more soundly.
- I'm not as defensive.
- I have more intimacy in my female and male friendships.
- Renewal is integrated into my lifestyle.
- I can say yes to myself and no to others without feeling guilty.
- My "body esteem" has improved.
- I have more clarity about my ministry, mission, and purpose.
- The content and substance of my life is a reflection of what brings me joy.
- I experience no more minor body aches and pains.
- I'm able to more quickly manifest desired outcomes and results.
- I express myself more.
- My bad habits have decreased.
- My complexion has improved.
- I am at peace.

And this is to name just a few.

Get to know each of the "RE" sisters personally, and invite her to take up permanent residence in your life.

92. *Integrate renewal into your life*

hat brings you joy is also what renews your mind, body, and spirit. Our challenge is to get in touch with what brings us joy and integrate it into our lives—*now*. Not wait until the kids are grown, until your next paycheck, until your next couple of days off, until you get married, until you get divorced, until you lose a few more pounds, *but now*.

If you were to examine the content and substance of your life right now, what would you find? *How, where, with whom* are you investing your energy? Would you find experiences of joy occurring regularly or rarely? Would you see yourself being "in pursuit of happiness" or actually *having* joy?

When you *integrate* renewal into your life, you move out that which isn't bringing you joy to make room for the relationships and experiences that do. You withdraw and shift your energy from what does not bring you joy and reinvest it in what does.

When you integrate joy into your life, you also learn to bring more joy to what is already present in your life. Integrating renewal into your workday may mean taking a lunch break instead of working through lunch; it may mean bringing a sack lunch instead of eating out to give yourself time to enjoy a more relaxed lunch in an empty conference room while you listen to your Walkman or Discman, or read a favorite book or magazine. Integrating renewal into your home life may mean taking a ten-minute "time out" when you get home before you shift into second gear checking phone messages, straightening up, or cooking dinner. It may mean turning off the TV, turning on some jazz, and lighting some incense while you wash dishes. Integrating renewal may mean replacing some of the morning showers you take with evening baths that allow you to stretch out, lay back, and let the warm, soothing water do therapy to your mind, body, and spirit.

You cannot find, save, or make time. Having renewal be a regular and consistent part of your life is not about trying to find, save, or make time.

We each have twenty-four hours available in a day. We must learn to *integrate* renewal into the fabric of our lives instead of waiting for the elusive "free moment." The challenge is to align your relationships, activities, and energy with what brings you joy and weave renewal into the fiber of your life.

Begin integrating renewal into your life—today.

93. *Become a sensuous woman*

I love those sixteenth-century paintings by the Italian artist Raphael that show voluptuous, radiant, smiling, curvaceous women, reclining naked in the grass or on a velvet couch with a look of sheer ecstasy on their faces as they eat a handful of plump, luscious grapes. I love the way Raphael painted these women gazing at you with a confident yet playful look in their eye that seems to say, "Welcome to *my* world." Raphael painted alive, alert images of women that show them delighting in their bodies and enjoying life. "Raphael's women" look like they don't give a damn about what anyone thinks about them. They are fully taking in life and are present to the rapture of the moment.

Becoming a sensuous woman is about being able to fully take in life— being alive, alert, and present. A sensuous woman is able to easily give and receive pleasure through her senses of sight, sound, touch, taste, and smell. Becoming a sensuous woman isn't about *doing* anything differently. It's about *being* differently, and allowing more of who you really are to come out and play. Your *nature* is to be sensuous. To allow your sensuous self to emerge, you have to *sssllllloooowww down*, exhale, listen to your body, and move with grace instead of jerky, jagged, sharp-edged movements.

I am grateful to all of the sensuous women that I have in my life—Lillie, Vicky, Glinda, Musinah, Tiffany, Maria, Staci, Maxine, Sharon, Linda, Anita, Priscilla, Teer, Faye, Fatimah, Marcia, Suni, Darice, Denise, Monvella, Veronica, Laurel, Marie, Mayet, Dielka, Delayna, Danni, Dorothea, Ruth, Meagan, Jewel, and DeShunda—to name a few. As I think about these sensuous women in my life, I've noticed certain similarities and recurring qualities.

A SENSUOUS WOMAN IS . . .

◇ Radiant

◇ Has clear, glowing skin

◇ Has discovered her distinct personal style (reflected in her clothes, hairstyle, etc.)

◇ Laughs frequently and easily

◇ Is very expressive

◇ Is comfortable touching or hugging others

◇ Moves her body with confidence

◇ Is magnetic

◇ Has presence when she walks into a room

◇ Moves with ease and grace

◇ Has a clear sense of self-identity and purpose

◇ Is very grounded and centered

◇ Smiles easily and laughs readily

◇ Is a size 6 to 26

◇ Is age 21 to 85

◇ Prays *and* meditates

◇ Loves herself

◇ Gives and receives compliments graciously

Is there such a thing as a formula for becoming a sensuous woman? Probably not, but there are some valuable insights that can be gained from the sensuous women that we know. To cultivate and bring forth the sensuous woman within, learn to take your time, slow down, discover your personal style, move with ease and grace, be interested in others, listen carefully, honor your boundaries, be present and alert, smile more, radiate positive energy, know your worth, loosen up, pay attention, laugh more, and pamper your mind, body, and spirit.

94. *Be bold, bodacious, and succulent (BBS)*

*Thriving is what was meant for us on this earth.
Thriving, not just surviving, is our birthright as women.*
—Clarissa Pinkola Estes

Thrival: thrival is to thrive as survival is to survive.
—Rachel Bagby

If you don't have the books *Succulent Wild Woman* or *Living Juicy* by the author who uses the pen name Sark, then I suggest you make your way to the library and check them out immediately or to the bookstore to purchase your personal copies. These books will liberate your spirit.

In *Succulent Wild Woman*, Sark defines succulent as "ripe, juicy, whole, round, exuberant, wild, rich, wide, deep, firm, rare, female." This is me. And this is you—in your natural "unsuppressed" state. Being a woman in touch with her joy and sacred power is being a woman who is bold, bodacious, and succulent (BBS). *Bold* means "vivid, courageous, forthright, spirited, and self-assertive," and *bodacious* means "remarkable and unmistakable." If this isn't you in all your glory, I don't know what is! I invite you to be who you really are, which is all of these things. I invite you to walk on your wild side and thrive!

Now, others may have told you or tried to convince you that you are something other than these things. They were simply misinformed. Next time someone asks you, Who do you think you are?! Try this reply: "Bold, bodacious, and succulent!" Sark tells us that being bold, bodacious, and succulent means "living untamed, juicy and abundantly" celebrating your unique qualities and your "marvelous imperfections." Giving yourself permission to have more outrageous adventures. Giving cheerfully but also "asking for what you need or want, regardless of the outcome." Being BBS means "letting your creative spirit rush, flow, tumble, leak, spring, bubble, stream, dribble out of you" while you are "learning to fall in love with you."

And most of all, being BBS means believing "you are enough, you have enough, you do enough." *Can I get an amen?!*

We've been playing small for far too long. We've been "toning it down" and shrinking so that others won't feel uncomfortable around us. We've been undervaluing our gifts, talents, skills, and abilities. We've been too polite and too accommodating. We've been "hiding our light under a bush" so that others won't be so shocked at our brilliance. We've discounted compliments, deferred our dreams, let others go first every time, and settled for the crumbs. We've doused the flames of our fiery ways, exiled daring deeds, and been forced to throw dirt on the glowing orange-hot embers of our sensuality. We've apologized for our loudness, brightness, boldness, and passionate ways. I say it's high time for us to stop apologizing for who we are and start being who and what we were created to be.

In words written by Marianne Williamson and spoken by Nelson Mandela at his 1994 inaugural address, Mandela speaks the truth about the chains that are holding our bold, bodacious, succulent selves hostage.

> *Our deepest fear is not that we are inadequate.*
> *Our deepest fear is that we are powerful beyond measure.*
> *It is our light and not our darkness that most frightens us.*
> *We ask ourselves, who am I to be brilliant,*
> *gorgeous, talented and fabulous?*
> *Actually, who are you not to be?*

> *Two, four, six, eight, who do we appreciate?*
> *Women who are BBS without apology!*

95. *Belly laugh*

I love myself when I am laughing.
—Zora Neale Hurston

Heads were turning. People were looking. Four black women in a very, very nice restaurant with mouths open wide, heads thrown back, and tears running down our faces—belly laughing! We didn't care what others in the restaurant thought. At that particular moment, it was *party over here.*

A few weeks earlier, I was in a hotel ballroom with forty-five people, interviewing and auditioning for a part-time training position. At the first break, we had the chance to mix and mingle and get to know the other candidates. I struck up a conversation with the Latino woman sitting next to me. Within minutes, we were sharing funny stories about our training experiences, and belly laughing! Our laughter seemed to get people's attention, like mentioning E. F. Hutton's name on those TV commercials. People started gravitating to us like moths to a flame or bees to honey. A few people actually walked up and politely interrupted, asking if they could join our conversation. They said it sounded like we were having just too much fun. We were.

In both of these instances, we were not *trying* to get attention. But that is what ended up happening. Unfortunately, hearing someone belly laugh in public has become a rare treat. Usually we hear an abbreviated chortle, or a muffled, corporate courtesy chuckle, but not laughter that comes from deep in your belly and makes your eyes water and your sides ache. Belly laughing becomes extinct in a culture where people become too self-conscious, too serious all of the time, too tense, terse, pessimistic, conformist, rigid, insecure, and *joy-less.*

We must find and create more opportunities to belly laugh. It keeps you healthier; releases muscular tension; and triggers the release of endorphins, the good-feelings hormones. Most important, belly laughing is *free!* Is the reason we don't belly laugh more because we don't have much to belly laugh about, or is it that we've become inhibited, or so concerned about seeming too wild or too boisterous? *So be it.* The most serious repercussions I've experienced so far are being accused of having too much fun.

Life is too short not to indulge in simple pleasures such as belly laughing. It's a *free* woman who is able to belly laugh.

ODE TO THE BELLY LAUGH

To belly laugh is a simple thing,
though for some it may seem a sin.
They might have to give up some of the pain
they have insisted they are in.

It is a free woman that can belly laugh
and let loose with all her being.
And in that moment, it would be joy
that others would be seeing.

This laugh could be the secret key
To liberating your soul
Releasing the pent-up energy
That you need to make you whole.

Self-conscious, insecure, a little uptight?
This laugh is a sight to see,
So throw back your head, open wide your mouth
And set your spirit free.

—djg

96. *No more jerky moves*

When I was feeling stressed, moving with grace would go straight out the window. I noticed this one morning when I was behind schedule for catching my flight at the airport. My husband dropped me off at the airport curb, and I dashed out of the car and bolted to my gate like O. J. Simpson in a Hertz commercial. I was yanking and jerking my carry-on bag along, rudely bumping into people, and half-running, half-walking through the concourse with a distorted scowl on my face, worried that I would miss my flight.

I ended up getting to the gate counter, confirming my seat assignment, and receiving my boarding pass with fifteen minutes to spare before the gate agent made the first boarding call over the loudspeaker. I took a seat to wait and to exhale. I needed to let my heart rate return to normal.

While I waited, my mind flashed back to how hastily I had jumped out of the car, without even giving my husband a goodbye kiss. And how I had swept through the airport like a human tornado. I noticed that when I kicked into this "rush mode," I got very self-centered, to the point that I became inconsiderate and impatient. It even affected how I moved—I got jerky.

Yes, *jerky*.

My movements got jerky, rough, and sharp. Instead of being smooth and graceful, my moves got jerky. *And jerky isn't pretty.*

And don't let a sister get angry or upset. We start snatching, yanking, and jerking all over the place. Could I have made my plane while maintaining grace, without the jerky moves? Could I have given my husband a kiss and moved quickly through the airport smoothly and gracefully? The answer was yes both times.

Now I catch myself. Especially when things get hectic, I try to move with grace, no matter what. Moving gracefully doesn't take any more time than moving with abrupt, sharp, jerky moves. Eliminating jerky moves means we have to stay aware of ourselves, our bodies, and our surroundings. Eliminating jerky moves also means that you strive to *not* let outside forces and circumstances fluster you and throw you off-center or off-balance. Being able to remain graceful in the face of stressful circumstances or situations means being able to stay grounded and centered.

Let's start a national movement—No More Jerky Moves. No More Jerky Moves.

JERKY
MOVES

97. Celebrate

aybe the reason certain events in our lives seem anticlimactic is because we don't celebrate them enough. We complete a big project, do a good job, lose twelve pounds, register for school, stay clean and sober, without anything to recognize or acknowledge the accomplishment. We need to stop waiting for a holiday, birthday, graduation, or wedding to roll around before we celebrate. A powerful woman celebrates because she declares that something is worth celebrating. She celebrates milestones, rites of passage, little victories, and personal triumphs, in either little or big ways.

This is how Empire Builders came about.

My training and consulting company teamed up with three other sister-owned companies to win a very competitive training contract for a large regional company. We were up against seven other very seasoned firms that had lots more experience than we did, so we were the long shots and the underdogs. We pulled out all of the stops and let our energy and brilliance flow, and our team won the contract! This called for a celebration. So I decided to have a celebration that would allow our team to share the excitement with other established black women business owners who were striving to grow their businesses, who would be inspired by our accomplishment. In my mind, we were inviting other women business owners to our celebration who also thought big and dreamed big—they, too, were empire builders.

The Empire Builders celebration, which was held at the home of one of the team members, was complete with candles, soft jazz, wine and cheese, champagne, broccoli and cheese quiche, fresh strawberries, sweet 'n sour teriyaki chicken wings, Caesar salad, raspberry cheesecake, and fresh-brewed Kenyan coffee for dessert. Each of the ten women who attended the Empire Builders celebration was delighted and honored to have been invited.

Before proceeding with dessert, we gathered together in the living room to explain the purpose of the gathering. The details of the strategy we devised were shared with the other business owners, as well as the contract dollar amount and the details of the contract negotiations. We then had each guest introduce herself, explain her business, and then share a recent business triumph with the rest of the group. After we completed the "circle of triumphs," we toasted to our collective successes.

When my girlfriend Cheryl turned 50, she brought it in with a bang. She decided to have a birthday celebration and invite friends to celebrate with her who were 45 years of age or older. Though it was her 50th birthday celebration, she decided to celebrate it by honoring her friends. Cheryl made a unique, handmade invitation for each guest, and decorated her home with beautiful silver and gold garlands, candles, balloons, and gold glitter dust. She fixed a scrumptious five-course meal and seated all of her friends at her long, formal dining room table to enjoy it. Cheryl invited me to join the celebration after dinner as the "after dinner" surprise. She asked me to lead the group through a miniseminar that would support her theme of turning 50. As I parked my car and walked up to Cheryl's front door, I could hear the music, laughter, and lively conversation slipping out of the open windows. These ladies were having a ball!

For the miniseminar portion of the evening, I decided to lead the ladies through a simple game I called "The Imaginary Backpack." I asked each woman to imagine that she was going on a trip into the next fifty years of her life, and all she could take was a backpack. Ladies were asked to reflect upon the first forty to fifty years of their lives, and decide upon the one quality, value, or character trait that they wanted to take with them in their backpacks. The Imaginary Backpack game proved to be the perfect finale to an already magical evening.

Life is short. Celebrate the little triumphs and the personal victories that have special meaning to you. *Celebrate good times, c'mon!*

98. Build your own powerhouse

One of the many blessing from my first book, *Sacred Pampering Principles*, is the hundreds of cards, phone calls, letters, and gifts I received from readers from across the country. My book was a gift I was giving to other women, and they, in turn, gave gifts back to me! I was delighted that my "gift" would touch so many lives and spur such a flurry of loving responses.

There were times when I would have the opportunity to personally return a particular phone call or letter that really touched me, and as a result a new friendship often developed. The following thoughts are courtesy of Hattie Finn-Carter, a reader-turned-friend in northern California. She was kind and gracious enough to allow me to share some of her words of wisdom with you. As I read and reread her stimulating and provoking words of wisdom, it occurred to me that Hattie was sharing insights and instructions for *building your own powerhouse. You* are the powerhouse because your power is housed in you.

When you build your own powerhouse, you recognize that you are always "under construction" in one form or another. You are always working on yourself—clearing away and removing the debris of old beliefs, thoughts, and ways of being that compromise your sacred power and steal your joy. Yes, you and I are divine works-in-progress and women-in-process of *becoming.* As you continue to build your own powerhouse, let the following words feed your soul. Let them in-power you.

1. What someone else thinks about you is not more important than what you think about yourself.
2. You cannot change other people. You can change yourself, then other people must change how they respond to you.
3. You are not a victim, and it is okay to be scared.
4. In the right moment, at the right time, you will be shown what to do, told what to say . . . until then, you must be still and love and honor yourself so you can hear the voice when it speaks through you and to you.
5. Giving is our way of demonstrating our belief in the abundance of life, along with the goodness of God, and that which is ours by divine right.
6. Free yourself from dead things.
7. Free your heart from fear of hurt or harm.
8. You are good enough, smart enough. You are enough.
9. Faith transforms confusion into order.
10. You need no validation that does not issue from within.
11. Spirit is at your beck and call 24/7.
12. The storm will pass over.

13. Know you already "have it."
14. Submit to peace of mind.
15. The foundation of life has already been laid for you.
16. Forgiveness is totally releasing without condition, remorse, or guilt.
17. Practice pleasure.
18. Have no unjust expectations.
19. Choose right action every time.
20. Listen to your inner signals.
21. Step into your life.
22. Embrace the opportunities disguised as challenges.
23. Be your own best friend.
24. Be spontaneous and open to change.
25. Show love and compassion.
26. Release blame.
27. Let it stay simple.
28. Stop resisting and receive.
29. Mistakes can be corrected. Problems can be solved.
30. Choose, choose, choose.

Thank you, Hattie.

Build on, Sister, build on.

99. Be ready

When I ran track and field in high school, preparation was a large part of the process—perfecting my form in practice, weightlifting to improve my strength and endurance, and running laps and ladders to develop my cardiovascular capacity. On the day of the track meet, there was still more preparation—psyching myself up mentally, being sure to stretch out adequately so that my muscles were limber and warmed up, and sharpening my track cleats before screwing them into the bottom of my track shoes.

But when I took off my sweats and stepped up to the starting block at the starting line, it was no longer about preparation: *it was about being ready.* When the official shouted, "Runners, take your marks, get set, go!" and shot off the gun with a loud *pop*, being ready was what was important. If I didn't take off and start running when that gun went off, then all of my preparation and planning would have been irrelevant, useless, futile, in vain. My preparation could not replace the running of the race. I had to get set and GO!

The decades of the 1980s and 1990s, in my estimation, were about preparation. The new millennium requires that we *be ready. ARE YOU READY?*

Being ready is about saying "Yes!" when the opportunity you've been asking for, hoping for, and praying for presents itself.

Being ready is about stepping up to the plate when you are asked to stretch, grow, try something new, or expand into your *dis*comfort zone.

Being ready is about being willing to access the necessary resources, make the necessary connections and contacts, and ask the right questions to make "it" happen, whatever "it" is for you.

Being ready is about being able to be spontaneous, being able to pick up and go if you have to, respond on short notice, being able to be relaxed and at ease even when you don't have all the details and all of your questions haven't been answered.

Being ready is about knowing that you are the answer, you are the one. If not you, then who?

Being ready is about rising to the occasion.

Being ready is about saying, "I'll find out," instead of "I don't know."

Being ready is about being flexible and adaptable even when it's not looking like you want it to look.

Being ready is about being spiritual enough to admit when you make a mistake, misunderstand, misinterpret, miscommunicate, or mess up.

Being ready means you understand the power of self-reflection and telling the truth, and you practice both.

Being ready means you hear Life's call to participate, and you answer yes!

How do you know if your consciousness is ready? To find out, check out your current reality. What is showing up—in your finances, with your body, with your goals, with your aspirations, in love relationships? What you have in your current reality is a reflection of your consciousness. If your consciousness is ready, it will manifest. If your consciousness is ready, you will be able to create and attract the fulfillment of what you desire in these certain areas of your life.

The new millennium requires that you be a ready woman, not just a prepared woman. Are you ready for prosperity, health, good lovin', to stop struggling, ripe opportunities, fulfilling relationships, more joy and power in your life? Are you ready to receive the blessings God has in store for you? If you give God a cup to fill, She will. If you give God a bucket to fill, She will. It's time to trade in your cup for a bucket.

100. *Expand your joy threshold*

For most of us, joy has been so squeezed out of our lives that we can tolerate it only in small doses. Or our joy thresholds are so low that experiencing joy in more than one area of our lives at a time can send us into "Tilt." We get so used to conflict, struggle, and hardship that we feel more at home "in strife" or struggling than we do "in joy."

Thank goodness that we cannot overdose on joy. We are designed and "wired" for it. My hope is that *All the Joy You Can Stand* has brought you closer to experiencing joy in all parts of your life. Not just some parts—all parts. *It is possible.* Besides, you deserve nothing less. Joy is your birthright. Joy is your nature. So let it in. Let it in.

At a sisters gathering in Colorado, we were discussing some of the challenges we had experienced in our lives, and one of the women pointed out, "God never gives you more than you can handle." She was referring to challenges we encounter, and when most people cite this statement, they, too, are speaking of challenges. We tend to forget that this works both ways— God never gives you more *blessings* than you can handle, either!

When I was a little girl in Sunday school, we used to sing a song that said, "I've got joy, joy, joy, joy down in my heart." Now, it is time for us to have joy down in our bodies, down in our finances, down in our minds, down in our relationships, down in our thoughts, down in our beliefs, down in our families, down in our affairs, down in our spirits, and down in our souls. Yes, all the joy you can stand.

Let it in, let it in, let it in.
You deserve nothing less.

101. *Embrace your power*

Said the woman to her Inner Power,
"Come out, come out, wherever you are."

AND IT DID.

We Want to Keep in Touch with You!

How to Connect with Debrena Jackson Gandy

Visit the author's Web site at www.DebrenasWorld.com to request her as a speaker, check out her calendar of events, be uplifted by her *Pampering Zone* newsletter, e-mail her, or purchase her exclusive line of INpowerment products from her online AfroScentrics Boutique.

You can arrange to bring the *Sacred Pampering Seminar* or the *All the Joy You Can Stand Workshop* to your area. To book Debrena Jackson Gandy for keynotes, seminars, workshops, lectures, and retreats, you can also contact Twanda Hill, her Speaking Coordinator. Twanda Hill can be reached at 12822-37th Avenue South, Seattle, WA 98168, phone 206-248-6072, fax 206-244-2740, or via e-mail at TwandaHill@aol.com.

Do you want to be added to Debrena Jackson Gandy's newsletter mailing list or her personal e-mail list? Or do you have a testimony or comment to share about how this book has affected your life? You can do this through her Web site or you may opt to mail or fax your name, address, phone number, and comments *directly* to Debrena Jackson Gandy at 23814 14th Avenue South, Suite 100, Seattle, WA 98198, phone 206-878-8163, fax 206-824-8973, or via e-mail to Debrena@earthlink.net. (She reads each card, letter, and e-mail, personally.) Thank you.